Ezra Pound's Chinese Friends

Ezra Pound's Chinese Friends

Stories in Letters

EDITED AND ANNOTATED BY
ZHAOMING QIAN

OXFORD
UNIVERSITY PRESS

OXFORD
UNIVERSITY PRESS

Great Clarendon Street, Oxford OX2 6DP

Oxford University Press is a department of the University of Oxford.
It furthers the University's objective of excellence in research, scholarship,
and education by publishing worldwide in

Oxford New York

Auckland Cape Town Dar es Salaam Hong Kong Karachi
Kuala Lumpur Madrid Melbourne Mexico City Nairobi
New Delhi Shanghai Taipei Toronto

With offices in

Argentina Austria Brazil Chile Czech Republic France Greece
Guatemala Hungary Italy Japan Poland Portugal Singapore
South Korea Switzerland Thailand Turkey Ukraine Vietnam

Oxford is a registered trade mark of Oxford University Press
in the UK and in certain other countries

Published in the United States
by Oxford University Press Inc., New York

© Zhaoming Qian 2008.

The moral rights of the authors have been asserted
Database right Oxford University Press (maker)

First published 2008

British Library Cataloguing in Publication Data

Data available

Library of Congress Cataloging in Publication Data

Data available

Typeset by SPI Publisher Services, Pondicherry, India
Printed in Great Britain
on acid-free paper by
Biddles Ltd., King's Lynn, Norfolk

ISBN 978-0-19-923860-6

1 3 5 7 9 10 8 6 4 2

© 2008 Previously unpublished letters and writings of Ezra Pound by courtesy of Mary de Rachewiltz and Omar S. Pound, used by permission of New Directions Publishing Corporation, agents.
Photos used by courtesy of the Beinecke Rare Book and Manuscript Library, the Harry Ransom Humanities Research Center, and New Directions Publishing Corporation, agents.
© 2008 Postscripts of Dorothy Pound by courtesy of Omar S. Pound.
© 2008 Scenes from Ezra Pound's screen book by courtesy of Mary de Rachewiltz.
© 2008 Letters and photographs of Carsun Chang by courtesy of Diana Chang and June T. F. Chang Tung.
© 2008 Letters and photographs of Tze-chiang Chao and C. H. Kwock by courtesy of C. H. Kwock.
© 2008 Letters and photographs of Achilles Fang by courtesy of Ilse Fang.
© 2008 Letters and photographs of P. H. Fang by courtesy of P. H. Fang.
© 2008 Photograph of Angela Jung Palandri by courtesy of Angela Jung Palandri.
© 2008 Letters and photograph of F. T. Sung by courtesy of Hongru Song.
© 2008 Letters and photograph of Fengchi Yang by courtesy of Lionello Lanciotti.
© 2008 Writing of William McNaughton by William McNaughton.
© 2008 Compilation, introductions, annotations, translations, and additional editorial matter by Zhaoming Qian.

Grateful acknowledgment is given to New Directions Publishing Corporation for permission to use the following copyrighted works of Ezra Pound: Excerpts from *Ezra Pound's Poetry and Prose: Contributions to Periodicals*, copyright © 1991 by the Trustees of the Ezra Pound Literary Property Trust; excerpts from *The Cantos of Ezra Pound*, copyright © 1934, 1937, 1940, 1948, 1956, 1959, 1962, 1963, 1966, and 1968 by Ezra Pound, reprinted by permission of New Directions Publishing Corporation; *The Great Digest, The Unwobbling Pivot, The Analects*, from *Confucius*, edited by Ezra Pound, translated by Ezra Pound, from *Confucius*, copyright © 1947, 1950 by Ezra Pound, reprinted by permission of New Directions Publishing Corporation.

Book cover from Ezra Pound's *Shih-Ching: The Classic Anthology Defined by Confucius* appears courtesy of Harvard University Press, Copyright © 1954, 1982 by the President and Fellows of Harvard College.

To Barry Ahearn,
George Bornstein,
and
Marjorie Perloff

CONTENTS

LIST OF ABBREVIATIONS

General

ACS	autograph postcard signed
ALS	autograph letter signed, followed by numeral indicating number of leaves of the original, e.g. ALS-3 = autograph letter signed consisting of three leaves
ANS	autograph note signed
TL	typed letter unsigned, followed by numeral indicating number of leaves of the original, e.g. TL-2 = typed letter unsigned consisting of two leaves

Libraries and Collections

AJP	Private collection of Angela Jung Palandri, Eugene, Oregon
Beinecke	Beinecke Rare Book and Manuscript Library, Yale University
Brunnenburg	Ezra Pound Library, Brunnenburg, Italy
HRHRC	Harry Ransom Humanities Research Center, University of Texas at Austin
Lilly	Lilly Library, Indiana University
LL	Private collection of Lionello Lanciotti, Rome, Italy
PHF	Private collection of P. H. Fang, Belmont, Massachusetts

Published Writings of Ezra Pound

Canto	*The Cantos* (14th printing; New York: New Directions, 1998) (references are to canto and page number.)
LE	*Literary Essays*, ed. T. S. Eliot (1954; New York: New Directions, 1968)
Personae	*Personae: The Shorter Poems*, ed. Lea Baechler and A. Walton Litz (1926; rev. ed. New York: New Directions, 1990)
Poetry and Prose	*Ezra Pound's Poetry and Prose: Contributions to Periodicals*, 10 vols., ed. Lea Baechler et al. (New York: Garland, 1991)
SP	*Selected Prose, 1909–1965*, ed. William Cookson (New York: New Directions, 1973)

Published Translations of Ezra Pound

Classic Anthology	*Shih-Ching: The Classic Anthology Defined by Confucius* (1954; Cambridge, Mass.: Harvard University Press, 1982)
Confucius	*Confucius: The Great Digest, The Unwobbling Pivot, The Analects* (1951; New York: New Directions, 1969)

Published Letters of Ezra Pound

Letters in Captivity   *Ezra and Dorothy Pound: Letters in Captivity, 1945–1946*, ed. Omar Pound and
                         Robert Spoo (New York: Oxford University Press, 1999)
Pound/Japan   *Ezra Pound and Japan: Letters and Essays*, ed. Sanehide Kodama (Redding
                         Ridge, Conn.: Black Swan, 1987)
Pound/Theobald   *Letters of Ezra Pound and John Theobald*, ed. Donald Pearce and Herbert
                         Schneidau (Redding Ridge, Conn.: Black Swan, 1984)

Works by Others

Gallup   Donald Gallup, *Ezra Pound: A Bibliography* (Charlottesville: University Press of
              Virginia, 1983)
Legge   James Legge, *The Chinese Classics*, 7 vols. (1865; Hong Kong: Hong Kong
              University Press, 1960)
Mathews   R. H. Mathews, *Mathews' Chinese–English Dictionary* (1931; Cambridge, Mass.:
              Harvard University Press, 1944)
Terrell   Carroll F. Terrell, *A Companion to The Cantos of Ezra Pound* (Berkeley and Los
              Angeles: University of California Press, 1980)

LIST OF FIGURES

INTRODUCTION

Pound is the inventor of Chinese poetry for our time.

T. S. Eliot[1]

I predict that the next century will see, even be dominated by, a dialogue between the U.S. and China in which Pound's poetry will take on an importance and weight not obvious at the moment: that not only has he woven a new wholeness, at any rate potential wholeness, out of European and American, but also of Chinese, elements.

Tom Scott[2]

No literary figure of the past century—in America or perhaps in any other Western country—is comparable to Ezra Pound (1885–1972) in the scope and depth of his exchange with China. To this day, scholars and students still find it puzzling that this influential poet spent a lifetime incorporating Chinese language, literature, history, and philosophy into Anglo-American modernism.

A package of notes and manuscripts Pound received from the widow of the American orientalist Ernest Fenollosa (1853–1908) in late 1913 first opened his eyes to the Imagist strength of Japanese Noh drama, Chinese classic poetry, and the Chinese written character. His 1915 volume *Cathay* from Fenollosa's Chinese poetry notes paved the way for his transition to high modernism. It also earned him recognition as "the inventor of Chinese poetry for our time." This first success led to his inquiry into Confucianism. In Guillaume Pauthier's French version of the Confucian Four Books (*Les quatre livres*) he discovered a philosophy that would correct Western civilization.[3] Consequently, Confucius recurs again and again in Pound's long poem *The Cantos*. His Canto 13 is a eulogy of Confucius' respect for the individual. Cantos 52–71 juxtapose early Republican America with China from Confucius' ideal kings Yao and Shun to Qing emperors Kangxi and Yongzheng as a way to suggest the right forms of government. Cantos 85 and 86 pay tribute to the Confucian tenets found in *Shu jing* or the Book of History, and Cantos 98 and 99 to Kangxi's "Sacred Edict." In the 1940s and early 1950s, Pound translated into English three of the Confucian Four Books and all 305 odes of the Confucian Book of Odes.[4]

How well did Pound know Chinese? How did he go about rendering Chinese texts into English? He is known to have owned a set of Robert Morrison's

[1] T. S. Eliot, introduction, *Selected Poems of Ezra Pound* (London: Faber and Faber, 1928), xvi.

[2] Tom Scott, "The Poet as Scapegoat," *Agenda*, 7/2 (1969), 57.

[3] Guillaume Pauthier, *Confucius et Mencius: Les quatre livres de philosophie morale et politique de la Chine* (1846; rpt. Paris: Librairie Garnier Frères, 1910).

[4] Ezra Pound, trans., "Confucius: The Unwobbling Pivot & The Great Digest," *Pharos*, 4 (Winter [1946] 1947); "The Analects," *Hudson Review*, 3/1 (Spring 1950); *The Classic Anthology Defined by Confucius* (Cambridge, Mass.: Harvard University Press, 1954).

multivolume *Dictionary of the Chinese Language* since 1914, carried a small Shanghai Commercial Press Chinese–English dictionary to the Disciplinary Training Center outside Pisa in 1945, and purchased a copy of *Mathews' Chinese–English Dictionary* around 1947.[5] Did he learn the Chinese language from dictionaries? Was he guided exclusively by eighteenth-to nineteenth-century orientalists' versions in his various Chinese projects?

Among the archival materials kept at the Beinecke Library of Yale University and the Lilly Library of Indiana University are over two hundred letters and postcards Pound received from his Chinese friends—F. T. Sung (1883–1940), Fengchi Yang (1908–70), Achilles Fang (1910–95), Veronica Huilan Sun (b. 1927), Carsun Chang (1886–1969), C. H. Kwock (b. 1920), Tze-chiang Chao (1913–c.1985), David Wang (1931–77), and P. H. Fang (b. 1923). Did Pound seek guidance from any of them? Those who have written about Pound and China have failed to address this fundamental question.[6] No one was able to do so until a few years ago since the letters Pound wrote to the above and other Chinese were sealed or had not been found.[7]

This book brings together 162 revealing letters between Pound and his Chinese friends, eighty-five of them newly opened up and none previously printed. Accompanied by my introductions and notes, these selected letters make available for the first time the forgotten stories of Pound and his Chinese

[5] See Robert Morrison, *A Dictionary of the Chinese Language, in Three Parts* (Macao: The Honorable East India Company Press, 1815); Zhang Tiemin, *Chinese–English Dictionary* (Shanghai: Commercial Press, 1933); R. H. Mathews, *Mathews' Chinese-English Dictionary* (Shanghai: China Inland Mission and Presbyterian Mission Press, 1931; rpt. Cambridge, Mass.: Harvard University Press, 1944).

[6] See Wai-lim Yip, *Ezra Pound's Cathay* (Princeton: Princeton University Press, 1969); John Nolde, *Blossoms from the East: The China Cantos of Ezra Pound* (Orono, Me.: National Poetry Foundation, 1983); Zhaoming Qian, *Orientalism and Modernism: The Legacy of China in Pound and Williams* (Durham, NC: Duke University Press, 1995); Mary Paterson Cheadle, *Ezra Pound's Confucian Translations* (Ann Arbor: University of Michigan Press, 1997); Ming Xie, *Ezra Pound and the Appropriation of Chinese Poetry* (New York: Garland Publishing, 1999); and Feng Lan, *Ezra Pound and Confucianism* (Toronto: University of Toronto Press, 2005). Cheadle is the only critic to have devoted some attention to Achilles Fang's impact on Pound. Nevertheless, relying on one side of their correspondence Cheadle's discussion of Pound and Fang is unavoidably less than satisfactory.

[7] In 1999 Mrs Ilse Fang lifted the seal her late husband Achilles Fang (1910–95) had fixed to 108 letters Pound wrote to him between 1950 and 1958. This breakthrough was followed by my discovery of six letters and a postcard of 1939–41 from Pound to Fengchi Yang in the private collection of Lionello Lanciotti (Rome). Pound's 1955-8 correspondence to David Wang was considered lost after Wang's mysterious death in 1977. Fortunately, in the mid-1970s Wang left a photocopy of the correspondence with Hugh Witemeyer. In 2003 Witemeyer graciously donated this photocopy (perhaps the only copy of the correspondence) to the Beinecke Library of Yale University. Meanwhile, Pound's surviving Chinese friend Angela Jung (Palandri) kindly permitted me access to six letters Pound wrote to her in 1952 and two letters Pound's companion Olga Rudge wrote to her on behalf of Pound in 1967. Furthermore, three postcards inappropriately filed in the Beinecke and Lilly Pound Archives escorted me to an "unknown" friend of Pound (P. H. Fang), a "lost" sourcebook, and two additional Pound letters. Once the newly-found Pound correspondence joined the Chinese friends' correspondence in the Pound Archives, the fascinating stories of Pound and his Chinese friends came to light.

friends. They illuminate a dimension in Pound's career that has been neglected: his dynamic interaction with people from China over a span of forty-five years from 1914 until 1959. This selection will also be a documentary record of a leading modernist's unparalleled efforts to pursue what he saw as the best of China, including both his stumbles and his triumphs.

This project has been conceived as a companion volume to *Orientalism and Modernism: The Legacy of China in Pound and Williams* (Durham, NC: Duke University Press, 1995) and *The Modernist Response to Chinese Art: Pound, Moore, Stevens* (Charlottesville: University of Virginia Press, 2003). Whereas my previous studies forgo personal dramas in favor of intertextual and inter-arts criticisms, this volume brings the influence of China into a lively and powerful social context. Rather than making their way through another critical work, readers will be able to hear Pound and his Chinese friends speak for themselves through their correspondence. And instead of weaving fragments of their exchanges into a study, I keep my critical opinions within my introductions to ten coherent dialogues. Pound's own words and his Chinese friends' words, rather than those of any critics, will make the most convincing arguments about Pound and China.

This book will matter to those who are interested in Ezra Pound as well as to those among the wider public who are interested in literary modernism and East Asian humanities. Catching exceptional glimpses of Pound's private dialogues with the Chinese, his shifting visions of China, and the evolution of his China-related works, *Ezra Pound's Chinese Friends* will stand to change the way we think of Pound and China, and modernism and China.

Scholars such as Carroll Terrell have identified Séraphin Couvreur's trilingual and James Legge's bilingual Book of History (*Shu jing*) as sources of Pound's Cantos 85–7; and Joseph Rock's monographs on the Naxi (Na-khi) ethnic group in China have been identified as guides for the Naxi passages in Cantos 101, 104, 110, 112, and 113.[8] But the correspondence included here will testify to the active involvement of his Chinese friends in these projects. Just as educator Pao Swen Tseng (1893–1978) offered Pound an oral translation of eight Chinese poems that led to his Seven Lakes Canto (Canto 49),[9] so Harvard scholar Achilles Fang prepared his use of *Shu jing* in Cantos 85–7 and Lijiang native P. H. Fang first introduced him to the Naxi rites of *Thrones* (1959) and *Drafts and Fragments* (1969). Relevant letters will also reveal that poet-translator Tze-chiang Chao, rather than Professor Lewis Maverick, dup up for Pound's Canto 106 the

---

[8] See Terrell, 466–7, 652–3, 713. See also Séraphin Couvreur, *Chou King* (Paris: Cathasia, 1950); Legge, iii; Joseph Rock, "The Romance of ²K'a-²mä-¹gyu-³mi-²gkyi, A Na-khi Tribal Love Story," *Bulletin de l'École Française d'Extrême-Orient*, 39 (1939), 1–155, plus 157–213; and "The ²Muan ¹Bpö Ceremony or the Sacrifice to Heaven as Practiced by the ¹Na-²khi," *Monumenta Serica: Journal of Oriental Studies of the Catholic University of Peking*, 13 (1948), 1–160.

[9] Angela Jung Palandri, "The 'Seven Lakes Canto' Revisited," *Paideuma*, 3/1 (Spring 1974), 51–4. See also Zhaoming Qian, *The Modernist Response to Chinese Art: Pound, Moore, Stevens* (Charlottesville: University of Virginia Press, 2003), 123–4.

seventh-century BC economist Guan Zhong (Kuan Chung). Before Pound
acquired a copy of Maverick's *Economic Dialogues in Ancient China* (1954), Chao
had already provided him with translations of Guan's sayings, biography, and a
chronology of the Chinese legalist tradition initiated by him.[10]

Among Pound's Confucian translations only *Ta Hio: The Great Learning of
Confucius* (1928) and *Confucius: Digest of the Analects* (1937) were made without the
aid of a Chinese.[11] In retranslating two of the Confucian Four Books into Italian
he obtained assistance from Fengchi Yang.[12] As to his late Confucian translations, Achilles Fang contributed more than a "Note on the Stone-Classics" to
The Great Digest & The Unwobbling Pivot (1951) and an introduction to *The Classic
Anthology Defined by Confucius* (1954).[13] He oversaw the production of the two
books from cover designs through corrections of romanized spellings and lining
up Chinese characters with English translations.

The letters will convince the reader that the exchange between Pound and
China was richer and more complex than often portrayed in modernist studies.
It is not always true that Anglo-American modernists and their Chinese coun-
terparts echo more than they differ. The anti-Confucian stance of F. T. Sung, for
instance, alienated Pound. During their meeting in London, Sung handed over
to Pound an article in English that criticized Confucian teachings. Despite his
disapproval Pound arranged to have it published in the London *Egoist*. This
article, along with a British orientalist's anti-Confucian piece, sparked Pound
into writing his first pro-Confucian essay, "The Words of Ming Mao 'Least
among the Disciples of Kung Fu-Tze'" (1914).[14] The opposite directions Pound
and his first Chinese contact took signal the complexities of East/West dialogue.

Although one may assume that the Chinese correspondents all speak respectfully, this shouldn't lead us to think they would not contradict Pound on
questions of principles. For example, Fengchi Yang, an "enemy alien" in
Mussolini's Italy, never flinched from resisting Pound's fascism. For two and a
half years the two debated in correspondence about China's war against Japan.
Every time Pound observed something provoking, Yang would jump to a blunt

[10] Lewis Maverick, ed., T'an Po-fu and Wen Kung-wen, trans., *Economic Dialogues in Ancient
China: Selections from the Kuan-tzu* (Carbondale, Ill.: Maverick, 1954).
[11] *Ta Hio: The Great Learning of Confucius* (Seattle: University of Washington Bookstore, 1928) was
based on Guillaume Pauthier's *Les quatre livres de philosophie morale et politique de la Chine*. Pound's
guide for *Confucius: Digest of the Analects* (Milan: Giovanni Scheiwiller, 1937) was James Legge's
bilingual edition of *The Four Books* (Shanghai: Commercial Press, 1923).
[12] Ezra Pound, trans., *Confucio: Ta S'eu. Dai Gaku. Studio integrale* (Rapallo: Scuola Tipografica
Orfanotrofio Emiliani, 1942); *Chiung Iung: L'Asse che non vacilla* (Venice: Casa Editrice delle Edizioni
Popolari, 1945).
[13] Achilles Fang, "A Note on the Stone-Classics," in *Confucius*, 11–15. Achilles Fang, Introduction
to *Classic Anthology*, xi–xviii.
[14] Ezra Pound, "The Words of Ming Mao 'Least among the Disciples of Kung-Fu-Tse,'" rpt. in
Poetry and Prose, i. 320.

rebuttal. Similarly, the Pound–Achilles Fang correspondence is best viewed as a prolonged, contentious dialogue between two learned men. It affords an unpredictable tale of collaboration and strife. Domineering as he was, Pound could be surprisingly flexible. Though his tone was always warm and civil, Achilles Fang frequently proved to be unyielding in his positions. He could be caustically critical of Pound's interpretation of one Confucian term and unexpectedly open to his definition of another. The most breathtaking letters between Pound and Achilles Fang perhaps occur in 1956–8 when their friendship was strained by the delays in the publication of a three-way, scholar's edition of the Confucian Book of Odes.

The letters gathered here document how much Chinese Pound understood at any given point. In September 1928 he confessed to his father that although he knew how the character worked, he could not read a Chinese poem: "For Cathay I had a crib made by Mori and Ariga . . . For your book Miss Thseng . . . read out the stuff to me" (Letter 8). Hugh Kenner told us that Pound's forte in 1936 was "looking up characters one by one in Morrison."[15] As late as 1941 he could do little more than that. On 7 November of that year he wrote: "I have had to think half a night to come up with an equivalent of the fire underneath what Morrison calls 'house'" (Letter 22). By 1951, nevertheless, he was able to read *Shu jing* in the original, "at least recogniz[ing] a few terms without having crib on next page" (Letter 31). *Shu jing* was one of many Chinese classics Achilles Fang sent him that spring. From *Shu jing* and *Yi jing* (Book of Changes) he moved on to *Tang Song qian jia shi* (Poems by a Thousand Tang and Song Poets) and *Chu ci* ('Southern Anthology'). A year later, he began borrowing Chinese anthologies also from Angela Jung. "[N]ot a lot all @ once as I still read very slowly," he stressed in a letter to her of 29 February 1952 (Letter 65). There are letters showing that by February 1957 he still had trouble comprehending writings such as Yongzheng's expansion of Kangxi's "Sacred Edict." He tried to get David Wang to translate into English Yongzheng's text, which he found "very damnbiguous" (Letter 149).

The letters selected for this volume also record Pound's engagement with Confucius during the early 1940s and throughout the 1950s. They not only disclose what editions Pound used and how much he understood at any one moment but also highlight the circumstances of his Confucian translations. Around 1940 Pound undertook to retranslate the Confucian Four Books into Italian. After finishing *Da xue* or *Ta S'eu* (1942) he originally planned to move to the fourth book, *Mencius*. It was Fenchi Yang's friend Sig. Tchu (Zhu Ying), who persuaded Pound to take up *Zhong yong* or *Chiung Iung* (1945) instead. As previous scholarship has shown, Pound was working on an Italian version of *Mencius* in May 1945 and his interest shifted to the third Confucian book, *Lun yu* or *The Analects,* when he was taken into detention outside Pisa.[16] In 1951–2, Achilles Fang succeeded in bringing his attention back to *Mencius.* Although Pound never resumed his translation of the fourth Confucian book, he incorporated some key Mencian notions into his *Rock-Drill* cantos. This volume includes letters illuminating Pound's otherwise baffling uses of the Mencian doctrine of "four TUAN" or the four virtuous beginnings of human nature. In the early 1950s Achilles Fang also prevailed on Pound to expand his reading of Confucius beyond the Four Books. It is true that after going over some of the "Thirteen Classics" with Achilles Fang, all Pound got to say was *"All answers are in the FOUR BOOKS."* But as it turned out, the opening *Rock-Drill* cantos center on *Shu jing,* which Achilles Fang hailed as "the liber librorum."

The correspondence calls into question several stereotypical assumptions about Pound's Confucianism. Some Pound scholars have pointed to Pound's Confucian studies during World War II as being responsible for his fascism.[17] Their opinion is based solely on Pound's misleading labeling of Confucian teachings as "totalitarian" and "fascist."[18] Drawing on Confucian works including those translated by Pound, Feng Lan has refuted this oversimplification.[19] The Pound–Yang correspondence will reinforce Lan's contention. In 1940–1 Pound's fascism grew so offensive that Yang began backing out from their correspondence. It was their mutual interest in the Confucian Four Books that saved it. As a Confucian, Yang saw Pound's enthusiasm for Italian fascism and his zeal for Confucianism as two separate preoccupations. Having learned of Pound's reading of the Four Books, Yang encouraged him to "occupy [himself] with this subject" (Letter 21), apparently with the intention of attracting him away from fascism.

Another problem in Pound scholarship is the tendency to overemphasize his exclusion of and hostility to Taoism and Buddhism. Pound was radically biased against Taoism and Buddhism during the 1930s and 1940s. Starting from the early 1950s, however, he opened himself up to non-Confucian Chinese traditions. In November 1951, after reading Arthur Waley's version of Taoist founder Laozi, he asked Achilles Fang: "Does Lao contain ANYTHING useful that is NOT in the Four Books (and their preludes, the Shih [Odes] and the Shu)?" (Letter 82). Seizing this opportunity, Fang brought up Laozi's most vocal proponent, Zhuang Zhou, as being "of great importance to sensible Confucians" (Letter 83). Between 1953 and 1956, moreover, Pound intermittently

---

[16] Hugh Kenner, *The Pound Era* (Berkeley and Los Angeles: University of California Press, 1971), 470. Ronald Bush, "Confucius Erased: The Missing Ideograms in The Pisan Cantos," in *Ezra Pound and China,* ed. Zhaoming Qian (Ann Arbor: University of Michigan Press, 2003), 163–92, esp. 167–8.

[17] See, e.g. Cheadle, *Ezra Pound's Confucian Translations,* 81.

[18] For Pound's labeling of Confucius as "totalitarian" and "fascist," see *SP,* 85; *Guide to Kulchur* (1938; New York: New Directions, 1970), 279; and Romano Bilenchi, "Rapallo 1941," *Paideuma,* 8/3 (Winter 1979), 431–42, esp. 435.

[19] Lan, *Ezra Pound and Confucianism,* 216–17.

chatted with P. H. Fang about the mysterious Naxi rites that fuse Confucian ancestral worship with Taoism and Buddhism. Their conversations, along with Joseph Rock's descriptions of the Naxi rites, inspired Pound's haunting poetry about the "wind sway" ceremony that focuses on possibilities of life after death, a departure from Canto 13, where Confucius is quoted as saying "nothing of the 'life after death.' "[20] Going over all of this material makes it easy to understand why in the mid-1950s Pound would admit his oversight to William McNaughton: "There's no doubt I missed something in Taoism and Buddhism. Clearly, there's something valid, meaningful, in those religions."[21]

No stereotypical portrayal of Pound's China is more widespread than his association with an approach that dismisses phonetic elements in the Chinese language. This association has to do with Pound's promotion of Fenollosa's essay "The Chinese Written Character as a Medium for Poetry" (1919, 1936).[22] For George Kennedy this essay is "a small mass of confusion" based on a "complete misunderstanding" of the Chinese language.[23] For James Liu it is responsible for the fallacy "common among Western readers outside sinological circles, namely, that *all* Chinese characters are pictograms or ideograms."[24] The aim of Fenollosa's essay is to push for concrete, natural thinking and writing as suggested by the primitive Chinese character. Nowhere in his essay does Fenollosa claim that *"all* Chinese characters are pictograms or ideograms." What he states is that *"a large number of the primitive* Chinese characters, even the so-called radicals, are shorthand pictures of actions or processes" (emphasis added).[25] Fenollosa does not altogether deny the existence of sounds in the Chinese character. Instead he stresses that the Chinese character "speaks at once with the vividness of painting, and with the mobility of sounds."[26] But yet in the second half of the past century the critical opinion of Kennedy and Liu

[20] For Emily Mitchell Wallace, Canto 110/797–8 "focuses not on the manner of death or ways of dying, but on ways of responding to the death of a loved one and to the possibilities of life after death." See Wallace, " 'Why Not Spirits?'—'The Universe Is Alive': Ezra Pound, Joseph Rock, the Na Khi, and Plotinus," in *Ezra Pound and China*, ed. Qian, 213–77, esp. 252.

[21] See William McNaughton, "A Report on the 16th Biennial International Conference on Ezra Pound, Brantôme, France, 18–22 July, 1995," *Paideuma*, 27/1 (Spring 1998), 130.

[22] Ernest Fenollosa, "The Chinese Written Character as a Medium for Poetry," ed. Ezra Pound, *Little Review*, 6/5–8 (1919). Ernest Fenollosa, *The Chinese Written Character as a Medium for Poetry*, ed. Ezra Pound (London: Stanley Nott, 1936).

[23] George Kennedy, "Fenollosa, Pound, and the Chinese Character," *Yale Literary Magazine*, 126/5 (1958), 26–36.

[24] James J. Y. Liu, *The Art of Chinese Poetry* (Chicago: University of Chicago Press, 1961), 3.

[25] Ernest Fenollosa, *The Chinese Character as a Medium for Poetry*, ed. Ezra Pound (1936; rpt. San Francisco: City Lights Books, 1968), 9.

[26] Ibid. Thanks are due to Haun Saussy, who called my attention to passages in Fenollosa's manuscript (at Yale) about the sounds and rhythmical patterns of Chinese verse, which EP elected to drop when he published it in 1919. See *Fenollosa/Pound, The Chinese Written Character as a Medium for Poetry: A Critical Edition*, ed. Haun Saussy, Jonathan Stalling, and Lucas Klein (New York: Fordham University Press, 2008).

was echoed and reechoed until Fenollosa's name, along with Pound's, became synonymous with the so-called pictographic approach, an approach that refuses to recognize phonetic elements in Chinese.

Defenders of Fenollosa and Pound assert that the essay is intended not for philologists and students of the Chinese language but for poets and students of creative writing. In Pound's words, Fenollosa "did not claim that the average Chinese journalist uses this instrument as a 'medium for poetry' but that it can and has been so used."[27] This argument is valid, but it cannot clear away the condemnation of Pound's disregard of Chinese sound in favor of its pictorial quality. The correspondence in this volume will bring our attention to the changes in Pound's understanding of the Chinese language. After all, he did not ignore the value of Chinese sound throughout his career.[28]

Elsewhere I have shown that in the late Cantos Pound's use of Chinese is both pictographic and phonetic.[29] Cantos 85–9 and 96–8 are replete with Chinese characters accompanied by their phonetic symbols. Canto 99 experiments with English–Chinese mixed alliteration. Canto 110 even offers a single-line poem in Chinese syllables: "yüeh$^{4.5}$ | ming^2 | mo$^{4.5}$ | hsien^1 | p'eng^2." The correspondence will confirm that in the early 1950s Pound made strenuous efforts to learn the pronunciation of Chinese characters. In a letter of February 1951 to Achilles Fang, Pound inquired, "What could save infinite time and labour fer pore mutts trying to learn a little chinese, esp/ SOUND" (Letter 32). In another letter to Fang (February 1952) he expressed his regret for not having done so earlier: "For years I never made ANY attempt to hitch ANY sound to the ideograms, content with the meaning and the visual form" (Letter 56). Later that year, when Angela Jung reminded him that he had belittled the usefulness of Chinese sound, he protested: "one's opinions change ... He should not be held responsible for what he said or wrote decades earlier."[30] During that period Pound was also trying to learn some conversational Chinese from visiting Chinese student Veronica Huilan Sun. In a letter to Fang (12 October 1951) he made an attempt to distinguish between the Shanghai dialect and the so-called Mandarin Chinese: "Very hard for senile ignoramus to attain vocal fluidity. What does Ni hao ma? [How are you?] sound like in the North Kepertl [Beijing]?

---

[27] EP's 1958 typescript entitled "Mori's Lectures on the History of Chinese Poetry" kept at Beinecke. For a French version, see EP's note to Mary de Rachewiltz, trans., *Catai* (Milan: Strenna del Pesce d'Oro, 1960), 45.

[28] Pound discovered the existence of Chinese sound in the mid-1930s, though he did not recognize its importance until about 1950. On 11 March 1937 he told Katue Kitasono: "When I did *Cathay*, I had no inkling of the technique of sound, which I am now convinced *must* exist or have existed in Chinese poetry." See EP, *Selected Letters 1907–1941*, ed. D. D. Paige (1950; New York: New Directions, 1971), 293.

[29] Qian, *Modernist Response to Chinese Art*, 217–20.

[30] Quoted in Angela Jung Palandri, "Homage to a Confucian Poet," *Paideuma*, 3/3 (Winter 1974), 307.

A rose of Shanghai pronounces: 'manchu,' in way almost impos / disting / fr / 'damn yankee' " (Letter 80).

One further evidence of how hard Pound worked at the detail of Chinese sound and sense is a typescript of forty-five pages entitled "Preliminary Survey," which he sent to Achilles Fang in January 1951 (Beinecke; see Appendix below). "It is even permitted us to suppose that the original Chinese speech was not only inflected but also agglutinative," he contended. As a poet he was looking for sound symbolism. Even with practically no access to archaic Chinese pronunciation, he speculated: "Despite exceptions a good many ch sounds can be read as indicative of place or of motion . . . YUAN in a number of cases has clearly to do with circling, enclosing . . . MEI and MENG are in certain cases dark, from definite black ink to young ignorance." Fang did not think much of O. Z. Tsang's *Complete Chinese–English Dictionary* (1920), upon which Pound based his abandoned survey. However, he admired Pound's interpretation of the Confucian word chih (zhi) 止 as "the point of rest" and "the hitching post sign": "[Y]our interpretation of 止 seems to solve a number of knotty problems in Kung's book" (Letter 30).

It is Pound's China-related cantos and Confucian translations that draw me to these letters. And these letters will in turn lead the reader back to these same cantos and translations. Two cases in point are *Rock-Drill* and *Thrones*. These two works contain some of everyone's favorite modernist lyrics, but not everyone has understood them very well. The most reliable commentaries on them are in these letters. In 1952–8, when *Rock-Drill* and *Thrones* were being shaped, Pound communicated with his Chinese friends almost daily. A wealth of Chinese materials they discussed made their way into these cantos. *Ezra Pound's Chinese Friends* should be read in conjunction with them. The characters, concepts, and other Chinese references covered in specific contexts frequently anticipate those of the *Rock-Drill* and *Thrones* cantos; consequently the exchanges clarify most if not all of the late cantos' Chinese obscurities.

Pound befriended not some ordinary Chinese individuals but a group of outstanding Chinese scholars and poets. Among them were some of China's most eminent educators of the past century. F. T. Sung was one of the first Chinese to teach mineralogy at Beijing University.[31] Pao Swen Tseng, who founded a girls' college in Hunan, central China, in 1918, may well have been China's first female college president. Carsun Chang, a renowned political science professor and Confucian thinker, was China's delegate to the 1945 United Nations Conference, signing the "Charter of the United Nations." Before joining Harvard in 1947 to work on a Chinese–English dictionary project,

---

[31] Cui Yunhao, "Woguo jinxiandai kuangwuxue jiaoyu de chansheng yu fazhan" (The Origin and Development of China's Mineralogical Education), *Zhongguo dizhi jiaoyu* (Geological Education in China) (1995), ii. 69–72. Thanks are due to Chunchang Li for calling my attention to this article.

Achilles Fang had already enjoyed a reputation as a formidable scholar of Chinese among Western students in Beijing. The rest of the group either had been or would shortly afterward become university professors. Their respective relationships with Pound and contributions to his visions of China are summarized in my introductions to the chapters into which the letters are divided.

NOTES ON THE TEXT

Approximately four hundred letters, postcards, and telegrams between Ezra Pound and his Chinese friends have been found in three Ezra Pound archives and three private collections. Printed here are 162 of them. In making a selection, I have tried to focus on those with significant information about the way Pound sought guidance from his Chinese friends; the literary, cultural, and political exchanges between Pound and these friends; and the shaping and publication history of Pound's works.

Excerpts from four letters Pound wrote to his parents Homer and Isabel Pound (Beinecke) have been included to document his 1928 encounter with Pao Swen Tseng, who offered Pound translation of eight Chinese poems that contributed to Canto 49.

Pound's letters to F. T. Sung and Carsun Chang are unfortunately lost. To fill up the gaps, I have included in chapter 1 on Pound–Sung Pound's introductory note to Sung's *Egoist* article and in chapter 6 on Pound–Chang two letters C. H. Kwock wrote to Pound on behalf of Chang and a memoir of Pound and Carsun Chang by William McNaughton.

All but four letters from Pound to his parents (Letters 4–8) and two letters from Achilles Fang to Pound (Letters 28, 38) are reproduced in full. What have been deleted from Letters 4–8 are irrelevant passages, and what have been omitted from Letters 28 and 38 are lengthy Latin/French quotations whose sources are given in notes. Deletions and omissions are designated by the mark [...]. Fifteen letters in Italian (Letters 9–23) are followed by English translations within square brackets.

The selected items are numbered in chronological sequence. The headings, closings, and signatures of all the letters and postcards have been regularized. The dates and return places within square brackets are from internal evidence or from postmarks.

In transcribing the selections, my aim has been to make them accurate and readable. Non-standard spelling, punctuation, and capitalization, whether intentional or accidental, have been reproduced. To tidy up such deviations would destroy the original flavor. Editorial clarifications and translations of foreign words are inserted between square brackets. Pound's and his friends' own inserts are placed within angle brackets.

Annotations of figures, places, and works are at the end of most items. In addition, a biographical glossary has been compiled in order to reduce the number of notes in the body of the text.

Pound used several different systems of romanized spellings of Chinese characters. These include the French system adopted by Guillaume Pauthier and the English (Wade) system adopted by James Legge and R. H. Mathews. In my introductions and notes, except for established usage, I give the pinyin spellings along with Pound's and others' versions. Frequently used Chinese names and titles are indexed in the variant forms with cross-references.

I am deeply grateful to Mary de Rachewiltz and Omar Pound, without whose active involvement and support this book would not have been possible. I am thankful to Diana Chang, C. H. Kwock, Ilse Fang, P. H. Fang, Lionello Lanciotti, Angela Jung Palandri, and Hongru Song, without whose warm hospitality this volume would not have been so rich.

I wish to thank Mary de Rachewiltz for guiding me to Fengchi Yang's literary executor Lionello Lanciotti; Angela Jung Palandri for introducing me to Carsun Chang's daughter Diana Chang; and Gary Gach for putting me in touch with Carsun Chang's and Tze-chiang Chao's friend C. H. Kwock. Emily Mitchell Wallace certainly did know that by sharing with me a newly unearthed letter from Joseph Rock to Pound she would lead me to three neglected cards in two Pound Archives, which in turn led me to the forgotten Pound's friend P. H. Fang. Through strenuous efforts Chunchang Li traced the grandnephew of Pound's first Chinese correspondent F. T. Sung. Despite my resolution, I have failed to locate every single one of the book's copyright holders. Upon notification my publisher and I would be pleased to correct the omissions in the next edition or reprint of this work.

I greatly appreciate the assistance of many research libraries and individuals. Special thanks are due to Linda Briscoe Myers, Assistant Curator of Photography at the Harry Ransom Humanities Research Center (University of Texas at Austin); Yingxing Xie, Librarian at the Tunghai University Library (Taiwan); Saundra Taylor, Curator of Manuscripts at the Lilly Library (Indiana University); and Patricia Willis, Curator of the Yale Collection of American Literature at the Beinecke Rare Book and Manuscript Library (Yale University). My profound thanks go to Hugh Witemyer, who provided the only surviving copies of Ezra Pound's letters to David Wang.

William McNaughton was unusually generous with his time and knowledge of Pound and his St Elizabeths circle, helping me with the details of my annotations. I am thankful to him also for contributing to this volume a memoir of "What Pound and Carsun Chang Talked about at St Elizabeths."

I am indebted to all Pound scholars. Donald Gallup's *Ezra Pound: A Bibliography* (Charlottesville: University Press of Virginia, 1983); Carroll Terrell's *A Companion to The Cantos of Ezra Pound* (Berkeley and Los Angeles: University of California Press, 1980); and Omar Pound's and Robert Spoo's *Ezra and Dorothy Pound: Letters in Captivity, 1945–1946* (New York: Oxford University Press, 1999) were indispensable guides. Other invaluable aids were Ilse Fang's "Bibliography of Achilles Fang," *Monumenta Serica*, 45 (1997); Roger Jeans' *Democracy and Socialism in Republican China: The Politics of Zhang Junmai[Carsun Chang] 1906–1941*

(Oxford: Rowman & Littlefield, 1997); Lionello Lanciotti's "Un carteggio inedito di Ezra Pound," *Catai*, 1/2 (1981); Angela Jung Palandri's "Homage to a Confucian Poet," *Paideuma*, 3/3 (1974); Pao Swen Tseng's *Huiyilu* (Taipei: Longwen Publishing House, 1989); Emily Mitchell Wallace's " 'Why Not Spirits?'—'The Universe Is Alive': Ezra Pound, Joseph Rock, the Na Khi, and Plotinus," in *Ezra Pound and China*, ed. Zhaoming Qian (Ann Arbor: University of Michigan Press, 2003); and Hugh Witemeyer's "The Strange Progress of David Hsin-fu Wand," *Paideuma*, 15/2 & 3 (1986).

Articles based on my research for Chapters 3 and 10 have appeared in *Letterature d'America* (Rome) and *Modernism Revisited: Transgressing Boundaries and Strategies of Renewal in American Poetry* (Amsterdam: Rodopi, 2007). I thank Cristina Giorcelli (editor of *Letterature d'America)* and Viorica Patea (co-editor of *Modernism Revisited)* for their feedback.

Without the aid of four remarkable colleagues I would not have been able to deal with three foreign languages in the Pound–China exchanges. Tanya Stampfl and Patricia Cockram spent numerous hours helping me translate into English fifteen letters and cards in Italian. Massimo Bacigalupo gave generously his time and expertise in Pound and Italian culture. Rayford Shaw assisted me with Greek and Latin quotations.

For their assistance I am grateful to Aleli Astok (California Institute of Integral Studies), Marcella Spann Booth, April Caprak (Burke Library, Hamilton College), Ida Chen (Tunghai University), Sheila Connor (Arnold Arboretum Library), John-Emmett Cooley (Catholic University of America), Nancy Cricco (New York University), Igor de Rachewiltz, Erika Dowell (Lilly Library, Indiana University), Daniel Gonzalez, David Gordon, Sarah Hartwell (Rauner Special Collections, Dartmouth College), Panchita Hawley, Anjiang Hu (Sun Yat-sen University, China), Jill Hughes, Steve Jones (Beinecke Library, Yale University), Everett Lee Lady (University of Hawaii), Zidan Li (Sun Yat-sen University, China), Federico Masini (University of Rome), Dennis Palmore (New Directions Publishing Corporation), Judith Pardo, Andrew Qian, Tim Qian, Jane Stoeffler (Catholic University of America), Shenru Tu, Don Walker (University of the Pacific), Jeffery Yang (New Directions Publishing Corporation), and Tao Yang (East Asian Library, Yale University).

As always, my wife May was a source of inspiration and comfort. She encouraged me to resurrect the forgotten stories of Pound's Chinese friends and supported the trying quest faithfully till its completion.

This six-year project was completed in the wake of Hurricane Katrina. Thanks should go to Wendy Stallard Flory, Christine Froula, David Quint, Yulin and Haun Saussy, Ronald Schuchard, and Patricia Willis, who supported me in various ways when I was displaced by the Storm. With library privileges at Emory and a Visiting Fellowship at Yale I was able to continue my research and writing in the fall of 2005.

I owe a debt of gratitude to Ronald Bush, David Moody, and Haun Saussy, who read the entire manuscript in draft form and offered valuable scholarly suggestions. Marjorie Perloff read an early version of the general introduction. Massimo Bacigalupo read a chapter. Special thanks are due to them as well as to George Bornstein and Claude Rawson for their wise counsel.

The preparation of this book was also aided by a University of New Orleans Research Professorship and a Franklin Research Grant from the American Philosophical Society. I am thankful to Daniel Albright, Linda Blanton, George Bornstein, Robert Cashner, John Cooke, Wendy Stallard Flory, Susan Krantz, Cristanne Miller, Ira Nadel, Marjorie Perloff, Peter Schmidt, Peter Schock, and Patricia Willis for their incredible friendship and support.

Finally, I wish to thank my editor Andrew McNeillie for his enthusiasm. Thanks are also due to my research assistant Daniel McBride, who helped with indexing, and to Jacqueline Baker, Fiona Smith, and Rowena Anketell, who saw this volume through the press.

I

F. T. Sung's China Plan for Pound
"China is interesting, VERY"

In 1968, during an interview for an Italian documentary, Ezra Pound expressed his regret at not having been to China. When asked, "Is this a disappointment for you, not to have seen China, which inspired you so much?" he replied, "Yes, I have always wanted to see China" (*Poetry and Prose*, x. 317). In this exchange, Pound was no doubt sadly reminded of his unfulfilled 1914 plan to travel from London to Beijing to be reunited with his parents.

The man who invited Ezra Pound and his father to visit China was Far-san T. Sung (Song Faxiang 宋 發 祥, 1883–1940). With BS and MS degrees from Ohio Wesleyan University (1903, 1906) and the University of Chicago (1907), Sung had taught chemistry and mineralogy at Beijing University (1908–12). After the Sun Yat-sen Revolution that overthrew China's last emperor in 1911, Sung joined the government of the Republic of China (see Fig. 1.1). In late December 1913, as Inspector General of Mints under the Chinese Ministry of Finance, he visited the Philadelphia branch of the US Mint, where he met deputy assayer Homer Pound and offered to find him a job in China. To this Ezra Pound responded on 4 January 1914: "China is interesting, VERY" (Beinecke). Two weeks later Sung traveled to London and made the same offer to Ezra, enabling him to write cheerfully to his father: "We may yet be a united family" (ibid). Ezra Pound's enthusiasm for China is no surprise. That winter he had gotten wise to Confucianism from Guillaume Pauthier's French translation of the Confucian Four Books (*Les quatre livres*, 1846; rpt. 1910) and he had been exposed to Chinese poetry through Herbert A. Giles' *A History of Chinese Literature* (1901). Moreover, he had received from Mary Fenollosa her late husband's notes on Chinese classic poetry and Japanese Noh drama in order to edit two anthologies—*Cathay* (1915) and *"Noh" or Accomplishment* (1917).

Upon his return to Beijing, Sung began corresponding with Pound: "I have already sent two inquiries for a position for you in China and have seen a few men and [will] see if I can make them give you a good position" (Letter 1). In his next letter, however, he admitted that finding a suitable job for Pound was not as easy as he had thought. Pound certainly would not want to be a translator.

Besides, he and Dorothy Shakespear were getting married. The China plan would have to be called off.

Sung turned out to be a caustic critic of Confucius. Interestingly, his criticism of Confucianism appears in an article Pound arranged to have published in the London *Egoist*, 1/6 (16 March 1914), 1/7 (1 April 1914), 1/10 (15 May 1914). In the article ("The Causes and Remedy of the Poverty of China") Sung compared China negatively with America, admiring American economists' adherence to the principle of production and consumption and denouncing the Confucian admonition against material "desires" and "appetites." The Chinese had been taught to be "satisfied in poverty," he contended, "hence the present poverty."

There is little doubt that Pound did not agree with Sung. His disapproval is evident in his introductory note to the article:

The following MSS. was left with me by a Chinese official. I might have treated it in various ways. He suggested that I should rewrite it. I might excerpt the passages whereof I disapprove but I prefer to let it alone. At a time when China has replaced Greece in the intellectual life of so many occidentals, it is interesting to see in what way the occidental ideas are percolating into the orient. We have here the notes of a practical and technical Chinaman. There are also some corrections, I do not know by whom, but I leave them as they are. (*Poetry and Prose*, i. 229)

By stating that "I might excerpt the passages whereof I disapprove," Pound articulated his skepticism about Sung's analysis of the causes of China's poverty. And by referring to China as a nation that had in the new century "replaced Greece in the intellectual life of so many occidentals," he squarely challenged Sung's negative assessment of China's place in the modern world.

Sung's anti-Confucian article led Pound inevitably back to a scrutiny of Pauthier's Confucian Four Books. Confucius' admonition against material appetites, he would find out, was not for the general public but for future government administrators. After reading William Loftus Hare's "Chinese Egoism" in *Egoist*, 1/23 (1 December 1914), Pound got a chance to respond implicitly to Sung. In his article Hare contrasted Confucius unfavorably with the third-century BC hedonist philosopher Yang Zhu. For Yang Zhu, Hare reported, a person's joy was in the world's materials. Confucius, with an everlasting reputation, never had a day's gaiety, whereas King Jie and King Zhou "had the joy of gratifying their desires," which "no infamy can take away." Sung was astute enough not to associate his anti-Confucianism with Yang Zhu. Nevertheless, like Yang he aimed his assault at the sage's indifference to material gratifications. In "The Words of Ming Mao 'Least among the Disciples of Kung-Fu-Tse'" (*Egoist*, 1/24 (15 December 1914); rpt. *Poetry and Prose*, i: 320), Pound derided the denigrators' dependence on "all things save [the human mind]," whose thirst for knowledge and aesthetic pleasures Confucius held to be vital to the fulfillment of life. Overtly a critique of Hare's tribute to Yang Zhu's self-indulgent egoism, Pound's first essay on Confucius also served as a rejoinder to Sung's overemphasis on material appetites at the cost of Confucian teachings.

Like his fellow American expatriate Henry James, Pound hated despotism and believed the importance of "recognition of differences, of the right of differences to exist" (*LE*, 298). In Pauthier's Confucius he seems to have found a philosopher, a cultural hero, who shared their modernist values. While affirming social responsibility the Chinese sage also stressed the relevance of individual dignity. To Pound such a philosopher could serve as an antidote against evils in the West. In "Imaginary Letter VII," which would appear in the March 1918 issue of the *Little Review,* he would condemn Christianity as having been reduced to one principle, " 'Thou shalt attend to thy neighbour's business in preference to thine own,'" thus hampering individuality and freedom of speech. Backing up this criticism would be an English version of an excerpt from the Confucian *Analects*. In it Confucius would be shown to value four of his disciples' diametrically different responses to his question, "What would you do" if recognized? His translation based on Pauthier would in 1924 be turned into verse, forming a pivotal part of Canto 13, the Confucian Canto.

Without any knowledge of the degree to which Confucianism had been corrupted, Pound unavoidably wondered how China could remedy its problems—what Sung described as "the corruption of the internal administration, the weakness of our army, the deplorable condition of our finance, and the misery of the people"—by abandoning its Confucian tradition. To Pound nothing seemed wrong with Confucian teachings. Sung and his fellow Chinese modernists just had to distinguish Confucianism from the political system of old China.

It is ironic that at a moment when the Chinese modernists were breaking from Confucianism in their search for a modern nation, Pound as their Anglo-American counterpart was moving in a contrary direction, reclaiming the humanist values of the Confucian tradition. From his initial engagement with China, Pound took a stance that was dramatically different from his predecessors and peers. Whereas other Westerners, as Edward Said has asserted, explored the Orient "for dominating, restructuring, and having authority over [it]" (*Orientalism* (New York: Random House, 1978), 3), Pound looked to China for an alternative to modernity. This attitude would puzzle—even shock—Sung and his contemporaries in their attempt to replace Confucianism with a Western model.

In the next few years, as Pound journeyed toward an imaginary China (see Fig. 1.2), inventing Li Bo in *Cathay,* Confucius in "Imaginary Letter VII," and Song Yu (Sō-Gyoku) in ur-Canto 4 (1919), his interest in F. T. Sung waned. On 23 January 1919, for some unknown reason, he wrote Sung perhaps his last letter, which is acknowledged in the latter's reply of 16 March 1919. In that reply, Sung, then appointed political adviser to the Chinese president's office, once more spoke of his China plan for Ezra Pound: "Do you still think of coming to China? If so, I would like to make arrangements for your coming" (Letter 4).

Fig. 1.1. F. T. Sung, 1914. From *Who's Who in China* (Shanghai: *China Weekly Review,* 1931). (Yale University Library)

Fig. 1.2. EP in London, 1916. (Beinecke)

1   *Sung to EP (TLS-1; Beinecke)*

31 Hsin Kai Lu
Peking
China
Via Siberia
Feb. the 8th [1914]

My dear Mr Pound:

I am writing you a line to tell you that I have received the package which you kindly forwarded to me. Enclosed please find a cheque for one shilling, which I hope will cover yours that you had advanced for me in Registration fee and stamps.

I returned to Peking on the 31st Ult. I expected to go to [the] South immediately upon my return, but I found it is not possible for me to do so until later. So I am settled in Peking for a few months.

My present address is 31 Hsin Kai Lu, Peking.

I will send you a copy of [an] English book dealing with Chinese affairs as soon as my baggages [baggage] come which have been sent by freight from New York City.

I have already sent two inquiries for a position for you in China and have seen a few men and [will] see if I can make them give you a good position. They ask me to get your academic records, etc. So if you will be kind enough to send it [them] to me, it will be a great advantage. I think I can get a fairly good position for you. We will see what can be done.

Hoping to hear from you and with best wishes,

I am,   Faithfully yours,
                          [signed] Far T. Sung

[Longhand postscript:] If there is any mail for me, please forward it to me at the above address. S.

2   *Sung to EP (TLS-1; Beinecke)*

E 31 Hsin Kai Lu
Peking
Via Siberia.
April 14. 1914.

My dear Mr Pound:

I have sent you a copy of [a] book on "Passing the Manchu" by parcel post some few days ago. I hope you will soon receive it. When you get through with it, please return it to me.

Now in regard to your coming out to Peking, I have been trying very hard to get a suitable position for you but so far I have not been able. I have found a position about 200.00 = £20 per month as a translator. If you feel like it, please let me know. It might be all right for you for the beginning, but I am rather afraid that you do not like it. I am looking for a good position for you.

Have you finished the papers that I handed over to you while in London? If so, please send it to my sister. Her address is Miss Mildred Y. Sung, 50 Nevins Street, The Harriet Judson, Brooklyn, N.Y., USA. I am sure she will appreciate what you have done for her.

Do you know any Chinese in London? My brother-in-law is now in London. I think he lives in 42 Hillfield Road, West Hampstead, London, N.W. His name is Dr. W.C. Chen who is working also in the newspaper work, I think. I have no letters from him yet. I hope you will call on him mentioning my name. I am sure he will be very much interested in you and your work. He used to be the chief Editor of Peking Daily News which I have shown you while in London or your father has sent it to you, I think.

If I can be of any other service to you, please let me know. I have been hoping to hear from you and do hope to have your letter soon.

With best wishes, I am,

Faithfully Yours,
[signed] Far T. Sung

3 *Sung to EP* (TLS-1; Beinecke)

31 Hsin Kai Lu
Peking
July 3rd, 1914.

My dear Mr Pound:

Accept my congratulations for your happy union and newly married life. I wish you great success.

I am sorry that you have changed your plan that you are coming to Peking to join me. I hope sometime in the near future you can come to pay me a visit.

I may return to London this fall, if I can arrange it. Please do not plan to go to Spain. If you want to have a trip, better come to China.

In regard to the article on "China's poverty," I thank you for its having published in that paper which is owned by you.

I would like to ask you to finish that speech for my sister as early as you can and send it to her. Her address is Miss Mildred Y. Sung, 50 Nevins Street, Brooklyn, NY. Put in as much funny stories as you can for illustrations. I certainly appreciate your kindness and troubles in helping me so much and if I can reciprocate in any way, kindly let me know at any time. Perhaps your Mrs. want[s] some thing from China and if so, please let me know.

I hope you have received my book which I sent you quite a long time ago.

Hoping to hear from you occasionally and with best wishes, I am,

Faithfully Yours,
[signed] Far T. Sung

your happy union: EP married DP (1886–1973) in London on 20 April 1914. See *Ezra Pound and Dorothy Shakespear: Their Letters 1909–1914*, ed. Omar Pound and A. Walton Litz (New York: New Directions, 1984).

that paper which is owned by you: *The Egoist* published in London from 1914 to 1919. It was founded by Dora Marsden (1882–1960) and edited by Harriet Shaw Weaver (1876–1961) with Richard Aldington (1892–1962), Hilda Doolittle (1886–1961), and T. S. Eliot (1888–1965) successively as subeditor.

4   *Sung to EP (TLS-1; Beinecke)*

1 Shih Chia Hutung
Peking
Mar 16, 19

Dear Mr Pound:

Your most welcome letter of 23/1/1919 was duly received with many thanks. I am glad to learn that you are keeping well and happy in your work.

Did you ever meet Dr W C Chen in the Chinese Legation in London? He is my brother-in-law and I think is teaching in the University of London. I am sure he will be very glad to meet you.

I may go abroad again some time next year. If so, I will write you in advance. My wife talks of going to the States this summer and probably goes to London to see her brother. Nothing has been definite yet.

When you write to your father at Philadelphia, please remember me to him. I am still remembering what a nice time I had with him while in his city.

I have moved to 1 Shih Chia Hutung two years <ago> and now settled here definitely. I would like to have these articles of mine published in your magazine some years ago. I have never received them <before>.

Do you still think of coming to China? If so, I would like to make arrangements for your coming.

With best wishes, I am,

Most sincerely yours,
[signed] Fartsan T. Sung

2
Miss Tseng and the Seven Lakes Canto
"Descendant of Kung and Thseng-Tsu"

One day in early 1928, in the middle of reading the galleys of *Ta Hio: The Great Learning of Confucius* (1928), his retranslation of the first of the Confucian Four Books, Pound remembered a picture book with Chinese and Japanese ideograms that he had seen at his Aunt Frank's Manhattan boarding-house. Had his parents retrieved the book? Yes, they had. By late February the old book traveled across the Atlantic to Rapallo, Italy, where Pound had moved in 1924. Decades later, in a discarded fragment for *The Cantos,* Pound would identify this volume as the source of the Seven Lakes Canto: "and my gr aunt's third husband | received in ms | from a friend | the 49th canto" (Beinecke).

Now in Pound's daughter Mary de Rachewiltz's collection, the relic is a fourteen-fold screen book made by a nineteenth-century Japanese artist. It consists of eight ink paintings, eight poems in Chinese, and eight poems in Japanese, mutually representing eight classic scenes about the shores of the Xiao and Xiang Rivers in Hunan, central China (see Figs. 2.1 and 2.2). While Pound was completely comfortable with translating the visual details into verse, he was not able to decipher the eight Chinese poems drawn in three calligraphic styles, not even with the aid of Robert Morrison's multivolume *Dictionary of the Chinese Language.*

By curious coincidence, a friend of Dorothy's was hosting a visitor from China, "a returned missionary" on her way to an international missionary conference in Jerusalem. Dorothy promptly went up the hill to see her. Although the visitor was leaving the next day for Jerusalem, she said if Pound could wait until she stopped by Rapallo again on her way back to China, she would be happy to look at the eight untranslated Chinese poems. Ezra was struck by the visitor's ancestral background. She was a descendant of Confucius' disciple Zeng Xi (Thseng-sie or Tseng Hsi). In April, when *Ta Hio* was out, he would be able to show Miss Tseng his version of "The Explanation of Thseng-Tseu [Zeng Xi]" (in ten chapters) following the Testimony of Confucius. A few years earlier, he must have told her, he had re-created a dialogue between her ancestor and his master in Canto 13, the Confucian Canto:

And Thseng-sie desired to know:
  "Which had answered correctly?"
And Kung said, "They have all answered correctly,
  "That is to say, each in his nature."

(Canto 13/58)

The visitor, Pao Swen Tseng (Zeng Baosun 曾 寶 蓀, 1893–1978), turned out to be the right person to interpret the eight Chinese poems for Pound (see Fig. 2.3). She was from Xiangxiang, Hunan, the Seven Lakes region. From her Pound could have learned practically everything about China's tradition of "mak[ing] pictures & poems on that set of scenes" (Letter 6), a tradition carried on even as far as Korea and Japan. More interestingly, Miss Tseng was also a poet. Among her published poems in Chinese are "Xiangxiang" and "Changsha," depicting the very scenes of the screen book. Educated at Mary Vaughan, a missionary school in Shanghai, and the University of London's Westfield College, Miss Tseng spoke perfect English. Moreover, she was the founding president of a girls' college in Hunan called Yifang. She would remain in that capacity for twenty-three years from 1918 to 1938 and from 1946 to 1949.

We know of no correspondence between Pound and Miss Tseng. However, certain details of their encounter and the fruit it bore can be gleaned from other sources. On 17 May 1928 Pound told Glenn Hughes of the University of Washington that he had "Conferred with descendant of Kung and Thseng-Tsu [Zeng Xi] just before leaving Rapallo" (Beinecke). From this we can infer that the meeting between the two took place in mid-May 1928. A transcript of Miss Tseng's oral translation of the eight Chinese poems has been found in an unmailed letter Pound wrote to his father on 30 July 1928 (Letter 7).

The greater part of the Seven Lakes Canto, as I have argued in *The Modernist Response to Chinese Art*, is based on Pound's exchanges at once with the screen book's eight pictures and with Miss Tseng's oral translation of the eight poems. Nonetheless, the poet of *The Cantos* could never forget his first collaboration with a Chinese poet and scholar:

> For the seven lakes, and by no man these verses:
> Rain; empty rain; a voyage,
> Fire from frozen cloud, heavy rain in the twilight
> Under the cabin roof was one lantern.
> The reeds are heavy; bent;
> and the bamboos speak as if weeping.
>
> Autumn moon; hills rise about lakes
> against sunset
> Evening is like a curtain of cloud,
> a blurr above ripples; and through it
> sharp long spikes of the cinnamon,
> a cold tune amid reeds.

Behind hill the monk's bell
borne on the wind.
Sail passed here in April; may return in October
Boat fades in silver; slowly;
Sun blaze alone on the river.

. . . .

(Canto 49/244)

After moving to Taiwan in 1949, Miss Tseng assisted her brother Yueh-nung Tseng (Zeng Yuenong, 1893–1986) and others in founding the now prestigious Tunghai University (see Fig. 2.4). In April 1957 Pound learned that Miss Tseng had traveled to the United States. He at once wrote to David Wang in New York City: "Do get Miss Tseng's news while she is in N. Y." (Beinecke). Wang contacted Miss Tseng's delegation but she had already left (Letter 156 n.).

The excerpts from EP's letters to his parents included here have been published before, 5, 6, and 8 in Angela Jung Palandri, "The 'Seven Lakes Canto' Revisited" (*Paideuma*, 3/1 (1974)), and 7 in Hugh Kenner, "More on the Seven Lakes Canto" (*Paideuma*, 2/1 (1973)) and Richard Taylor, "Canto XLIX, Futurism, and the Fourth Dimension" (*Neohelicon* (Budapest), 20/1 (1993)).

Fig. 2.1. "Night Rain" from EP's screen book. (Mary de Rachewiltz)

Fig. 2.2. "Autumn Moon" (right), "Evening Bell" (center), "Sailboats Returning" (left) from EP's screen book. (Mary de Rachewiltz)

Fig. 2.3. Pao Swen Tseng, 1928. (Tunghai University Library)

Fig. 2.4. Pao Swen Tseng and Yueh-nung Tseng, 1955. (Tunghai University Library)

5 *EP to Isabel Pound* (TLS-1; Beinecke)

Via Marsala, 12 Int. 5
Rapallo
1 March [1928]

Dear Mother:

[...]

D[orothy] is up a mountain with a returned missionary. Yes Chinese book arrived, berry interestin', returned missionary promises us a descendant of Confucius on a month or so, who will prob. be able to decipher it.

[...]

[signed] E

6 *EP to Homer Pound* (ALS-2; Beinecke)

Wien
30 May [1928]

Dear Dad:

[...]

Translation of chinese poems in picture book is at Rapallo.

They are poems on a set of scenes in Miss Thseng's part of the country. Sort of habit of people to make pictures & poems on that set of scenes.

[...]

[signed] Ez

7 *EP to Homer Pound* (TL-3; Beinecke)

Via Marsala, 12 Int. 5
Rapallo
30 July. [1928]

Dear Dad:

[...]

Chinese book reads as follows, rough trans.

Rain, empty river,

Place for soul to travel

(or room to travel)

Frozen cloud, fire, rain damp twilight.

One lantern inside boat cover (i.e. sort of shelter, not awning on small boat)

Throws reflection on bamboo branch, causes tears.
/ / / / / / /
AUTUMN MOON ON TON-Ting Lake
West side hills
screen off evening clouds
Ten thousand ripples send mist over cinnamon flowers.
Fisherman's flute disregards nostalgia
Blows cold music over cottony bullrush.

Monastery evening bell

/ / / / /
Cloud shuts off the hill, hiding the temple
Bell audible only when wind moves toward one,
One can not tell whether the
summit, is near or far,
Sure only that one is in hollow of mountains.
/ / / / / / / / / / / /
Autumn tide,
AUTUMN TIDE, RETURNING SAILS
Touching <green> sky at horizon, mists in suggestion of autumn
Sheet of silver reflecting ~~the~~ all that one sees
Boats gradually fade, or are lost in turn of the hills,
Only evening sun, and its glory on the water remain.
/ / / / / / / / / / /
Spring in hill valley
Small wine flag waves in the evening sun
Few clustered houses sending up smoke
A few country people enjoying their evening drink
In time of peace, every day is like spring.
SNOW ON RIVER
Cloud light, world covered with <milky> jade
Small boat floats like a leaf
Tranquil water congeals it to stillness
~~In Sai Yin there dwell people of leisure.~~
The people of Sai Yin are unhurried.
/ / / / / /
Wild geese stopping on sand
Just outside window, light against clouds
~~Light clouds show in sky just beyond window ledge~~
A few lines of autumn geese on the marsh
                                        at their
Bullrishes have burst into snow-tops

The birds stop to preen their feathers.
&&&&&&
EVENING IN SMALL FISHING VILLAGE.
Fisherman's light blinks
Dawn begins, with light to the south and north
Noise of children hawking their fish and crawfish
Fisherman calls his boy, and takes up his wine bottle,
They drink, they lie on the sand
      and point to marsh-grass, talking.

Chinese book reads as follows: EP's typescript consists of three leaves. According to Richard Taylor, "Canto XLIX, Futurism, and the Fourth Dimension," at some point before March 1965, the last two leaves "were accidentally transposed," leading Hugh Kenner to transcribe the text (March 1965) in the order of A-B/F-G-H/C-D-E in "More on the Seven Lakes Canto."

8   *EP to Homer Pound* (TLS-2; Beinecke)

[Rapallo]

Sept. 1 [1928]

Dear Dad:

Given infinite time I MIGHT be able to read a Chinese poem, thass to say I know how the ideograph works, and <u>can</u> find 'em in the dictionary or vocabulary,

BUT I shd. scarcely attempt it unless there were some urgent reason. Also some of the script in that book was fairly fancy.

For Cathay I had a crib made by Mori and Ariga, not translation or anything shaped into sentences, but word for sign, and explanation with each character.

For your book Miss Thseng, descendant of Kung read out the stuff to me.

Am perfectly able to look up an ideograph and see what shade it can be given, etc.

BUT it za matr of time. wd be no point in it.

No I am not a sinologue. Dont spread the idea that I read it a zeasy as a yourapean langwidg.

[. . .]

E.

Mori and Ariga: see Glossary on Mori Kainan and Ariga Nagao respectively.

3
Yang as Pound's Opponent and Collaborator
"To sacrifice to a spirit not one's own is flattery"

In 1937–8 Pound regularly spent four to five hours a day learning Chinese. From James Legge's bilingual Confucian Four Books he moved on to the Confucian Book of Odes, *Shi jing*, in the original. "I MAY be able to read in time, at the rate of three lines a day," he told the Japanese poet Katue Kitasono, who sent him *Shi jing* in four volumes (*Pound/Japan*, 45). To write about China and to begin to translate the Confucian Four Books, Pound could not rely only on his own sets of Chinese–English dictionaries and Legge's bilingual Confucian Four Books. Starting from the late summer of 1939, almost every time he traveled to Rome, he would stop by the Italian Institute for the Middle and Far East (IsMEO) (see Fig. 3.1) to look up some Chinese materials, and it was there that he met the Chinese instructor Fengchi Yang.

Fengchi Yang(Yang Fengqi 揚 鳳 歧, 1908–70) had been an assistant professor of modern history at Beijing's Qinghua University (see Fig. 3.2). He came to Italy around 1935 to pursue a higher degree. When he and Pound first met in September 1939, Yang had just earned a doctorate in letters from the University of Rome and was beginning to teach Chinese at the IsMEO. As an "enemy alien," he would soon lose his job. It was not until the Italian fascist regime collapsed in 1944 that he was able to return to the IsMEO.

To continue a conversation at the IsMEO Library, Pound wrote to Yang on 2 October 1939. He was then seriously deluded about Japanese culpability for the war in China. His letters, like his 1941–3 radio broadcasts from Rome, are characterized by Italian fascism and anti-Semitism. In his first letter he tried to convince Yang that China's worst enemy was not Japan but "international usury" (Letter 9). Not hearing from Yang for ten months, Pound wrote again on 22 August 1940, this time questioning the moral foundation of the Nationalist Chinese leader Chiang Kai-shek: "I hear that Chiang Kai-shek was converted to Christianity, which seems WRONG for a Chinese" (Letter 10). While Pound's intention was to challenge Yang to a debate, he did not want to alienate him. So he quoted the Confucian epigram, "非 其 鬼 而 祭 之 諂 也" (see Fig. 3.3).

The phrase from Legge's bilingual Four Books would come back to his mind in mid-1945, and consequently it surfaces in Canto 77 with an English translation: "To sacrifice to a spirit not one's own is flattery."

In his reply Yang called Chiang "the greatest and bravest statesman"; because he was trying to save China, Chiang "always had the esteem of the Chinese people, and naturally also of our troops" (Letter 11). As to Chiang's moral principles, Yang explained, they were modern and democratic as set forth by Sun Yat-sen, the founding father of the Republic of China.

In his next letter Pound was careful to acknowledge his ignorance about Chinese reality. However, he irritated Yang by stating that "foreigners who have learned something from China have almost always had to INVADE it, later absorbing the culture" (Letter 12). Yang's rebuttal of this simplistic assertion was blunt: "It is not always true, as you said, that foreigners had to invade China to learn or take something from the country. For example, Korea and Indochina have absorbed Chinese culture without invading it" (Letter 13).

Subsequently, Pound wrote in a more reserved manner, as if apologizing for his earlier impertinence. In one letter he conceded that China had a just claim to its sovereignty. Yang influenced Pound toward a slightly better understanding of the conflict between China and Japan. This does not suggest, however, that Pound changed his political view. He still believed "春 秋 無 義 戰." The Mencian epigram is inscribed in Letter 16, just as its English translation is appended to Canto 78: "In 'The Spring and Autumn' | there | are | no | righteous | wars." More than several times what Pound said to Yang can be related to the Pisan Cantos (Cantos 74–84), whose Chinese quotations his Confucian studies during World War II anticipated.

While the politics of Pound and Yang diverged, their literary interests shared much common ground. Throughout the years 1939–42 Yang served as an informant. He helped Pound locate various Chinese books and identify numerous Chinese characters. His assistance became vital in 1941–2 when Pound took up translating into Italian two of the Confucian Four Books. Pound sent Yang part of his draft of the *Ta S'eu* (1942) for evaluation. As Letter 21 testifies, Yang approved not only Pound's Italian translation but also his inserted commentary. In his reply Pound could not resist repeating his usual observation about translation and about the "ideogram": "And in a classical and ancient text, I think one has to preserve the original meanings of the ideograms, and not to follow the formless and colorless value given words in a newspaper of today" (Letter 22). In that letter Pound also disclosed his intention to translate into Italian all four of the Confucian Four Books: first "Ta S'eu" and then "Mencius, one book at a time."

Pound's plan was cut short upon his arrest for making pro-fascist radio broadcasts from Rome. On 3 May 1945 he was "working on the Mencius when the Partigiani came to the front door with a tommy-gun" (*Letters in Captivity*, 113).

Fig. 3.1. EP in Rome, *c.*1941. (HRHRC)

Fig. 3.2. Fengchi Yang, *c.*1960. (Lionello Lanciotti)

ANNO
XVIII
VIA MARSALA 12-5
RAPALLO

« Liberty is not a right but a duty ».
m

22 Ag/

EZRA POUND

Caro Dottor Yang

     Dopo nostro incontro , ed avendo sapito da Valeri
che siete nazionalista , del partito di Chang Kai Chek , ho meditato
ancora una volta il testo

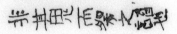

Poi incontrando alcuni Giapponesi a Roma, e poi meditando ancora ;
mi pare che essiste un modo di fare una pace con onore
per la Cina. Naturalmente non conosco le condizioni di oggi giorno
in Cina. Vorrei consultarvi , se vi interessa.

Ho sentito che Chang Kai Chek fu convertito al Cristianesimo;
che a ma pare un ERRORE per un Cinese. In somma un
cristiano potrebbe mettere un po in ordine ~~~~~~~~ le sue
idee, meditando il 學大 , forse un Confuciano
potrebbe derivare un stimolo dallo studio della teologia ~~~~~~~~
medioavale/ o qualche spinto per

ma NON per convertirse.

Una altra cosa ho sentito ma non so se sia vero. Mi e che voleva
stato detto che Chang NON potendo ottenere il morale dalle
sue truppe, coi testi della bibbia, ha ritornato al uso dei
testi confuciani.

E vero anche , o no ? che lo studio dei Quattro classici fu
sospeso nelle scuole col arrivo della Republica in Cina ?
Lo ho sentito , e i disturbe e ~~~~~ calamita susseguente non m hanno
sorpreso.

     Forse Chang non ha avuto tempo di riflettare sul

Fig. 3.3. Letter 10. (Beinecke)

9   *EP to Yang (TL-2; LL/Beinecke)*

Via Marsala 12.5
Rapallo
2 Ott [October 1939]

Illmo Dott Yang Fengchi

Caro Dottore Yang (se questo è il nome di famiglia, e Caro Dottore Fengchi se questo è il patronimico)

Non dubito dell'eroismo di Ch[i]ang Kai Chek, e sono stato tanto contento [di] incontrarVi perche volevo sapere precisamente il punto di vista della Cina interiore. MA

正 名

Non so se voi ed il Generale [si] rendono contro [conto] del grado in cui TUTTI i NOMI, tutte le parole sono stato falsificato nell'occidente. Le democrazie non lo sono, sono USUROCRAZIE.

Io credo che il peggior nemico della Cina non è <Giappone> ma 放 利 賬 specialmente quell'usura internazionale.

La rivoluzione Russa intendeva attaccare al capitale, ma invece fu pervertito e deviene [divenne] un attacco alla proprietà. Forse adesso Stalin incomincia a renders[i] conto.

Spero vederVi presto a Roma la settimana prossima, ed intanto vi prego di credere che quando dico pace con onore non intendo un onore vuoto. Ho una fede nell'immortalità della Cina e credo che nessun studente della storia può mancare d'averla ma ho visto mio paese trad[i]to; cioè ho appreso del tradimento settant'anni DOPO IL FATTO. Mi pare che quando possibile si deve evitare tali ritardi. Non so quando la penetrazione dell'usura internazionale nella Cina ha cominciato ad essere un pericolo per Voi; o in che grado voi [vi] siete resi conto della forza e natura della penetrazione.

[In]somma posso anche benissimo avere impressioni falsissimi della s[it]uazione, perché quasi nessuno nell'occidente ha mezzi [di] informazione; anche rudimentarii.

cordialissimi saluti ed a presto

[Dear Dr Yang (if that's your family name, and Dear Dr Fengchi if that's your patronymic):

I do not doubt the heroism of Chiang Kai-shek. I am glad to have met you because I wanted to know the point of view of the Chinese interior, BUT 正 名 [precisely named].

I don't know if you and the [Secretary] General are aware of the extent to which THE NAMES OF ALL THINGS, all words, have been falsified in the West. The democracies aren't democracies; they are USUROCRACIES.

China's worst enemy is not Japan but 放 利 賬 [usury], specifically inter-national usury.

The Russian Revolution intended to attack capital, but instead it was perverted and became an attack on property. Perhaps now Stalin is beginning to see it.

I hope to see you in Rome next week, and meanwhile I ask you to believe that when I say peace with honor I don't mean an empty honor. I have faith in the immortality of China and I believe that no history student can fail to have this faith, but I have seen the betrayal of my country; that is, I have become aware of the betrayal seventy years AFTER IT STARTED. It seems to me if possible we have to avoid such delays. I don't know how far the penetration of international usury into China has begun to be a threat to you or to what extent you are aware of the strength and nature of the penetration.

In any case, it's possible that my impressions are completely wrong because almost nobody in the West has access to information, even of the most rudimentary kind.

Best regards, I'll see you soon.]

(TL-2; LL/Beinecke): the second leaf of the original letter is lost. The passage from "[In]somma posso" (In any case) on is transcribed from its carbon copy (Beinecke).

Ch[i]ang Kai Chek: see Glossary on Chiang Kai-shek.

正 名 : Earliest introduced characters in *The Cantos* (Canto 51/252), 正 名 (pronounced *zheng ming* and meaning precise naming), are taken from *Analects*, 13.3 (*Confucius*, 249).

Generale: Secretary General Zhu (Segretario Generale Tchu). According to Achilles Fang to EP, 4 January 1951, Zhu Ying 朱 英 "now attached to the Chinese Legation at Vatican . . . a resident of Rome for the past 30 years or so" (Lilly).

10   EP to Yang (TLS-2; LL)

Via Marsala 12.5
Rapallo
22 Ag/ [August 1940]

Caro Dottor Yang

Dopo nostro incontro, ed avendo saputo da Valeri che siete nazionalista, del partito di Ch[i]ang Kai Chek, ho meditato ancora una volta il testo

非 其 鬼 而 祭 之 諂 也

Poi incontrando alcuni Giapponesi a Roma, e poi meditando ancora; mi pare che essiste [esiste] un modo di fare una pace con onore per la Cina. Naturalmente non conosco le condizioni di oggi giorno in Cina. Vorrei consultarvi, se vi interessa.

Ho sentito che Ch[i]ang Kai Chek fu convertito al Cristianesimo; che a ma [me] pare un ERRORE per un Cinese. In somma un cristiano potrebbe mettere un po' in ordine le sue idee, meditando il 學 大 [大 學], forse un Confuciano

potrebbe derivare un stimolo dallo studio della teologia medioevale/ o qualche spint[a] per 尚
志

ma NON per convertirs[i].

Una altra cosa ho sentito ma non so se sia vero. Mi è stato detto che Ch[i]ang NON potendo ~~arrivare al~~ <ottenere il> morale <che voleva> dalle sue truppe, coi testi della bibbia, ha ritornato al uso dei testi confuciani.

E [È] vero anche, o no? che lo studio dei Quattro classici fu sospeso nelle scuole col arrivo della Repub[b]lica in Cina? Lo ho sentito, di disturbi e calamità susseguente non m'hanno sorpreso.

Forse Ch[i]ang non ha avuto tempo di riflettare [riflettere] sul ritmo della storia della Cina? Forse vuol fare in dieci anni quello che avverà solamente in 160 anni?

Tutta questa lettera deve leggersi come interrogativa. A questa distanza non si può SAPERE. Ma qualche volta a distanza si vede una cosa che non sia visibile da vicino.

cordialissimi saluti
[signed] Ezra Pound

[Dear Dr Yang: After our meeting I learned from Valeri that you are a Nationalist, a member of Chiang Kai-shek's party, and I reexamined the aphorism 非 其 鬼 而 祭 之 諂 也 ["To sacrifice to a spirit not one's own is flattery"]

Then, after meeting some Japanese in Rome and after reexamining the aphorism, it appears that there is a chance of making an honorable peace with China. Of course I don't know the present situation in China. I want to consult you on this if you are interested.

I hear that Chiang Kai-shek was converted to Christianity, which seems WRONG for a Chinese. In any case, a Christian might get his thoughts in order, meditating the 大 學 [Great Learning]. Maybe a Confucian can get stimulus from studying medieval theology so a lift to 尚 志 [self-cultivation] but NOT to conversion.

I've heard something else and I don't know if it is true. I was told that since Chiang was NOT able to keep up the morale of his troops by using the Bible, he went back to using the Confucian texts.

Also, is it true or not that the study of the "Four Books" was suspended in schools with the coming of the Republic of China? I heard this, and the subsequent disturbances and calamities did not surprise me at all.

Maybe Chiang didn't have the time to think of the rhythm of Chinese history? Maybe he wanted to do in ten years what will only happen in 160?

One must read this whole letter as a question. At this distance one cannot KNOW. But sometimes at a distance one sees something which is not visible close by.

Best regards. Ezra Pound]

Valeri: Italian poet Diego Valeri (1887–1976).

非其鬼而祭之諂也: Quoted from *Analects*, 2.24 (Legge, i. 154; *Confucius*, 201). Cf. Canto 77/496:

非	7—not
其	one's own
鬼	spirit
而	and
祭	sacrifice
之	is
諂	flattery
也	bi gosh

大學: *Da xue*, first of the Confucian Four Books. See EP's English versions *Ta Hio: The Great Learning of Confucius* (1928) and *The Great Digest* (1947); and Italian version *Confucio: Ta S'eu. Dai Gaku. Studio integrale* (with Alberto Luchini, 1942). See also Glossary on Confucius.

尚志: *shangzhi*, "self-cultivation," quoted from *Mencius*, 7.1.33 (Legge, ii. 468). In "Mang Tsze" (1938) EP gives the Mencian characters after stating that "Dante's view upon rectitude rimes certainly with that of Mencius" (*SP*, 84).

11   *Yang to EP (ALS-3; Beinecke)*

Assisi

18.9.40

Illmo Professore Pound

Vi prego di scusarmi il ritardo con il quale rispondo alla vostra lettera del 22 agosto. Ritardo dovuto al lungo tempo impiegato dalla vostra. Vi sono grato del ricordo ma purtroppo non sono d'accordo con le vostre idee:

Per me Chiang Kai-shek è un grande uomo politico, il più grande e valoroso uomo politico che oggi ha la mia patria, uomo che vuole la m[i]a nazione grande e libera. Su ciò che riguarda la fede di Chiang verso Cristianesimo non mi posso pronunziare perché non la conosco. Ma la sua volontà per salvare la Cina è, senza alcun dubbio, grande e per questo egli ottiene sempre la stima del popolo Cinese e naturalmente anche quella delle nostre truppe le quali sono moralmente diciplinati nè colla bibbia nè col confucionismo, ma coi testi dei principii di Sun Yat-sen.

Gli Stati Uniti impiegarono otto anni per ottenere l'indipendenza ed in questi 160 anni non hanno avuto mai una grave minacia [minaccia] dalle potenze estere, invece la Cina?

Non date alcuna fiducia alle propagande giapponesi i quali non hanno rispettato mai l'onore della Cina. Se è vero come avete detto, [che] oggi il Giappone vuole fare con onore uno pace con la Cina, vuole dire che la nostra difesa in questi tre anni ha corret[t]o i[l] pregiudizio del Giappone!

Tornerò fra poco a Roma.

Saluti cordiali.

Yang Fengchi

[Dear Professor Pound: I want to apologize for my delay in responding to your letter of 22 August. The delay was caused by the long time it took your letter (to arrive). I am thankful that you remember me. Unfortunately, I don't agree with your ideas.

For me Chiang Kai-shek is a great statesman, the greatest and bravest statesman my country has today, a man who wants my nation to be great and free. Regarding the belief of Chiang vs. Christianity, I can't tell you anything because I don't know. But his will to save China is without doubt great. Because of this he has always had the esteem of the Chinese people, and naturally also of our troops. Morally our troops are disciplined neither by the Bible nor by Confucianism but by the texts of Sun Yat-sen's principles.

It took the United States eight years to win independence. For as long as 160 years it never had any serious threat from foreign forces. But what about China?

Don't trust Japanese propaganda because the Japanese have never respected the honor of China. If it's true, as you said, that Japan now wants to make an honorable peace with China, then this means that our defense in the past three years has remedied Japan's prejudice! I will return shortly to Rome. Regards, Yang Fengchi]

Sun Yat-sen: (1866–1925), father of modern China. The three great principles set forth by him are nationalism, democracy, and the people's livelihood.

12   *EP to Yang (TLS-2; LL)*

Via Marsala 12.5
Rapallo
2 Nov [1940]

Caro Dott Yang

Potete dire al Sig Segretario Generale Tcheou [Tchu] che io ho scritto due articoli (uno in inglese, uno in Italiano) ma non so quando (o si) saranno pubblicati.

È molto difficile capire perchè Wang Chin Wei non ha ragione; e perche Chiang Kai Chek non è sbagliato in suoi rapporti (magari se ci [ce] ne sono pochi e piccoli) colla finanza internazionale.

Siamo ignorantissimi. Certo manca una traduzione del volume (?secondo) della vacchia enciclopedia Cinese che tratta dell economia. (Non trovo il titolo in questo momento ma un intiero volume tratta della moneta e dei questioni economici) Poi il libro di Lihaoouen (<come il nome sta> scritto in francese) Toan-pen-tang-king sse-yao potrebbe meritare una traduzione?? <e il Ta-pao-lo, specialmente per miei studi>. Libri di questo genere non hanno bisogno, mi pare, d'edizioni bilingue, essendo la materia prosaica.

In somma i forestieri ch hanno appreso qualche cosa della Cina hanno quasi sempre dovuto INVADERE il paese, poi assorbendo la cultura. Essezione [Eccezione] fatto per alcuni gesuiti ch hanno riportato i libri di Confuzio, e di Menzio; ed il libro delle ceremonie (Li Gi) ed alcuni poesie in Europa.

Ho letto hieri [ieri] che [il] Giappone sta ameliorando i rapporti non solamente colla Russia, ma anche col Australia. Invece avrebbe dovuto ameliorare i rapporti colla Cina (totale) ovvero la Cina ed il Giappone avrebbe potuto convenire in trattati coi due paesi?

Il Giappone pubblica molte in inglese. Non so se la Cina pubblica informazione per l'estero in qualsiasi lingua europa? Non sarebbe possibile che L'Illustrissimo Sig Tcheou [Tchu] invita [inviti] Comm De Feo a discutere le possibilità dei [di] scambi culturali; cioè in particolare di traduzioni dal Cinese?

Con aggiunte di informazioni odierni?

cordialmente
[signed] Ezra Pound

[Dear Dr Yang: You may tell Mr Secretary General Zhu that I've written two articles (one in English and the other in Italian) but I don't know when (or if) they are going to be published.

It's very hard to understand why Wang Jingwei is not right; why Chiang Kai-shek is not wrong in his dealings in international finance (but perhaps these dealings are few and unimportant).

We are very ignorant. Of course, there is no translation of the (second?) volume of the old Chinese encyclopedia dealing with economics. (I can't remember the title right now, but an entire volume has to do with money and economic issues.)

Moreover, the Book of Lihaoouen (as it is written in French), Toan pen tang king sse yao, might be worth translating? and Ta-pao-lo, especially for my studies. It seems to me that works of this kind do not need bilingual editions because they are in prose.

Anyway, foreigners who have learned something from China have almost always had to INVADE it, later absorbing the culture. I make exceptions for those few Jesuits who brought back the books of Confucius and Mencius, the Book of Rites (Li ji), and some poems to Europe.

I read yesterday that Japan is improving its relations with Russia and Australia, although it should also improve its relation with China (all China). Or else China and Japan could have joined together to deal with the two countries?

Japan publishes much in English. I don't know if China publishes any information for foreign countries in any European language. Wouldn't it be possible for the most honorable Mr Zhu to invite Comm. De Feo to discuss the possibility of cultural exchanges, which means especially translations from Chinese, with the addition of updates? Regards, Ezra Pound]

Wang Chin Wei: Wang Jingwei (1883–1944), president of the Chinese Nationalist Party (1932–8), defected in 1938. He became puppet ruler of Japanese occupied China in 1940–4.

Toan-pen-tang-king sse-yao . . . Ta-pao-lo: unidentified.

De Feo: Luciano De Feo, the director-selector for the First Exposition of Cinematic Art held in Venice in 1932, was then Director General of the Italian National Institute for Cultural Exchanges (IRCE).

13   *Yang to EP (TLS-1; Beinecke)*

Roma

9, II, 40.

Caro Signor Pound

Vi ringrazio sentimente per la vostra lettera. Via mando, per informazioni, alcuni volumetti per mezzo dei quali spero sia possibile farsi un'idea chiara della politica nazionale giapponese. Per mezzo di essi forse potete convincervi che Wang Ching-wei ha torto e Chiang Kai-shek ha ragione. Per mancanza di spazio e le altre ragioni, è inutile intavolare per lettera una discussione come quasta [questa]. Insomma ogni paese ha diritto di essere libero e di poter vivere la sua vita (specialmente politicalmente).

Non capisco che libro sarebbe "Ta Pen Tang King SSe Yao" e "Ta Pao Lo": potete scrivermi i caratteri in cinese? Vido [Vedo] spe[s]so il sig. Tchou [Tchu]; egli mi ha detto che conosce molto bene il Comm. De Feo ed anche ha parlato, molto tempo fa, con lui riguarda agli scambi culturali fra i due paesi; ma per ora è quasi impossibile attuare qualunque idea in quel senso. Non è sempre vero, come avete detto, che i forestieri hanno dovuto invadere la cina per apprendere qualchecosa dal paese: per essempio la Korea e l'Indo-cina hanno assorbito la cultura cinese senza invaderla ed i Mongoli hanno una volta conquistato la Cina e non hanno appreso niente la [della] sua cultura. Il Giappone, come culturalmente, ha già imparato molto dalla Cina nei secoli passati, ma ades[s]o esso invade la Cina non è per apprendere qualchecosa culturale ma su le altre ragioni imperialistici i quali non possono essere compromes [s]i da un cinese che ama la propria indipendenza del sua paese.

Cordialmente

[signed] Yang Fengchi

[Dear Mr Pound: Thank you for your letter. For your reference I'm sending some pamphlets, which I hope will give you a clear idea about the nationalist politics of Japan. These may help to convince you that Wang is wrong and Chiang is right. Because of limited space and other reasons it's useless to start discussion like this in a letter. In any case every country has the right to be free, to be able to live its own life (especially politically).

I don't know which book would be "Ta Pen Tang King Sse Yao" or "Ta Pao Lo"? Could you write down the Chinese characters? I see Mr Zhu often; he told me that he knows Comm. De Feo very well. He talked to him a very long time ago about cultural exchanges between the two countries, but now it's almost impossible to do this. It is not always true, as you said, that foreigners had to invade China to learn or take something from the country. For example, Korea and Indochina have absorbed Chinese culture without invading it. The Mongols once conquered China and they didn't learn anything of its culture. Culturally Japan has already learned a lot from China in the past centuries. Now it's invading China and the reason for invading is not that it wants to learn anything culturally but for imperialist purposes that can't be accepted by a Chinese who loves the independence of his country. Regards, Yang Fengchi]

14   EP to Yang *(TLS-1; LL)*

Via Marsala 12.5
Rapallo
12 Nov. [1940]

Caro Dott Yang

Io sono d'accordo e rispetto profondamente vostro patriottismo e quello di Chiang K.S. ma, d'altra parte mi pare che La Cina non deve NULLA alla Lega di Nazioni, che la Cina non ha fatto subito alleanza colle forze costruttive dell Europa Nuova/ vuol dire che il Giappone ha stato più scaltro nella scelta d'alleati?

Poi il sistema dell usura DISTRUGGE sempre ogni paese che lo tollera. Vede storia della Banca S. Giorgio di Genova/ che mangiava tutto. Vendeva la Corsica alla Francia etc/

Io non discutto i diritti della Cina/ discuto solamente la politica più adatta per conquistarli o di conservali. Giappone certamente non va a Pekino in richerchia delle cultura. Ma sarebbe più commoda per le Cina se il Giappone avesse invece invaso l'Australia?

Le CONTINGENZE hanno, forse, costretto Chiang K.S. di fare le cose migliore al momento ch'egli ha agito/ questo non discuto; solo me preoccupo di vederlo, forse, fidare ad un sostegno di legno putrido.

Non posso GIUDICARE, posso solamente avere una curiosità. La Polonia voleva conservare un modo di vita del seicento. L'Abissinia era nell'anno 400 prima del mille.

Tutto questo accoglienza dei b[i]anchi "moderni" nella Cina, fu forse necessaria, visto le contingenze, ma ADESSO bisogna conoscere subito il sistema proclamata tre giorni fa da Hitler, già indicato da Funk e Riccardi.

Lasciamo da parte per il momento il Giappone, alla forza si contrappone la forza. Ma per AVERE la forza sufficiente? In somma, non parliamo del Giappone, parliamo della struttura economica INTERNA. e dei rapporti fra la Cina e l Europa nuova. La velocità degli eventi mi pare tale, ch'OGNUNO deve star sveglio.

con amicizia,
[signed] E. Pound

[Dear Dr Yang: I agree and I have the deepest respect for your loyalty to Chiang Kai-shek. But on the other hand it seems to me China owes NOTHING to the League of Nations. Because China didn't immediately ally itself with the constructive forces of New Europe, does it mean that Japan was shrewder in its choice of allies?

Besides, the system of usury DESTROYS every country that tolerates it. Look at the history of Banca St Giorgio, which swallowed everything. They sold Corsica to France. I am not discussing the rights of China. I am only discussing the most appropriate politics to win them or to protect them. Certainly Japan has not come to Beijing in search of culture. But would it be more comfortable for China if Japan had instead invaded Australia?

The CIRCUMSTANCES have perhaps compelled Chiang Kai-shek to do things as well as possible in the time when he acted. I have no doubt about this. But I am concerned that you might trust rotten wood to support you.

I can't JUDGE; I can only be curious. Poland wanted to protect the seventeenth-century way of living. Abyssinia existed in the year 400 before 1,000.

The acceptance of the "modern" banks in China was perhaps necessary given the circumstances. But NOW we need to pay immediate attention to the system Hitler proclaimed three days ago and which Funk and Riccardi have elucidated.

For the moment we side with Japan because force is needed against force. But how TO HAVE sufficient force? Anyway, we are not talking about Japan. We are talking about INTERNATIONAL economic structure and the relationship between China and New Europe. It seems to me that things are moving so fast that EVERYBODY has to stay alert. Amicably, E. Pound]

Banca S. Giorgio: a financial power with its own army that took control of Corsica from Genoa in the mid-fifteenth century. Corsica was annexed to France in 1769.
Funk e Riccardi: Walter Funk served as Minister for Economic Affairs in Nazi Germany from 1937 to 1945. Raffaello Riccardi served as Minister for Exchanges and Currency in Fascist Italy from 1939 to 1941.

15   *Yang to EP (TLS-1; Beinecke)*

Roma
14, 11, 40

Caro Signor Pound

Ho ricevuto le sue lettere e Vi ringrazio; anch'io Vi ho scritto, non so se V'è arrivata? Voi potete tenere tutti i volumetti che Vi ho mandato salvo quelli due sulla [sui] quali ci sta il timbro della biblioteca dell'Am[ba]sciata e Vi prego di ristituirmeli [restituirmeli] dopo avete letto.

"The China Year Book" dell'anno 1939 è un bel volume nel quale si può trovare le materie più recenti.

Un documento governativo come quelle Memoriale di Tanaka è una cosa importantissima nella storia diplomatica sino-giapponese; noi non dobbiamo dare lo stesso valore come quelle notizie del giornale le quale [quali], magare qualche volta dicono la verita (generalmente non [no]) ma è una verità mutabile e contemporanea. Dall'anno 1927 all'anno 1931 la Cina sequiva [seguiva] una politica pro-giappone se è doppo [dopo] che ha interrotto questa amicizia? Voi dite che prima l'invassione [dell'invasione] il Giappone non non ha datto fastidio alla Cina; io vi dico che sarà vero se quest'invasione significa quel la volta del settimo secolo.

E daverro ci farrebbe ridere se un inglese sta contro La trasportazione dell'oppio in la Cina, pero dobbiamo sapere che oggi non è il 1839!

Cordialmente
[signed] Yang Fengchi

[Dear Mr Pound: Thank you for your letters. I also wrote you a letter, but have you received it? You may keep all the pamphlets I have sent you except the two which bear the stamps of the Library of the Embassy, and I ask you to return them to me after you have read them.

"The China Year Book" of 1939 is a beautiful volume in which you will find the latest issues. A government document such as Tanaka's Memoir is something extremely important in Sino-Japanese diplomatic history. We must not give it the same value as the notices in the newspapers, which perhaps sometimes tell the truth (usually not), but it is a changeable and immediate truth. From 1927 to 1931 China had a pro-Japanese policy; it was later that it broke off this friendship? You say that before the invasion Japan did not give China trouble. I tell you that this is true only if you are referring to the invasion of the seventh century.

And it would really make us laugh if an Englishman was opposed to the opium traffic, but we have to realize that this is not 1839! Best regards, Yang Fengchi]

Tanaka: Tanaka Giichi (1863–1929), prime minister of Japan from 1927 to 1929, presented to Emperor Hirohito the militarist position that "[i]n order to conquer the world, we must first conquer China." *trasportazione dell'oppio*: see Letter 109.

16   EP to Yang *(TLS-1; LL)*

Via Marsala 12.5
Rapallo
17 Nov [1940]

Caro Dott Yang
    Libro di Tanaka molto interessante. Ma da il 1927.

Credo che Tanaka dà più fastidio OGGI ai giapponesi che 春
ai Cinesi. Insomma, antiquato quasi quanto Imperatore 秋
Guglielme II di Germania. 無
    Giappone mueve VELOCEmente 義
    Lunedi, Giappone, American canning factory. 戰
    fabbrica Americana per conserve in scattola.
    Giovedi, Giappone, stato corporativo.
    Bisogna pensare: che cosa Giappone STA per fare/bisogna pensare: che cosa
Giappone sta per pensare.
    la CINA 中 [國]
    Inghilterra per l'oppio, non solamente nel 1839 ma al congresso di 1923.
Roberto Cecil impediva riforma. Sempre con espressione pietistiche.
    Chiang K.S. eroe/ benissimo. guerriglia necessaria, solo modo possibile.
assinare [assassinare] necessaria/ Ma NON VA, cioé non è il futuro.
    Io non posso comprendere contingenze/etc. accett[o] TUTTO che è gia stato
fatto sino ad oggi. Ma DOMANI?
    Non è questione di che cosa è stato.
    È questione: che cosa PUO ESSERE alle ore 15 oggi alle ore 17 domani.
    League of Nations: porcheria, scrofaria. Funzione della Cina a Ginevra, per
quanto io ho potuto sapere: Ogni volta un delegato Cinesa parlava, ha ridotto al
assurdo le pretesa ed ipocrisia d gli Inglese e loro fantocchi.

[signed] Ezra Pound

[Dear Dr Yang: Tanaka's book very interesting. But from
1927. I believe Tanaka TODAY is more bothersome to the 春
Japanese than to the Chinese. In any case, almost as 秋
antiquated as Emperor William II of Germany. Japan moves 無
RAPIDly. 義
    Monday, Japan, American canning factory. 戰
    Thursday, Japan, cooperative state.
    We have to think: what Japan IS ABOUT to do/ We have to think: what Japan
is about to think.
    CHINA 中 [國]
    England for opium, not only in 1839 but also in the Congress of 1923. Robert
Cecil hindered reform. Always with pious expressions. Chiang Kai-shek was
very good. Guerrilla warfare necessary, only way possible. Assassin necessary/
But IT DOESN'T WORK, that is, it is not the future.
    I can't understand circumstances, etc. I accept EVERYTHING that has
already been done now until today. But TOMORROW? The question isn't
what has been; the question is what COULD HAPPEN at 3 p.m. today or
5 p.m. tomorrow.

The League of Nations: filth, pigsty. Function of China in Geneva as far as I have found out. Every time a Chinese delegate spoke, he revealed the absurd pretense and hypocrisy of the English and their puppets. Ezra Pound]

春 秋 無 義 戰: quoted from *Mencius*, 7.2.2 (Legge, ii. 478). EP's typescript for Canto 78 (Beinecke) has both the original and its English translation, though only the translation is printed in Canto 78/503:

In "The Spring and Autumn"
there
are
no
righteous
wars

Roberto Cecil: Edgar Algernon Robert Gascoyne-Cecil (1864–1958), president of the League of Nations Union (1923–45), authored *The Way of Peace* (1928).

17 *Yang to EP (TLS-1; Beinecke)*

Roma
21, II, 40.

Caro Sig. Pound

Molte grazie delle sue due magnifiche opere.

Mi devo scusare se non posso continuare la nostra discusione perchè da una parte ade[s]so sono troppo oc[c]upato, dovuto dall'apertura della università, e da l'altra parte non abbiamo l'aria adatta di parlare. Insomma, io posso dire così: se oggi alle 15 il Giappone ritira le sue truppe dalla Cina, domani alle 17 noi vediamo la vera pace, anzi, la vera cooperazione fra questi due paesi. Se non [no], qualunque cosa conclusa sarà una cosa falsa e non durerà! Se è difficile a capire perchè la Cina non si mette d'accordo col Giappone, sarà più difficile ancora a capire perchè i Giapponesi sono venuti in Cina.

La Cina non ha tanto fiducia per la Società delle nazione dopo la missione di Leedon. Come sono andate i delegati cinesi non sapevo, però ho parlato [con] qualcuno di loro che diceva [che] non c'era male.

A che anno si è unito il congresso d'oopio [d'oppio] a Ginevra? Al 1925 o al 1923? Non mi ricordo chi era il delegato ing., era Robert Cecil o Roberto F. Fitch? È pec [c] ato che non c'è nussun bolletino da consultare. Lasciamo andare le cose passate. Le vorrei dire soltanto che oggi questo commercio è monopolizato [monopolizzato] dai Giapponesi soli nelle zone occupate.

Tanti Saluti aLei e la Sua Signora!

[signed] Yang Fengchi

[Dear Mr Pound: Many thanks for your two magnificent works. I have to apologize that I can't continue our discussion because in the first place I'm too busy with the opening of the university and in the second place we don't have the proper atmosphere. In any case I should say this: If at 3 p.m. today Japan withdraws its troops from China, at 5 p.m. tomorrow we'll see peace; in fact real cooperation between these two countries. If not, whatever will have been resolved will be false and won't last! If it's difficult to understand why China does not make peace with Japan, it will be even more difficult to understand why Japan invaded China. China doesn't trust the League of Nations any more after the Leiden Mission. How the Chinese delegate did I never found out. But I have talked to some of them, who said that it was not bad.

What year did the Opium Control Board convene in Geneva, 1925 or 1923? I don't remember who the delegate was. Was it Robert Cecil or Roberto F. Fitch? It's a pity that there is no written document to consult. Let's leave out the past. I would like to tell you that today all trade has been monopolized by the Japanese alone in the occupied zones. Regards to you and your wife. Yang Fengchi]

la missione di Leedon: Leiden Mission.
Roberto F. Fitch: Unidentified.

18   *EP to Yang* (TLS-1; LL)

Via Marsala 12.5
Rapallo
24 Nov [1940]

Caro Dott Yang

Mi rincresce che siete troppo occupate etc. Sul <u>Meridiano di Roma</u> di oggi, troverete qualche parola scritta con intenzioni amichevoli verso la Cina.

E credo che sarebbe possibile di continuare la discussione sulle pagine di quella rivista, presentando le vedute veramente cinese [cinesi]; se Voi e il Sig Tchou [Tchu] avete voglia.

Un errore di stampa, non molte importante.. Si deve leggere "dai Bramini che <u>NON</u> si oppongono agli usurai."

[signed] Ezra Pound

[Dear Dr Yang: I am sorry that you are too busy, etc. In the *Meridiano di Roma* you'll find some articles written with friendly intentions toward China.

I think it possible to continue our discussion in the pages of this magazine presenting the true Chinese point of view; if you and Mr Zhu would like to do this.

A printing error, not very important. It should read "from the Brahmins who do <u>NOT</u> oppose usury." Ezra Pound]

Bramini: see EP, "I Bramini e l'usura," *Meridiano di Roma* (8 December 1940), 12.

19   *Yang to EP (ACS-1; Beinecke)*

Roma
22 Maggio [May] 1941

Caro Sig. Pound

C'è un articolo mio sulla civiltà romana, non so se potrò dare alla "Meridiano di Roma"? Sarei molto lieto se lei potrà presentarmi un posto su qualunque rivista di pubblicarlo.

Molti con [Con molti] saluti,
Yang Fengchi

[Dear Mr Pound: I have an article about Roman civilization. I wonder if I could submit it to the *Meridiano*? I would be very pleased if you could find space for me in any magazine for publication. Best regards, Yang Fengchi]

20   *EP to Yang (TL-1; Beinecke)*

[Rapallo]
[8 July 1941]

I Dio
Caro Dott YANG

Sono molto contento del vostro articolo sul Meridiano d'oggi. Cosi le cose procedono in ordine; Prima l'amicizia; poi la politica.

Non posso capire che significano le parole del nuovo trattato se ne [non] che il Giappone ritira la sua armata dalla Cina; come vostro desiderio.

Almeno con un tempo necessario. ed un po di tatto, delicatezza.

Nel frattempo spero che continuerete [a] fare capire ai lettori del Meridiano quanto profondo sia il pensiero, Anschauung Cinese, quanto parentela; e quanto commercio spirituale desiderabile.

amicizia

[God
Dear Dr Yang: I'm very pleased with your article in today's *Meridiano*. So things are proceeding in order, first friendship, and then politics.

I can't understand the meaning of the new treaty unless Japan withdraws its troops from China, as you wish.

At least within the necessary time. And a bit of tact, delicacy.

In the meantime, I hope you will continue to show the readers of the *Meridiano* how profound the Chinese Anschauung is and how similar or related; and how desirable this spiritual exchange. Amicably]

(TL-1; Beinecke): the original letter is lost. Our text is transcribed from its carbon copy (Beinecke).
vostro articolo: "Roma vista da un cinese," *Meridiano di Roma*, 8 (July 1941), 9.

21   Yang to EP *(ACS-1; Beinecke)*

Roma

5–11–41.

Caro Signor Pound

Ho letto gli ideogrammi che mi avete indicati. La vostra versione merita elogio; ed ugualmente interessanti sono le note che ad essa avete aggiunte. Voglio sperare che continuerete ad occuparVi dell'argomento.

Quanto a me, sono molto occupato in un lavoro affidatomi da G. E. Tucci. Cordiali saluti a voi e [la] signora,

Yang Fengchi

[Dear Mr Pound: I have read the ideograms you showed to me. Your version merits praise. Equally interesting are the comments you inserted. I hope you will continue to occupy yourself with this subject. As for me, I'm busy with something G. E. Tucci asked me to do. Regards to you and your wife, Yang Fengchi]

G. E. Tucci: see Glossary on Tucci, Giuseppe.

22   EP to Yang *(TL-2, Beinecke)*

[Rapallo]

7 Nov. [1941]

Caro Dott Yang

Vi ringrazio per va/ cartolina benevola/ma la versione è da rifare. Ero a Roma senza dizionario, ed ho fidato troppo a Legge; che era pieno di cristianità, e che non ha guardato gli ideogrammi. Tre o quattro versi sono forse a posto ma gli altri sono a [da] rifare.

Ho visto (cioè VISTO) l'ideogramma "sincerità"/perfezionamento o aggiustamento della parola al pensiero/Il TIGRE [虎] è importante/

ma io era lontano di capire la [lo] scoglia [scoglio]; e ho dovuto pensare mezza notte per arrivare ad un equivalente del fuoco sotto quello che Morrison chiama "casa" ma che sarebbe stato forse una tenda; e almeno una casa di forma poco svillupata [sviluppata].

Spero di fare un VERO lavoro prima di pubblicare il volumetto. Il collega Luchini è un tesoro, che ha veramente scrupoli per la parola italiana. Sino adesso i traduttori sono stato ipnotizzato [ipnotizzati] dal sostantivo, sempre cercando di legare l'ideogramma ad un[a] "parte"/sostantivo; verbo, ajjetivo [aggettivo]. Qua l'italiano ha più possibilità forse, che non l'inglese.

Cambiare "processo" a proseguendo e dove tradurrse [tradurre] si radica 'm [in] la mano che afferra la terra è la radice; la mano vegetale; non mano animale. Almeno, cosi mi pare/

E in un testo classico ed antico; mi pare che si deve conservare il senso originale degli ideogrammi; non cadere nel informe ed incolorito valore dato alle parole in un quotidiano di oggi.

Spero di rivedervi quando torno a Roma; ed anche d'avere vostro [la vostra] opinione sulla nostra versione. Facciamo adesso il Ta S'eu

Poi inizierò il Mencio, facendo un libro alla volta. Per quanto vedo/ta [la] vera tradizione è Kung/ Tseng/Mencio e [g]li altri sono irrelevanti; sovente interessante, ma non la linea diretta.

Certo quel commento al Cap. V. è fuori

che viene stampato

l'ambito etico. dove il Tseng manca

etc/ buon esito al vostro lavoro ed a presto, spero.

[Dear Dr Yang: Thanks for your beautiful postcard. But my version needs some revision. I was in Rome without a dictionary. I put too much trust in [James] Legge, who was full of Christian terms and didn't look at any ideograms. Three or four verses are probably okay, but I have to revise the others.

I saw (literally SAW) the ideogram "sincerità"/perfection or adjusting the word to fit the thought/

The TIGER [虎] is important/

But I was far from understanding the cliff; and I have had to think half a night to come up with an equivalent of the fire underneath what Morrison calls "house" but was more likely a tent; or at best a very underdeveloped form of house.

I hope to get some REAL work done before I publish my little volume. My collaborator Luchini is a great find because he is very meticulous with Italian words. Until now the translators have been hypnotized by the noun, always trying to link the ideograms to a "part"/noun, verb, adjective. Maybe the Italian language has more possibilities than English.

Change "process" to continuation and one has to translate the radical: the hand that grasps the earth is the root; the vegetable hand, not the animal hand.

At least it seems to me like this/

And in a classical and ancient text, I think one has to preserve the original meanings of the ideograms, and not to follow the formless and colorless value given words in a newspaper of today.

I hope to see you when you return to Rome; and also to hear your opinion about our version. We are now doing the Ta S'eo. Then we'll start the Mencius, one book at a time. As far as I can see, the true tradition is Kung/Tseng/Meng. The others are irrelevant; they are interesting, but not in the direct line.

Of course the comment that is printed in Chapter 5 is beyond the ethical scope, whether Tseng is missing, etc. Good luck with your work. I'll see you soon I hope.]

(TL-2; Beinecke): The original letter is lost. Our text is transcribed from its carbon copy (Beinecke).

Legge: James Legge (1815–97), *The Four Books* (Shanghai: Commercial Press, 1923). EP's copy of Legge's one-volume Four Books is kept at the Burke Library of Hamilton College.

Il TIGRE [虎]: Reference to the etymology of the character 慮 (consider). EP renders 慮 as "keep his head in the presence of a tiger" in *The Great Digest* (*Confucius*, 29). Cf. Canto 85/569: "and then consider the time | liú 慮."

Morrison: Robert Morrison (1782–1834), *A Dictionary of the Chinese Language, in Three Parts* (Macao: The Honorable East India Company Press, 1815). EP's and DP's copy of the multivolume dictionary is kept at the Burke Library of Hamilton College.

Luchini: Alberto Luchini, cotranslator with EP of *Ta S'eu*, was then director of the Department of Racial Studies and Propaganda under the Italian Ministry of Popular Culture.

Mencio: at the suggestion of Sig. Tchu (see Letter 49), EP moved on to *Zhong yong*, the second of the Four Books, instead. The result was *Chiung Iung: L'Asse che non vacilla* (1945), rpt. in *Confucio: Studio integrale & L'Asse che non vacilla* (1955).

23   Yang to EP (ALS-2; Beinecke)

Albergo d'Italia
Roma
15. 6. '42.

Caro Sig. Pound

Stamane quello amico (del ministero) mi ha telefonato dicendo che voi volevate qualche idiograma cinese, ma non ho capito bene le parole quindi non ho potuto rispondere [a] quello che mi domandava ed ora non so, se voi avete già trovato sul vocabolario o no; se vi ne ha bisogno ancora vi prego di scrivermi. Il Sig. Tchu è piaciuto quel suo libro di "Ta Hsiao" (大 學) e vorrebbe ancora alcune copie <per gli amici suoi> e se non vi dispiace vi prego di mandarai [mandare] altre 10 copie quando vi è comodo.

Tanti saluti cordiali dal Sig. Tchu e da me molte grazie e saluti cari,

Yang Fengchi

[Dear Mr Pound: This morning my friend (from the ministry) called to tell me that you wanted some Chinese ideograms, but I didn't catch the words, so I couldn't respond to what he asked. Now I don't know if you have found them in a dictionary; if you still need them, please write to me. Mr Zhu liked your book "Ta Hsiao" (大 學) very much and he would like more copies to give to his friends, and if it's no trouble to you I would like you to send me ten more copies when you have time. Regards from Zhu and many thanks, Yang Fengchi]

altre 10 copie: in a card of 30 July 1942 (Beinecke), Yang acknowledged receipt of ten more copies of *Ta S'eu* (大 學) from EP.

4
Achilles Fang and Pound's Bilingual *Confucius*
"All answers are in the FOUR BOOKS"

Brought from Italy to the United States, Pound was pronounced unfit for trial and committed to St Elizabeths Hospital in Washington, DC. During his first years of incarceration at the federal hospital for the criminally insane (1946–52), Pound was engrossed in Confucian translations, not writing any new cantos. Apart from making draft versions of *The Analects* (1950) and the *Odes* (1954), he prepared a bilingual edition of *The Great Digest & The Unwobbling Pivot* with reproductions of rubbings from the Tang Stone-Classics. It was Willis Meeker Hawley (1896–1987), a Hollywood bookseller and sinologist, who gave him the idea of the Stone-Classics. Pound had purchased Chinese books and dictionaries from Hawley, and in a letter of 6 October 1948, Hawley told him about "some of the Chinese deluxe editions which are made up of rubbings from monuments on which the classics were carved in the handwriting of famous calligraphers" (Lilly). Two years later, in August 1950, samples of the Tang Stone-Classics finally reached St Elizabeths (see Fig. 4.1). When Hawley offered to compose "a one page preface or post-face about the Stone Classics" (Beinecke), Pound chose to brush the proposal aside.

What Pound had in mind was someone with real authority to treat this topic. At the same time, a man who was ideally qualified for the task was also looking for Pound. That summer Pound's American publisher, James Laughlin of New Directions, forwarded to him a letter from a "Reverend Fang," suggesting consistent and correct spellings of Chinese names in Cantos 52–61. On 28 September 1950 that man wrote to Laughlin again to inquire about how "the remaining Cantos [would] turn out" and if some of them might "deal with modern China" (Lilly).

The man who inquired about *The Cantos* was Achilles Fang (Fang Zhitong 方志彤, 1910–95), whom the Harvard-Yenching Institute had hired in 1947 to work on a Chinese–English dictionary. Born of Chinese ancestry in Korea, Fang went to Shanghai, China to attend the American Baptist College before entering Qinghua University in Beijing where he earned a BA in philosophy in 1932. After two more years of graduate studies at Qinghua, he joined the Guangxi Medical College in South China as a Latin instructor (1934–7). Having also taught German at two colleges in Beijing (Catholic University and Deutschland-Institut) and edited the *Monumenta Serica: Journal of Oriental Studies of Catholic University,* Fang was overqualified for the job (see Fig. 4.2). Before long he understandably grew bored with the dictionary project and began pursuing a Ph.D. degree in comparative literature at Harvard. His chosen topic for a dissertation was Pound's *Pisan Cantos.*

Fang and Pound initially communicated through Laughlin, and by November 1950 Fang offered to compose a note on the Stone-Classics for Pound's bilingual edition of *The Great Digest & The Unwobbling Pivot* (1951). After making a draft, Fang decided to come down to Washington to meet Pound. Pound was overjoyed. Fang's visit to St Elizabeths on 27 December 1950 was described by Dorothy as "a pleasure—to both of us." It was a pleasure to Dorothy because she was relieved that after several years' isolation Ezra had "somebody to talk with, who understood some of his problems" (Beinecke).

This first meeting between Pound and Achilles Fang was immediately followed by vigorous exchanges of letters. The extant Pound–Achilles Fang correspondence consists of some 214 items, 108 from Pound to Fang and 106 from Fang to Pound. Considering their massiveness and importance I have given these letters two chapters: the letters of 1950–2 are reproduced in this chapter, and those of 1952–8 are presented in Chapter 7.

Many of the early Pound–Fang letters concern the Stone-Classics edition of *The Great Digest & The Unwobbling Pivot.* They reveal that Fang contributed more than just "A Note on the Stone-Classics" (*Confucius,* 11–15), which Pound found "very well written" (Letter 46). During their first meeting, Fang handed over to Pound a list of recommended changes in the romanization of Chinese names. Pound accepted them, conceding that they would "fit without ruining sonority" (Letter 27). As the edition was more complex than any other Pound books he had handled, Laughlin invited Fang to review the proofs, not only to "mark in pencil the changes in spelling" but also to "examine the proofs of the facing Chinese characters and see whether they were all right, and whether they were lined up properly" (Beinecke). Fang graciously complied with the request, a relief for both Laughlin and Pound.

The letters tell us a great deal about Pound's Confucian studies at St Elizabeths. As a fervent book collector, Fang took pleasure in sharing his own copies of Chinese classics with Pound. (Before his death Fang willed his collection to Beijing University, with an initial shipment of some 5,000 volumes.) Among those texts he sent Pound was *Shu jing* (Book of History) in the original, a source of *Rock-Drill* (1955), and at Pound's request Fang gave him an account of the "Thirteen Classics." After reading through some of these volumes, Pound came to a conclusion, which he repeated again and again in subsequent letters: "All the answers are in the FOUR BOOKS."

As a scholar Fang delighted in discussing Confucian terminologies with Pound. The two usually disagreed with each other on readings of Confucius and Mencius. Their debate on one issue could continue for weeks, even months. Occasionally Pound's interpretation would strike Fang as brilliant. One such example is Pound's definition of the Confucian word *zhi* 止, which prompted Fang to say: "your interpretation of 止 seems to solve a number of knotty problems in Kung's book" (Letter 30). The exchanges between Pound and Fang on concepts such as *jing* 敬 (respect) and "four TUAN" 四 端 (four virtuous beginnings of human nature) may appear tedious, but they have a bearing on Pound's late cantos. When read in conjunction with Letters 42, 44, and 58, Pound's uses of the "four TUAN" in Cantos 85, 89, and 99 recall and intensify his earlier references to the Confucian belief in *ren* 仁 or virtuous human nature.

As a dictionary compiler, Fang was able to answer Pound's trying queries about Chinese dictionaries, evaluating in specific terms their respective strengths and weaknesses. From the beginning Pound surprised Fang with his insight into the reorganization (in the seventeenth century) of Chinese diction-aries from a 540-root (radical) system to a 214-root system. For him the change was "one of [the] greatest intellectual acts in all history" (Letter 29). At Pound's urging, Fang investigated the development of Chinese dictionaries from *Shuo-wen* (100–21 AD) to *Kangxi* (1716), resulting in a working bibliography that illuminates the organizational changes (Letter 57).

Pound was of course curious to know what Fang might think of Fenollosa's essay "re/ the chinkese langwidG OR ideogram which is fer somethings the most precise and, in fact, only satisfactory medium for making certain statements" (Letter 37). His own view on the Fenollosan approach had under-gone some noticeable transformation. With *Mathews' Chinese–English Dictionary* he was able to study Chinese sound, even its tone. He would rhyme Chinese syllables with English syllables in *Thrones* (1959). In one of his letters to Fang, he wrote: "For years I never made ANY attempt to hitch ANY sound to the ideograms/content with the meaning and the visual form" (Letter 56).

The exchanges between Pound and Fang in 1950–2 encouraged them to continue their work together. During that period Pound was increasingly frustrated by his failed attempts to bring out an edition of the Confucian Odes with a Chinese sound key and a Chinese seal text. Fang offered to assist him in this complex project. The story of how the Odes project was going to strain their friendship will be uncovered in their late correspondence.

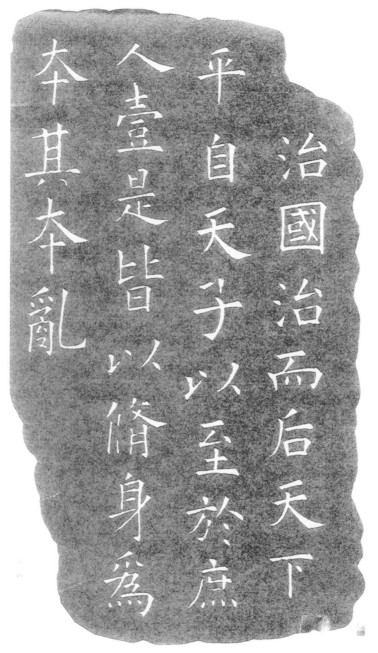

治國治而后天下
平自天子以至於庶
人壹是皆以脩身爲
本其本亂

Fig. 4.1. Sample of the Tang Stone-Classics. (Lilly)

Fig. 4.2. Achilles Fang with his daughter Madeleine, 1951. (Ilse Fang)

24   *Fang to EP (ALS-2; Lilly)*

23 Boylston Hall
Harvard College
Cambridge, Mass.
Nov. 26, 1950

Dear Dr Pound,

Many thanks for your kind letter. Now I can proceed and do that short note on Stone Classics. K'ienlung's edict does not contain anything very exciting; should I succeed in turning out a fairly readable version, I shall submit it for your inspection.

I hope to come to Washington around Christmas and have written to that effect to the Superintendent.

Yours respectfully
Achilles Fang

your kind letter: EP's message delivered by James Laughlin on 25 November 1950: "I sent your letter down to him and he replies as follows: 'All glory to the nobl Fang/whom shall be DEEElighted to see at any time gawd letZim git here. It is the T'ang text we are using.' He also likes very much the little snapshot you sent of the stones, and I hope we may keep this, and have it enlarged and use it for some of our publicity" (Beinecke).

short note: "A Note on the Stone-Classics" (*Confucius*, 11–15).

K'ienlung's edict: for Qianlong's preface to the Qing Stone-Classics, see Fang's version in *Confucius*, 13–15. Emperor Qianlong (1711–99) succeeded Yongzheng (Yong Tching of Canto 61) in 1736, who succeeded Kangxi (Kang Hi of Canto 60) in 1723.

25   *EP to Fang (ALS-1; Beinecke)*

S. Eliz
DC
2 Dec [1950]

But very necessary.
ancient awareness
& practice.
- - - - - - - - - - - - -
as to excitement, Dr Fang,
I had some.
very cordially yours
& hoping see you
soon.

EP

26   *EP to Fang (ALS-2; Beinecke)*

S. <u>Elizabeths</u> Hospital

Wash D.C.

[5 December 1950]

Dear Dr Fang,

Thanks so much for the foto.

I shall be delighted to see you if you manage to get to Washington.

Visiting hours any day from 1–4 P.M. but please write to Superintendent, S. Eliz, now & your name will then be on the visiting list and no time lost after your arrival.

It is the T'ang lettering, rubbings, but text as in Legge & opinions as per Yong Ching or Sacred Edict of Kang H(s)i.

gratefully yours

E.P.

the foto: see Letter 24 n.

Legge: see Letter 22 n.

Yong Ching or Sacred Edict of Kang H(s)i: F. W. Baller, ed., *Sacred Edict* (Shanghai: China Inland Mission, 1907), with Emperor Yongzheng's literary and Salt Commissioner Wang Youpu's colloquial expansions of Kangxi's Edict and Baller's English translation of the latter, source of Cantos 98–9.

27   *EP to Fang (TL-1; Beinecke)*

[St Elizabeths Hospital]

[Washington, DC]

[30 December 1950]

to FANG, Achilles

strictly anonymous communication.

Thanks very much.

Also the corrections will fit without ruining sonority.

★★

Probably no need to send the Stilwell and other book if you give me the titles, they can probably be got from library.

★★

BUT the next question is: which of the OTHER 13 classics can be got at? Neither Hawley nor Orientalia [Hummel] have mentioned any of them in their catalogues. The Four, the Odes, Spr/ and Aut, the Shu/ yes, got 'em. Also Li Ki, Couvreur. (Hummel sez call it LEE GEE)

What else can a man read? i.e. GET the original texts of?

★★

Meant to say that Giles "Strange Tales," one of the few evidences of civilized sinology. Fellow named Orr, or Ogg or something did decent trans/ of the Shu, as far as I can remember.

and take tranquility to feed my breath
然   the italians say: è pacifico [it's obvious]
犬 然   when a thing is acceptable without discussion
dog's man too active

Stilwell: *The Stilwell Papers,* ed. Theodore White (New York: Sloane Associates, 1948). During World War II Joseph W. Stilwell (1883–1946) was US chief of the joint staff in the China-Burma-India war zone.

13 classics: *Book of Odes, Book of History, Book of Changes, Book of Rites, Gongyang's Commentary, Guliang's Commentary, Zuo's Commentary, Rites of Zhou, Records of Rites, Book on Filial Piety, Analects, Erya,* and *Mencius.* For reference to "the 13 classics," see Fang's version of Qianlong's preface (*Confucius,* 15).

[Hummel]: Arthur William Hummel (1884–1975), director of the Library of Congress Orientalia Division (1928–54).

"Strange Tales": Herbert A. Giles (1845–1935), *Strange Tales from a Chinese Studio* (Shanghai: Kelly and Walsh, 1916), a version of *Liaozhai zhiyi* by Pu Songling (1640–1715).

然: see Letter 28.

28   *Fang to EP (TLS-4; Lilly)*

[Cambridge, Mass.]
January 3, 1951

Dear Mr Pound,

Thank you ever so much for your two "anonymous communications." As Mrs Pound might have conveyed to you how I enjoyed meeting you, "every minute of it" (as people in this country would say), I do not repeat myself here. Sometimes it's a pity that one remains a heathen, for one cannot draw upon the saying, "The Lord has been good to me."

What edition of the Shu [Book of History] have you got? I have here a copy of Legge, pirated, exactly identical with the Four Books you have: Chinese text, notes, etc. If you are interested in it, I shall be glad to mail it to you.

I believe Couvreur's Li Ki and Tso Tchouan (Tso's commentary on Spring and Autumn) are in the library there.

Li Ki may be considered as a Reallexikon or encyclopedia of ancient learning, while Tso Tchouan (anglice: Tso Chuan) is a model for later historians, who have a penchant for the anecdotal.

But the liber librorum [book of books] is the Shu. It is not so dull as most ignoramuses think but often very lively. And it has direct bearing on Kung and Meng [Mencius].

Legge's translation of the Shu is, it is humbly submitted, comparable to Giles' Strange Tales. Both the Presbyterian missionary and the British consul are heavy in style; so are the Shu and the Liao Chai Chih I [*Strange Tales*]. I mean, Legge's Shu is not bad at all.

As soon as you give me word, I shall mail the book post-haste. (A friend of mine here has a copy of Liao Chai Chih I; do you like to have it? He is willing to part with his duplicate copy.)

I wonder if you would like to read Edouard Chavannes' Les mémoires historiques de Sé-ma Ts'ien: a readable translation of Ssu-ma Ch'ien's Shih Ki, which very often reads like Herodotus. By the way, Ssu-ma Ch'ien has served as a model for most of the best prosateurs of China and Japan (and Korea and Annam). The last chapter in the last volume (Vol. 5) contains Kung's biography. (Chavannes' book is not complete; of the original 130 chapters he translated about half.)

Now I can see where you got that chen, circumflex. It is the mistake of Tsang's dictionary. The fact is, chen and chên do not make any difference; both are pronounced djən. The circumflex is meant to indicate that e is not pronounced e as in end but something like u in (American and not British) under. The proofreading of Tsang's book is at fault: e, when not in diphthongs, should have been made uniformly either ê or e.

Hope Fenollosa's "East and West" was not dreary reading. Tomorrow I am sending Williams' dictionary, which has the good point, inter alia, of distinguishing between k and ch.

Yours respectfully
[signed] Achilles Fang

Thank you for the new address of Peter Russell.
Very sorry to have caused you to write on Paige's editorship of Letters. Mr Horton might have spared you the pain by simply ignoring what I had to gabble out of sheer inadvertency. However, I am glad to get another anonymous communication. (When I see Macleish, I shall tell him that you had no hand in the editing of that book. May I show him your letter? I will not undertake anything rash without your permission, of course.)
I wonder if

> And they worked out the Y-king or changes
>> to guess from   (Canto LIII p. 12)

could be revised to

> And he etc etc

or to   Wen Wang etc etc   (for Wen Wang see p. 11),
for I should like to use the (revised) passage as motto for my Pisan-explication.
De Mailla 1.239–240 (s.v. 1142 av. Chr.) has:

Ouen-ouang (Wen-wang 文 王) resta trois ans dans les prisons de Yeou-ly (Yu-li 羑 里): [. . .]

Doesn't this describe E.P in Pisan?

(By the way, Wen-wang was thrown into prison by the last king of the Yin—also called Shang—dynasty, Cheou-sin (p. 12, i.e. Shou-sin 受 辛), who saw, and correctly, his Nemesis in this amiable man.)

A propos of 敬 (at the beginning of the Analects translation in Hudson Review and at the end of Canto LIX, London ed.), pronounced <u>king</u> (k unaspirated) or <u>ching</u> (Mandarin, which turns k and k' followed by i or ü into ch and ch', e.g. Hummel's LEE GEE). [...]

Speaking of the term 敬, Chu Hi once said:

My teacher Ch'eng I-ch'uan was the first to elucidate this term adequately. In recent years Ch'eng Sha-sui would refute his view, saying that ancient sages never spoke of the term 敬 in isolation but always spoke of respecting one's parents, respecting one's sovereign, or respecting one's elders (敬 親, 君, 長), the object being always attached to the verb. But this doesn't make sense. The sage (Confucius?) spoke of 修 己 以 敬 [cultivate oneself and be respectful], 敬 而 無 失 [be respectful and no fault] and 聖 敬 日 躋 [be respectful and advance daily]. Do not these instances prove that the term was used unattached? If, for argument's sake, we are to practise "respect" when we have parents, a sovereign, or elders, then should we be disrespectful when they are not about? ...

- - - - - - - - -

(By the way, will you please drop "respectfully" when you write to me; for you are an "elder" 長 to me.)

- - - - - - - - -

Isn't it remarkable that [Leo] Tolstoi should say "Simply, without any relation to anything definite"?

- - - - - - - - -

Do you suppose the term 敬 has any relation to reverentia in Maxima debetur puero reverentia [The greatest respect is owed to the boy]

(I'm quoting from Juvenal and not from Thackeray's The Newcomes)? or to

And Kung said

"Respect a child's faculties (Canto XIII p. 59)

- - - - - - - - - -

Karlgren (Analytical Dictionary of Chinese and Sino-Japanese, Paris 1923, p. 138, no. 396), s.v. 敬:

The seal shows this to contain, besides 攴 to beat, not <u>kou</u> 苟 but 句 and 羊: to 句 speak 羊 nicely (cf. 義, 善).

- - - - - - - - - -

By the way, Karlgren, no. 929, analyses your character 然 into "to 火 roast 犬 dog's 肉 meat." Speaking of dogs, I was a bit amused to notice, near Hartford, the sign-board "Uncle Ezra's Dog Farm," which forcibly reminded me of Congress Heights.

the Four Books you have: James Legge, *The Four Books* (Shanghai: Commercial Press, 1923).

Couvreur's Li Ki and Tso Tchouan: Séraphin Couvreur (1835–1919), *Li Ki* (Ho Kien Fu: Mission catholique, 1913) and *Tch'ouen ts'iou et Tso-tchouan* (Ho Kien Fu: Mission catholique, 1914).

Giles' Strange Tales: see Letter 27 n.

Ssu-ma Ch'ien: see Glossary on Sima Qian.

Tsang's dictionary: O. Z. Tsang, *A Complete Chinese–English Dictionary* (Shanghai: Lin Nan Middle School, 1920). EP's unfinished essay "Preliminary Survey" (see Appendix) is based on Tsang's dictionary. See Letter 30 n.

"East and West": Ernest Fenollosa (see Glossary), *East and West: The Discovery of America and Other Poems* (1893; New York: Crowell and Co., 1936).

Williams' dictionary: Samuel Wells Williams, *Syllabic Dictionary of the Chinese Language* (1950).

Peter Russell: see Letter 91 n.

Paige: Douglas Duncan Paige (b. 1924) interviewed EP and edited *Selected Letters, 1907–1941* (1950) while teaching at Wellesley College.

Horton: see Glossary on Horton, T. David.

MacLeish: see Glossary on MacLeish, Archibald.

De Mailla: see Glossary on De Mailla, Joseph-Anne-Marie de Moyriac.

Wen-wang: see Glossary on Wen, King.

敬: *jing*; cf. *Confucius*, 193: "敬 *respect for the kind of intelligence that enables grass seed to grow grass; the cherry-stone to make cherries.*" See also Cantos 85/575 and 98/711 where 敬 occurs without an object attached.

Ch'eng I-ch'uan: Cheng Yichuan (1033–1107), cofounder with Zhu Xi (see Glossary) of the Cheng-Zhu school of Confucian ethics.

Juvenal: Roman poet Juvenal (*c*.55–127 AD), *Satires* 14. 47.

Thackeray's The Newcomes: William Makepeace Thackeray (1811–63), *The Newcomes* (1853–5).

Karlgren: see Glossary on Karlgren, Bernhard.

29   EP to Fang *(TL-2; Beinecke)*

[St Elizabeths Hospital]
[Washington, DC]
[5 January 1951]

hnBL FANG

kindly NOT show letter to M[a]cLeish, but convey comfort ANonymously.

Ez/ haz CHOU; ideogram, latin and frog [French]/ Couvreur also Legge english. HERE

Li Ki in Rapallo. no need or desire for it in D.C. seeking CHINESE texts not yet chewed thru.

Young Igor <i.e. my son-in-law's kid brother> sends half dozen proverbs in his last letter.

Don't much want translations unless I can get the original at the same time. How can I tell what the style is if I have only the trans/??

Fenollosa's notes interesting, and HIS "style" OF the period.
***

no objection to hnBL Fang misquoting or improving "they" to "he" re the I CHING (or King) but I had in mind the successive returns, and wasn't setting up to be Ouen-ouang [King Wen]. and didn't get Mr Sung's edition, or see ideogramic text until I had got out of the gorilla cage into the hell hole.

As to RESPECT/there are degrees/I SUSpect Tolstoi and ALL goddam hrooshuns [Russians]/ seem to recall that Kung mentioned cases where respect was NOT required. Tolstoi? A Mihite? Or at any rate a slav/

will look up text and see what verb Kung uses in the case of the bloke aetat [aged] fifty who was still an ass. as distinct from the neo-nato. The neo-nato might be held to have some of the sense of the cherry-stone?

of course if the hnBL Fang is THAT MUCH older than a neonato??

Also/as change from seal to the 214 root system was cert/ one of [the] greatest intellectual acts in all history. I see no reason to exclude the idea that the 214 root system may occasionally have improved on the preceding.

The good Hawley will probably rise thru the ceiling, if such idea is ever mentioned in his vicinage.

as to Chu Hi and the Ch'eng.

I d/n well know that respect is sometimes used in specific ref/ and that when I had got to grass-seed and looked back to Italian version to see if I needed to revise, I found that I could NOT revise/ because it would not fit context/

BUT surely the term is pretty well isolated where Kung distinguishes between the Chun[g] [respecting one's sovereign] and the Hsiao [respecting one's parents] (if there is ANY use my trying to transliterate romanJikly anyhow between the gent and the piker.

(Hope Uncle Ezra's dawg farm aint an imitation of Amy's High-Lo kennels. Mebbe he got there first. (precedingly born)

Oh yes, once again, if I start answering back to Fang, and continue to read, then F/has already puttt down at least part of the answer. Canto XIII.

AND: them bloomink SWEEDES!!!!

Thanks for indicating the Stilwell which will rd/at 1st/op/and probably the Belden/as to White Papers?? is it safe? I once recd/ten vols/of U.S. treasury reports, read several pages and LOOK where it landed me.

CHOU: Séraphin Couvreur, *Chou King* (Paris: Cathasia, 1950), a Latin-French-Chinese edition of *Shu jing* (Book of History), source of Cantos 85–6.

Igor: see Glossary on De Rachewiltz, Igor.

Sung's edition: Z. D. Sung, *The Symbols of Yi King* (Shanghai: China Modern Education, 1934).

cherry-stone: see Letter 28 n.

214 root system: the 214-radical system first adopted by Mei Dingzuo in *Zihui* (Character Treasure, 1615). See Letter 57.

Hawley: see Glossary on Hawley, Willis Meeker.

Chu Hi and the Ch'eng: see Letter 28 n. and Glossary on Zhu Xi.

SWEEDES: see Glossary on Karlgren, Bernhard.

Belden: Fang sent EP a copy of Jack Belden's *China Shakes the World* (New York: Harper, 1949) to stir interest in modern China.

30   *Fang to EP (TLS-1; Beinecke)*

Cambridge, Mass.
January 12th 1951

Dear Mr. Pound,

Yesterday I had the temerity to mail you the Stilwell book; and this in spite of your injunction and Meng's advice (IV B xxiii, second sentence. Legge's version is very much perverted; a more sensible translation would be—"When to give and not to give are both equally proper, etc."). I already seem to hear you declaiming, Quo usque, o Achilles, abutere nostra patientia? [Abuse our patience, O Achilles, to what extent?]

Hope to send you the Belden book soon. I can't say whether it would be "safe" to read White Papers. 1054 pages of it cannot all serve the triple objective, ut doceat, ut moveat, ut delectet [to teach, to move, to delight]; and yet, part of the Annexes (pp. 413 sqq.) seems to be quite readable.

Thank you ever so much for two more anonymous communications. As for your notes, I am now writing down the ideograms. (I am afraid, some of the CH words have to be regrouped under K.) After they are retouched here and there, no "comments, castigatory, astringent, tolerant etc." would be needed. Please give me a bit more time for the work. Hope to use the plenipotentiary power judiciously.

Thank you sincerely for the three A books. Adams is fascinating; Agassiz is a little heavy; as for Alighieri's Paradiso, I should not forget that Eliot profited by your advice. If a bloke happens to have a name beginning with B, would you prescribe him Boccaccio, Baudelaire, and Browning-Sordello? (Excuse this flippancy.)

It is true that the first word in "Respect a child's faculties" stands for 畏 and not 敬; but Kung surely was using the two terms synonymously. At any rate, in [*Analects*] XVI viii (p. 177), 畏 seems to stand for 敬.

By the way, your interpretation of 止 seems to solve a number of knotty problems in Kung's book. I've been looking through commentaries, but so far failed to come across any that lays emphasis on that term. Please accept my congratulations. I shall not fail to expand on this aspect of Your Confucianism.

Respectfully yours
[signed] Achilles Fang

I have here a few texts (易 [Book of Changes], 書 [Book of History], 詩 [Book of Odes], 孝 經 [Book on Filial Piety]) belonging to my wife, who is willing to part with them. As soon as I hear from you, I shall mail them to you.

Stilwell book: see Letter 27 n.
Belden book: see letter 29 n.

your notes: "Preliminary Survey" (see Appendix). In the winter of 1950–1 EP used O. Z. Tsang's *Complete Chinese–English Dictionary* (1920) as a guide to speculate about sound-symbolism in primitive Chinese. He didn't use *Mathews' Chinese–English Dictionary* because Hawley had warned of its "scrambled romanization" (12 January 1947, Lilly). For Fang's criticism of Tsang's dictionary, see Letter 28.

Adams: see Glossary on Adams, Brooks.

Agassiz: see Glossary on Agassiz, Louis.

your interpretation of 止: see Appendix. Cf. *Confucius*, 232: "*There is no more important technical term in the Confucian philosophy than this chih* (3) *the hitching post, position, place one is in, and works from.*" 止 appears in Canto 85/563, 573 and Canto 87/591, 596.

31   EP to Fang *(TL-2; Beinecke)*

[St Elizabeths Hospital]
[Washington, DC]
[18 January 1951]

Hnbl FANG

two rolls Chou Change [Book of Changes] arrived S. Liz/ 4 other presumable rolls of something also recd/ at Tenth Place [DP's apartment]. Enjoyable sight.

regret

inform

hnbl F/ that some goddam worm has been at respected pages. Problem? shd/ one (i.e. Ez) attempt to treat worst worm-holes with crass occidental stickum

as per sample

or wd/ it do more harm than good. and shd/one trust sd/goddam worms now deceased and not likely to gnaw while Ez peruses or after shake-up?

Evidently overlooked commas in your letter and thought change—odes some other text. No harm done save "disturbo" to Fang, and pleasant to read from nicely printed text.

at least recognize a few terms without having crib on next page.

Iggurunt man wanting to know what ELSE one shd/ read after material that Legge has already trapsed through? Fg/ realize the very fragmentary state of Ez' formation,

Not read ANY guide or history of Chinese literature since closed Giles history Ch/ Lit/ about 1909. Had Fenollosa's notes and selections and thaZZZall.

AND take it Bhud and Taoists bamboogroving ad lib/ thru a good deal of it??

Of course there is enough in the 4 BOOKS and the Odes to occupy any normal male for a life time,

but frailties of idle curiosity assail from time to time.

Will certainly READ the Chinese MORE and see MORE in this edtn/ than in the Shanghai bilingual.

Enjoying the simpatico but not infallible Stilwell. Too bad he knew nothing of Europe, and, as you say, 仁 [humanity].

Later: yes, yes, very fine. Will try to work Sun Li-jen in somehow. If the ass of a pub[lishe]r/ wd. put a SCALE (miles, parsangs or whatever, on his MAP!!!)

p. 292/translation? unconscious? have I got to look up that ideogram with a DAWG in it?   獲

incidentally our damn SWEEDE dont seem to differentiate 犬 &犭

ad interim/ and strictly anonYmouse.

Mr (Sumner?) Wells Williams dont like that one either.

verry good INK used on that Y Ching [Book of Changes].

Giles history: Herbert A. Giles (1845–1935), *A History of Chinese Literature* (New York: Appleton, 1901).

Fenollosa's notes: see Glossary on Fenollosa, Ernest.

Shanghai bilingual: Z. D. Sung, *The Symbols of Yi King* (1934).

Sun Li-jen: in *The Stilwell Papers* Sun Liren is referred to as Stilwell's favorite Chinese army commander.

獲: in *Analytic Dictionary* (1923) Bernhard Karlgren defines 獲 *huo* (#120) as "catch, seize, obtain." 獲 surfaces in Canto 85/567.

Wells Williams: see Letter 28 n.

32   *EP to Fang (TL-1; Beinecke)*

[St Elizabeths Hospital]
[Washington, DC]
[5 February 1951]

Hnbl/ FANG

strictly anonymous communication.

What could save infinite time and labour fer pore mutts trying to learn a little chinese, esp/ SOUND. would be (without waiting to make perfect word-book) to print RADICAL index, now pages 1179/80 of Mathews, as pages 1180 and 1181, THAT IS so that one could see them ALL without turning the page every time one wants one on the other side as at present.

AND <pages 1181–1221> print with the sounds and tone numbers. enough space could be made by omitting heading and the "colloquial designations." p 1180

plenty of meanings I know, but have to look up the sound to understand metric in 1000 family/

Mathews is certainly VERY good on groups.

as ref/ "balanced expression 7 word"

"meet the moon coming off", all verbs theatre words.

Spose if weren't so goddamlaZy I cd/ find out when etc/ the 1000

might also investigate obstacles to PRINTING above item.

Mathews: R. H. Mathews, *Mathews' Chinese–English Dictionary* (Shanghai: China Inland Mission and Presbyterian Mission Press, 1931; rpt. Cambridge, Mass.: Harvard University Press, 1944).

1000 family: Tang Song qian jia shi (*Poems by a Thousand Tang and Song Poets*). In 1951 Fang sent EP a set in four volumes.

33   *Fang to EP (TLS-1; Lilly)*

[Cambridge, Mass.]
Feb 10, 1951

Dear Mr Pound,

On February 16, Friday (9–9:30 P.M.), Ass. Prof. Richard Ellmann (quite a nice chap) and A. F. are to talk 'unrehearsed and live,' over the Harvard Yard radio (which cannot be heard beyond Harvard dormitories). Subject: Ezra Pound's Cantos. I am expected to elucidate, if I can, your Confucianism.

Have you any special message that I may quote in the course of my talk? Your greetings to the Kremlin, 'tell them to read cantos' (as the author of Eimi reports), is hardly necessary. I think your cantos are being read at Harvard; how intelligently, that is another question, of course.

If a public message is not to your liking, will you at least give me some strictly private suggestions?

Yours respectfully
[signed] Achilles Fang

P.S.: Yesterday I mailed you the Jack Belden book.

Richard Ellmann: Richard Ellmann (1918–87) would join Northwestern (fall 1951), Yale (1968), and Oxford (1970).
Jack Belden book: *China Shakes the World* (1949).

34   *EP to Fang (TL-1; Beinecke)*

[St Elizabeths Hospital]
[Washington, DC]
[10 February 1951]

O FANG

in ignorance of wot't'ell the Achilles is doing re/ alledged dictionary/ and of position of 1000 family selection.

Does the sd/ Achilles want stray observations?

per es/ re difference between one dawg and another, i.e. the shaggy dawg and the friend of man? or in SEVEN WORD no. 45/ the vurry nice contrast of chih and szu/   知

backed by position of chih as derived or putt in arrow [矢] category not mouth [口] category rad[ical]/

no find in dic/   暮

significance clear but noise in doubt.

1000 family selection: see Letter 32 n.
SEVEN WORD no. 45: see Letter 32 on "balanced expression 7 word" in *Mathews' English–Chinese
    Dictionary.*
暮: see Letter 36.

35   EP to Fang *(TL-1; Beinecke)*

[St Elizabeths Hospital]
[Washington, DC]
[13 February 1951]

FANG

can be NO direct message from bug-house. EVERYthing useful can be clearly derived from published works.

1. all answers are in the FOUR BOOKS, i.e. all answers re/ conduct. E.P. translating and publishing Confucius in italian/ E.P.'s DIFFERENCES from Fascist theory and practice, PUBLICATION of same permitted in Italy. in brief: J. Adams and the U.S.A. Constitution.

Leahy (Admiral) "I was there"/showing Petain wanted: something between U.S. Constitution and Mussolini's first proposals.

Can Fang indicate new Bill of Rights pubd/ in England, as program? perhaps not in this talk but as topic of future curiosity.

Note appalling IGNORANCE, foetid in Hull and Leahy, but present also in Mme de Chambrun AND Stilwell, the latter fine value, BUT unaware of Europe, balance of power in Europe, European history also moral fury vs/C[hiang]. K. Chek, who under no obligation to prefer excessive Russia to a victorious Germany. Naturally no sympathy with Charlie [T. V.] Sung and his gang.

Gentle curiosity re/ LATER developments of Gesellism, cd/ be touched LIGHTLY, more in nature of enquiry as to what Mr P/ believes.

Write Rev. Henry Swabey, Lindsell Vicarage, Chelmsford, Essex, England, for proposed Bill of Rights/ useful subject for some stewed-dent's thesis re/"on which he leans." Hnbl/ Fang not LEAN on ANY asst/ profs.

the FOUR BOOKS: the four quintessential Confucian books *Da xue, Zhong yong, Lun yu,* and *Mencius.*
    See Glossary on Confucius. See also Letter 22 n.
Leahy: Admiral William Daniel Leahy (1875–1959) was President Roosevelt's chief of staff (1942–5).
Petain: Philippe Pétain (1856–1951), premier of the Vichy government, was tried and convicted
    in 1945.
Hull: Cordell Hull (1871–1955) was US Secretary of State from 1933 to 1944.
Mme de Chambrun: José Laval, daughter of French head of state Pierre Laval (1883–1945), married
    René de Chambrun in 1935.
Charlie Sung: T. V. Soong (1894–1971), Chiang Kai-shek's brother-in-law, was his finance minister
    from 1928 to 1933 and foreign minister from 1942 to 1945.
Gesellism: the monetary theories of the German businessman and economist Silvio Gesell
    (1862–1930).
Henry Swabey: see Glossary on Swabey, Reverend Henry.

36   Fang to EP (TL-2; Beinecke)

[Cambridge, Mass.]
[February 1951]

RE 暮, <u>mu</u>⁴.

- - - - - - - - -

This ideogram is a mistaken vulgar variation of 莫, which is [not] pronounced <u>mo</u>⁴ (in the sense of "do not", like μή) but <u>mu</u>⁴ (in the sense of "evening" or "late" as in The Analects XI xxv, 7, p. 112 暮). The K'ang-hsi dictionary (i.e. the dictionary compiled under the auspice of that emperor) and all later dictionaries list 暮 under 日 and 莫 under 艸.

- - - - - - - - - -

As for 莫,

The oracle-bone inscriptions of the Yin (Shang) dynasty write it both as 𦱴 (the sun among four grasses) and as 𣊟 (among four trees).

In bronze inscriptions of the Chou dynasty, the second form (four grasses) alone is found.

The first etymological dictionary Shuo-wen chieh-tzu 說文解字 of Hsü Shen 許慎 (second century A.D.; exact date not known) does not list 暮; instead it gives 𦱴, under Radical 艸. (This dictionary employs 540 Radicals.)

The dictionary Yü-p'ien 玉篇 of Ku Yeh-wang 顧野王 (519–581) records 暮 under Radical 542 日. (This dictionary uses 542 Radicals.)

- - - - - - - - - - - -

Whether 莫 was originally written 𣊟 or 𦱴 (as on the scroll in your room), it is to be considered as <u>the</u> correct form. 暮 cannot but be considered as a mistaken variation.

- - - - - - - - - -

> Hey Snag wots in the bibl'?
> wot are the books ov the bible?
> Name 'em, don't bullshit ME.
>   莫   OÝ TIΣ

a man on whom the sun has gone down

...   [Canto 74/450]

May one read "ME" as the pronunciation of 莫 <<u>mo</u> or <u>mu</u>>? ME at the same time reminds one of μή, which in turn makes one think of ού. And OÝ TIΣ, "Odessey", → "a man on whom the sun has gone down". Of course, the lower part of 莫 should represent neither 大 [big] nor 人 (man) but two grasses (艸); but does that matter???? non mihi [nothing].

Written two weeks or so ago, but got lost all this while among the pile of Poundiana on my desk.

Shuo-wen chieh-tzu: see Glossary on Xu Shen.
scroll in your room: a scroll of calligraphy by the etymologist Shen Jianshi, a gift from Achilles Fang.

37 *EP to Fang (TL-4; Beinecke)*

[St Elizabeths Hospital]
[Washington, DC]
[March 1951]

what has the hnbl/FANG to say to thick-headed occidental re/ the chinkese langwidG OR ideogram which is fer somethings the most precise and, in fact, only satisfactory medium for making certain statements, and IS in others the most damblasted and DAMbiguous modus loquendi, wot yu cant bust open with a meat AX??

[人] man
[煙] mist
[寒] cold < not example of ambiguity/>
[橘] orange
[柚] pumelo/

mean the blighter's face is all scrunched up like a[n] orange?? or wot the HELL?? Further fantasies fer child's guide to quick-chink:

numbers from yr/ beelUvvid' Mathews'.

[舍] she, 5699/shed
[甘] kan as in CANdy and sugar CANE
[恨] 2095/ hen, as in french haine.
[落] lo, 4122/low, and LOC as in location.
[書] su 5509/SUper
Lan 3807, as in LANiard [纜]
[浮] fou, 1906, as in frog/fou
[理] li, 3864, LIning (here only to the eye, not to ear)

I suppose that indistinguishable left-component, plus 3 mouths signifies Gavin Douglas' "blaisterand bubb"/ but still cant find which rad[ical]/ it is used for.

[臨] lin perfectly easy once one had the [臣] ch'en rad/

thought I HAD tried it, anyhow, but eye very untrained and no nack for running up and down columns.

VERY stupid of me not to see the sun under the grass/ but had finally done so.   [暮]
  ★★

the melopoeia, or part that matters TO ME, seems to resist all vagaries of dialect.
  ★★

now this pumelo? can the id/ refer to familiar tree (i.e. fam/ in Rapallo) the uncultivated orange, looks like an orange, but no taste and inedible (or at least until famine times.)

could that line mean: hearths cold, oranges reverted

i.e. to wild and useless state, from lack of care? probably the yu [柚] cannot mean mock-orange/ and this probably useless barbarian conjectured. a one-eyed wind with three mouths, three whoofs, blowing 3 ways makes more (//more mare's nests). Will remember that blooming "lin" [臨] from now on.

Cdn't be expected to know Sieh [謝] was proper name (as hadn't looked at commentary)

2630 [謝], a, b, c, d, wot a twister

any more data re Belden himself?

Belden might be improved??? question.

He is O.K. in loathing the Dewey, Luce, Fortune swine, BUT only objects to smear when aimed at pinks and commies. He is illiterate re/K'ung. Obviously Chiang K-S did NOT (p 425) practice the Confucian doctrine of ANYthing.

doubt if B[elden]/ ever read the text of K'ung even in Legge. also a bit of know-it-all when he generalizes, but good re/ what he has seen. Also still dodges fact that Roose was Roose. less competent than Chiang? and wd/hv/ made worse mess in C[hiang]'s circumstances. A swine of the smeariest.

Erigena is sd/ to hv sd/ "authority comes from right reason" have never spotted the chapter and verse where he says it, but had v. limited time for the search.

the Ta S'eu (or HIO, or whatever trans/lit/approx you use) knocks the tar out of almost every assumption B/ makes re K'ung, tho doubtless he is accurate enough re/ what Chiang or the mutts pretended was Confucian.

Bunting is howling for a bilingual oriental series (all oriental langs/) like the Loeb greek, latin. Might be tea time subject of talk with Harvard weaklings????

A. F. ever glance at Erigena or Avicenna? just to see that there have been nice minds outside the Middle Kingdom. But only one K/

Did I say Santayana half admitted: "no philosophy, only philo-epistemology since," I forget when, possibly Leibnitz, possibly Ocellus. I think I drew him by saying: since Ocellus: Sin, jih, jih sin [Day by day make it new].

Kindergarten mnemonics for sound. Do I know the sound of 60 id[eogram]s/??

Further mnemonic trifles/

shu¹ [殊] 5851/kill, very

as we say "dead right, dead certain"

***

re FOUR grasses, trees, etc/ I repeat: the reorganization from 500 down to 214 radicals was one of [the] greatest intellectual acts of all time. Lacking in english (so far as I know) a clear and adequate report on what actually happened/ did it need 1000 scholars or 40 or six?

Cannot rule out a priori the possibility that they did not simply DERIVE, but that they made new combinations of abbreviated root-pictograms with new connotations.

Sin jih jih sin

A.F. rad[ical]/ card gives rad/ 136 [舛], as confuse.

is there any specific known evidence that rules out idea of "opposites" i.e. waxing and waning moon

Some review OUGHT to print an A.F. account of the reorganization DOWN to 214 unless it wd/ interrupt A.F.'s more pressing commitments.

E. hasn't SEEN any hist/chin/lit/ since he read Giles in some internat/lit/ series, over 40 years ago. Do not recall that he (G/) had given a thought "entertained a thought" (Mat. yü 7622, 3 [寓 意]) to the amount of thought needed to reorganize the rad/ system.

***Also lot of fuss re,/ <u>exact</u> rhyme/ whereas inexact syzogy, SHADINGS of sound, one of most useful devices for melody, not only shifts of do, re, mi etc/ but also of fengs, fangs, fins, fons, etc. no reason to suppose we waited fer Bill Yeats to start use of it.

**

already noted (?) lo [落] as in low, lower//

spanish ll, fluids, etc. one of [the] most common associations in numerous languages.

[人] man...[柚] pumelo: a line from "On the Northern Tower" (秋 登 北 楼) by Xie Tiao 謝 眺 (464–99). In a letter to EP of 2 March 1951 (Lilly) Fang copied out the poem with a sound key illustrating its rhyme scheme and tonal arrangement.

Gavin Douglas: Gavin Douglas (1474–1522), Scottish translator of Virgil's Aeneid.

Dewey: Jack Belden holds that Republican presidential candidate Thomas Dewey (1902–71) and Time-Life-Fortune publisher Henry Luce (1898–1967) endorsed Chiang because of shared anti-Communist sentiment.

Belden... (p 425): Belden refers to Chiang as a dictator.

Bunting: the British poet and translator Basil Bunting (1900–85) first met EP in Paris c.1923.

the Loeb greek, latin: a series of Greek and Roman classics with translations published in England by Heinemann and in America first by Macmillan and then by Harvard University Press.

Erigena: the Irish-born theologian John Scotus Erigena (c.815–c.877) is listed in Cantos 74, 83, and 87.

Avicenna: Ibn Sīnā (c.980–1037), Persian author of nearly 240 books. EP owned a copy of his Metaphysics Compendium (1926).

Santayana: see Glossary on Santayana, George.

Leibnitz: EP writes about the German philosopher Gottfried Wilhelm Leibnitz (1646–1716) in Guide to Kulchur (1938; New York: New Directions, 1970), 74 as follows: "After Leibniz, the precedent kind of thought ceased to lead men."

Ocellus: the Pythagorean philosopher Ocellus (5th century BC) is listed in Cantos 87 and 107.

38   Fang to EP (TLS-3; Lilly)

[Cambridge, Mass.]
3/14 [1951]

Dear Mr Pound,

The rad/card was not made by A.F.; it was done some years ago, when A.F. was still in Peking, by the ignoramuses here for the confusion of poor students. Of course, rad/ 136 [舛] does not mean "confuse." The cardinal meaning of that ideogram might be found in the last entry under that ideogram in Mathews: DISCREP-ANCY, from which ideas like "opposing, perverse, disobedient, error, disorder, confusion, contradictory" can be derived. Anciently the id/ was written 舛

Now, Hsü [Xu] Shen thinks the pictogram stands for two persons lying back against back 對 臥, but later etymologists disagree with him and assert that the pict/ represents two things placed back against back. At any rate, the funda-mental meaning is "discrepancy" or "overlapping." I have failed to find any evidence supporting the idea of "opposites," etc.

Since I am at it, allow me to disillusion you about Mathews. This dictionary is full of errors, even after revision. Almost every third sentence (I mean, entry) is either erroneous or misleading. Take the phrase 寓 意; it never means "to entertain a thought." <"to entertain a thought" or "to give a thought to..." would be 留 意.> NEVER. Lit. it means to house a thought in a thing, in which "in a thing" is either expressed or implied. Or shall I say, "to charge a thing with one's thought"? It is often used in the sense of "allegory"; in some contexts it means something <quite like> POSSUM's [Eliot's] objective correlative. E.g. in speaking of the Eulogy of Oranges supposedly written by Ch'ü Yüan (jap. Kutsugen or Kutsu Gen) critics say he was making use of yü-i [寓 意]; the orange was a mere allegory. When T'ao Yüan-ming (Toenmei) wrote

悠 然 見 南 山

"Calmly I see the Southern Hills,"

he is supposed to have taken recourse to yü-i: it was immaterial whether he actually saw the hills, for the important thing is that his mind was at peace. Objective correlative?

When students can make use of vernacular dictionaries I always advise them to throw Mathews out of the window. The best v. dictionary is 辭 海.

I like your analysis of 臥; Hsü [Xu] Shen's is very weak, nor is there any satisfactory explanation. I think yours can be maintained.

Yesterday I forwarded the galley proofs of Stone-Classics, with the necessary ideograms.

Yours respectfully
[signed] Achilles Fang

For the moment I cannot squeeze out a minute and write on the development of radicals. However, I shall keep this subject in mind.

I am sincerely grateful to you for introducing me to Erigena and Avicenna. For the moment I am studying the Oirishman. "Authority comes from right reason," occurring in many of your writings, has intrigued me quite. In fact the entire chapter (De divisione naturae, liber primus, cap. 69; Joannis Scoti opera quae supersunt omnia,/1853, ex typis Migne, au Petit-Montrouge,—publ. as a vol. in Patrologiae cursus completus,/column 513) is quite interesting. [...]

"No philosophy, only philo-epistemology since ... " What Santayana said to you is unfortunately true. In college A.F. "majored" in "Western" philosophy (my thesis was on Leibnitz and his Monalology); but all the philosophy I had was centred around epistemology. (It is so also here at Harvard.) Only that nowadays they do not even touch on the theory of knowledge,—now it is all symbolic logic. So much so that anybody who does not draw upon the first half of the first volume of Russell and Whitehead's Principia Mathematica is not even considered as a professional philosopher. (Neo-Realism) A.F. has given up "philosophy" for good, and is glad of it.

After Erigena I hope to take out Avicenna.

Hsü Shen: see Glossary on Xu Shen.
Ch'ü Yuan: see Glossary on Qu Yuan.
T'ao Yüan-ming: see Glossary on Tao Qian.
辭 海: Cihai dictionary, ed. Shu Xincheng et al. (1936).
your analysis of 臥: in a letter to Fang of 28 February 1951, EP describes the "SLEEP ideogram" 臥 as "bureaucrat [臣] faced by member of the general public [人]" (Beinecke). See also SP, 81.
Leibnitz: see Letter 37 n.
Principia Mathematica: Bertrand Russell and Alfred Whitehead, Principia Mathematica (1910–13).

39   EP to Fang (TL-1; Beinecke)

[St Elizabeths Hospital]
[Washington, DC]
[April 1951]

Fang
    moderately frivolous enquiry re/ being called er JU [爾 汝] Mencius Seven lower [2.] 31.3.
    ?? expression like "Hi there!
    Hey you."
    idiomatic?
    did I ask if any clear work on chinese pronouns in any occidental lang?
    probably better go on observing cases.
    Everything needed is in the 4 Books.
    One keeps noticing ideograms that one had failed to concentrate on.
    Gt/ bore not having odes text in seal, meaning DONE, not floating in promise.
    Kimb/ cursing Hawley fer incomprehensible reasons and cunctating.

benedictions
anon

er JU: in a letter to EP of 5 April 1951 Fang confirms: "爾 汝 in the Meng passage should mean
'Hi there!', 'Hey you!' (or even 'Hey Mao', or Hey johnny')" (Beinecke).
Kimb/ cursing Hawley: see Glossary on Kimball, Dudley.

40   *Fang to EP (TL-1; Beinecke)*

[Cambridge, Mass.]
June 11, 1951

Dear Mr Pound,

The whole will look very impressive in press-proof. You and Hawley must
have given sample pains to the work.

In order to facilitate my work of correlating Ch. and Engl. pages I cut the long
galley sheets into pages and numbered them red; hope the printer will not be
confused.

Here and there I modified your romanizations, not to make them conform to
the standard system but to make them consistent.

Other suggestions (done in ink) you will find on appropriate pages; I beg you
not to get offended at the liberty I've taken.

I notice that the sequence of the two books is altered; I like the change, for
the Ch. always speak of Hsio-Yung [Digest-Pivot] and not Yung-Hsio [Pivot-
Digest].

Pp. 111–113–115 are missing; I'm waiting for them. As soon I get them I shall
forward them to you. With regard to these pages, I suggest that

—Shi King, III, 1, 5, 3.

be inserted after the Ode in Chung Yung XII, 3, and

—Shi King, I, 15, 5, 2.

after XIII, 2.

Yours respectfully

Thank you very much for the Italian papers.

Shi King, III, 1, 5, 3 . . . Shi King, I, 15, 5, 2: these suggestions were not taken.

41   *EP to Fang (TL-1; Beinecke)*

[St Elizabeths Hospital]
[Washington, DC]
[10 October 1951]

To the Hnbl/ FANG
    P.S. to ms/

If the Hl/ Fang has any more spare copies of extracts from Hav/ YenChing/
wd/ he in benignity send 'em to

Mary de Rachewiltz

Schloss Brunnenburg, Merano, Italy

marked simply "For Igor,"

that is for her young "brother-in-row"

who knows more chinese than her father BUT whom I shd/ like to have
stimulated to KEEP HIS MIND ON the subject.

benedictions.

extracts: Igor de Rachewiltz recalls receiving from Fang extracts from *Shu jing* (Book of History)
and *Mencius*.

42   *EP to Fang (TL-1; Beinecke)*

[St Elizabeths Hospital]
[Washington, DC]
16 Oct 51

Lacking energy, very hard keep eye fixed on page, ergo may have missed
something. Suppose chinese have indexed 4 books/but may not be copy of
index at HaaaVUDD? Wd/ notes like following be any used to Hnbl/ FANG?

Convinced it is more important to understand the 4 Books than to understand chinese language, OR let us say UNLESS a man understand the ideograms
IN the 4 Books, he never will understand chinese language, or ideogram/and
cert/ much more important to grasp the grams in the 4 bks/ than to remember
many thousand minor and derivative characters /?

敬

Curious that so basic a sign, one so essential to grasp Confucian Anschauung
shd/ appear only 3 times in Ta S'eu and 4 in Chung Yung.

Ta S/ III, 3, twice/VII, 1.

Chung Y/ <u>XX, 13</u> <at first sign might seem weaker use than in Ta S'eu/ but it
isn't, on further reflection.>/XXXI 1 & 3/XXXIII, 3.

****

note tuan/Chung Y/ VI/XII, 4 端 [tuan]

****

Has Fang noted the important defining of   至

Chung Y/ XII 4, from the top   一

to   厶

the bottom.   土

dont trust me not to have skipped and missed something. haven't yet been
thru Analects/ and WHATTA DAMN nuisance that printer not getting me my

bilingual stone AND the seal char/ odes so I can GIT ON and improve my damtrans/lations. how lousily low the noncoherence and muttishness of ALL murkn endamndowments.

Ta S/ III, 3, twice/VII, 1: "於 緝 熙 敬 止 *Coherent, splendid and* **reverent**"; "為 人 臣 止 於 敬 *As a minister, in* **respect**" (*Confucius,* 40–1); "之 其 所 畏 敬 *if they are filled with reverence and* **respect**" (*Confucius,* 54–5).
Chung Y/ XX, 13: "敬 大 臣 則 不 眩 *he who* **respects** *the great ministers will not be led astray*" (*Confucius,* 156–7).
XXXI 1 & 3/XXXIII, 3: these sections are omitted in *Confucius.*
tuan/Chung Y/ VI/XII: "執 其 兩 端 用 其 中 *followed the middle line between these inharmonic* **extremes**" (*Confucius,* 106–7); "造 端 乎 夫 婦 *has its* **origin** *in ordinary men and women*" (*Confucius,* 118–19).
the important defining of 至: "及 其 至 也 察 乎 天 地 *in its* **entirety**, *a rite addressed to heaven and* earth" (*Confucius,* 118–19).

43 *Fang to EP (TLS-1; Lilly)*

[Cambridge, Mass.]
Oct. 20, 1951

Dear Mr Pound,

Once more my gratitude for If This Be Treason, esp. the paragraphs dealing with Céline, who (please be prepared for a shock) I had never read. Naturally I read through most of his works this week. I'm now having the book photostated for my Poundiana collection, which is the pride of my humble library.

Yes, I immediately mailed the three offprints to Igor.

Thank you for your note on 敬. It is, as you say, Rather curious that the ideogram occurs not too frequently in the Pivot and Digest in despite of the fact that these two books are permeated with the concept of reverentia. Nor is it less interesting to note (I assure you I don't intend to be patronizing) that you have independently come to lay emphasis on this sign, independently of the so-called neo-Confucianists of the Sung dynasty. I wish you would write something on it a bit more extensively. (Some of the neo-C. even cooked up a ritual around that idea: when they sat down to read—reread—K'ung's books, they would first wash their hands, put on their headgears—like women in church service, men had to wear their hats if they wanted to show respect, in China—and burn incense sticks.)

As for the four tuan, Mathews got it—indirectly—from Mencius, p. 79 of your (and my) copy. Poor Mathews. S.v. 6541, 1 and 2 are misleading: "a clue." They should mean rather "inkling," "a loose thread or two," "the barest beginning." 3 seems to be correct, but seldom used. 4 also is misleading, for it is a synonym of 1 & 2. 5 (a part) means really "an aspect," "a phase." No quarrel with 6; only that "troubles; disturbances" are to be understood in a more special sense; for the term rather means "much ado" as a constitutionally indolent man would

understand it. 7 (to make a pretext) should read "to take . . . as a pretext for . . ."
Sorry to be so nasty to old Mathews, but he was a MERE missionary.

By the way we have here a verbal concordance of the Four Books (done by a
Jap., by the name of Morimoto, who also published a sister volume, that of the
Five Classics), a number of v.c. (published by Harvard-Yenching Institute at
Peking) of Yi [Book of Changes], Shih (Odes), Shu [Book of History], Analects,
Mencius, Chuang-tzu, indices to Li-chi (Liki)[Book of Rites], Chou-li [Rites of
Zhou], I-li [Records of Rites], v.c. of K'ung's Ch'un-ch'iu [Spring and Autumn]
and its three commentaries (Tso-chuan, Kung-yang chuan, Ku-liang chuan), etc.
etc. Indeed, we are equipped with thousand and one tools as well as authentic
texts which no Ch. scholars a generation before had dreamed of: only that we
are not so learned as those old-fashioned gents.

(If it means anything to you,) I am at one with you about how the Dixionary
should be made. (Frankly, however, I do not see what earthly use has a Ch. dix.
to anybody, if it is to imitate the NED, and we are told to imitate that model. If
the thing is ever to be completed, it will run to 100 times 13 vols.)

As I communicated to Mrs Pound, I am expecting my book on China of
220–264 early next year. (I notice you dealt [with] the period in a few lines.)

Yours respectfully
[signed] Achilles Fang

If This Be Treason: If This Be Treason (Siena: Tip. Nuova, 1948).
Céline: among the works of Louis-Ferdinand Céline (1894–1961) are Voyage au bout de la nuit (1932),
    Mort à crédit (1936), and Mea Culpa (1936).
four tuan: see Letters 42 and 44.
the thing: the Harvard-Yenching Chinese–English dictionary, a project dismissed in January 1957.
my book on China of 220–264: The Chronicle of the Three Kingdoms (Cambridge, Mass.: Harvard
    University Press, 1952).

44   EP to Fang (TL-2; Beinecke)

[St Elizabeths Hospital]
[Washington, DC]
[October 1951]

Achilles/
    Yes. I noted those four tuan in Mencius p. 78/9
    II, 1, vi, 5
    manhood/equity/ceremonies, propriety/knowledge 白 adds to 知
    which is cert/ NOT love, duty, propriety, knowledge.
which four wd/ have some profundity. taking love as 親 <but this might be
simply caritas. save for the tree, lower left> but what ideogram translated
"duty"? it is not merely dagger-thru-heart as usual I dongiVVadam who said

it first. Even yr/ prize package Karlgren hit a bullseye in a foot note re/ relative lights of fire and water/shine outward, shine inward. Not saying he knew what he was printing, but he printed it.

Yes, I thought there must be a concordance/ or several shots at it.

I dont think my suggestion re/ order of english words opposite the ideograms wd/ necessarily mean much greater bulk in a dictionary/possibly the contrary.

Await yr/ exposition of 220–264. Having no memory hv/ no idea who was WHO at that time/ but cd/ look it up in child's guide Three Kingdoms/ confusion?? Plus a dab of aesthetics? Have just come on a civilized german. Chlodwig Hohenlohe 1819–1901 (or mebbe he died a year or so later.)

Knr [Hugh Kenner]/ sez Thoreau quotes Kung (dunno if consciously or not)

Never hv/ seen NED, and have never felt desire to do so but mebbe that is an error? much as I disbelieve it. The main purpose of endowments, empiricly viewed, is to sabotage curiosity.

Hold ON damBIT/

the Mencius is taking four OTHER things as the TUAN or what Mat/ lists as the FOUR TUAN

waaal. cant hold up this note forever/will hv/ to inspect them unfamiliar terms   hand
           work
           broom
           heart

no thats all over the shop. Menc/ "2nd/ intensity" sage mountain (TOP, go up) but tuan itself orderly pile hand grip going down (Sherlock) deserving of contemplation.

Legge. Legge. Legge/////UGH

alZo, upper centre LOOKS alike in   羞

                and   義

BUT is it?

mi manca testo seal [I don't have the seal text]
sans which, one guesses, and likely to be betiched by derivation.

four TUAN in Mencius: the Mencian concept of four tuan is fitted into Canto 85/565:

THE FOUR TUAN[1]

端

or foundations.

and it recurs in Cantos 86, 89, 93, 97, and 99.

manhood/equity/ceremonies, propriety/knowledge: Legge renders 仁 義 禮 智 in *Mencius*, 2.1.6.5 as "benevolence," "righteousness," "propriety," and "knowledge" (Legge, ii. 202–3).

白 *adds to* 知: 日 (light) added to 知 (to know) is 智 (sense of right and wrong), the last of the "four TUAN."

love, duty, propriety, knowledge: under 6541 端, Mathews lists seven meanings (see Letter 42) plus 四
端 (four tuan): "love, duty, propriety, and wisdom."

Karlgren: Bernhard Karlgren, *Analytic Dictionary of Chinese and Sino-Japanese* (1923).

yr/exposition of 220–264: see Letter 43 n.

Chlodwig Hohenlohe: Chlodwig Karl Viktor (1819–1901), *Memoirs of Prince Chlodwig of Hohenhohe-Schillingsfüerst* (1906).

Knr [Hugh Kenner]/ sez Thoreau quotes Kung: Thoreau quotes *Analects*, 2. 17 in *Walden*: "Confucius
said, 'To know that we know what we know, and that we do not know what we do not know,
this is true knowledge.'" See *Walden* in *The Norton Anthology of American Literature*, ed, Nina
Baym (New York: W. W. Norton & Co., 2003), vol. B, 1812.

羞 *and* 義: 羞 (shame) is used in *Mencius*, 2.1.6 to define 義, the second *tuan*: "羞 惡 之 心 義 之 端
也 The feeling of **shame** and dislike is the principle of **righteousness**" (Legge, ii. 203).

45   *EP to Fang (TL-1; Beinecke)*

[St Elizabeths Hospital]
[Washington, DC]
[21 November 1951]

O FANG

The focus of energy on getting the goddam obstacles OUT of the way???

Until Ez got STONES bound up facing yankwords various points not clear to Ez.

continual observation, mind free from unnecessary bothers, aids observation
T'ang stone calligraphy.

Conceivable that Chiang Heng calligraphy somewhat resembled very admirable by no mean ordinary T'ang.

Elimination of unnecessary strokes/DISTINCTION between forms which
are NOT (biGum) clearly visible in other calligs/ and prints.

All this demanding repeated observation by senile correspondent/BUT

goDDDAMMIT the WORST impediment to Ez learning a little more is the
NON-presence of ODES bound facing the SEAL text/

until that, no way to answer various wild guesses/ AND . . . also the question
of whether when the possibly greatest intellectual operation in history, the
metamorphosis from seal to square character/whether the blokes who squared,
followed precedent ALWAYS, or in several (?quite a few) cases improved the
combination of signs.

All of which not a querry to be answered "straight off the bat" as Muss
[olini]/sd/re/elimination of taxes by having money represent work done.

benedictions.

P.S. wotTheHell I mean IZ: does Fang see any way to accelerate the Laughlin,
Kimball etc/ to GIT bloody ON with printing the ODES?

The T'ang had ALREADY attained a graphic representation eliminating various
ambiguities (to say nothing of the satisfactory proportion of the graphs).

DAWN the sloppy callig/rz and type cutters who have degenerated from this level.
[In DP's hand:] and, P.S. what kind of stone has been used?

Chiang Heng: the calligrapher of the Qing Stone-Classics.
Laughlin, Kimball: see Glossary on Laughlin, James and Kimball, Dudley.

46   EP to Fang *(TL-1; Beinecke)*

[St Elizabeths Hospital]
[Washington, DC]
[25 November 1951]

INcidentally Monsieur FANG

your preface is very well written, and the translation from CH'ien-Lung thus showing that familiarity with the classics in one language, especially that of the Middle Kingdom, conduces to admirable use of another.

I trust the imperfections of the artigianato [artisan, craftsman] will not unduly disturb you, perfection cannot be attained by mere ten months of not stepping on gas.

yours fraternally

I TRUST the egregious Laughlin has caused his slaves to post copies to you simultaneously with his sending them hither.

your preface: "A Note on the Stone-Classics" with a translation of an extract from Qianlong's 1794
   preface to the Qing Stone-Classics (*Confucius*, 11–15).

47   Fang to EP *(TLS-1; Lilly)*

[Cambridge, Mass.]
Nov 28, 1951

Dear Mr Pound,

Just received a copy of the PIVOT. It looks very good; I like to believe that New Directions has not brought out a more perfect book. In fact, a student writing his thesis here was so attracted to it that he had to buy a copy.

I have just written Laughlin asking him why the printing of the Odes is delayed and offering to help Kimball out. Meanwhile if you tell me what sort of a seal text you are having printed, I may be able to send you that text from the library here, provided we have it. Will you please send me the sample sheet you showed me last year?

I am afraid I can't satisfy Mrs Pound's justifiable curiosity: the books I consulted do not say what sort of stone was used. Perhaps granite? or is it marble?

I have here a copy of Legge's Shu-king [Book of History], pirated, looking exactly similar to your Four Books. If you are interested in this Liber Librorum [Book of Books] of China I shall mail it to you immediately.

Yours respectfully
[signed] Achilles Fang

Kimball: see Glossary on Kimball, Dudley.

48   *EP to Fang (TL-1; Beinecke)*

[St Elizabeths Hospital]
[Washington, DC]
[6 December 1951]

鳳 [phoenix]
O FANG (FENG)
TWO years ago the BLOODY Kimball HAD all the fotos/ of lesser seal odes (sd/ to be foto/d) fr/ only seal text in this dummy/sphere.

AND he measured out the sample page/ about 9 by 6 to take translation <TO FACE the seal text, divided strophe by strophe indicating articulation of the ODE> AND the romanj [sound key] spaced out to indicate a POSSIBLE, or at least interesting scansion of the SOUND of the blinkink text (not in archaic, save one or two spots where one wanted the onomatopoeia of the plop of the fishtails.)

also NOT uniform, BEcause wanted a diagram to test conjecture that the variations took place in a dimension that does NOT interfere with the prosody and tone leading.

AND gramPAW canNOTTTTT git on profitably, with his meditation on the Shih [Odes] UNTIL he has it bound up in this CONvenient form.

UNTIL STONE klassikcz are face to face with the yanki's thus like certain points continue (continued) to avoid senile eye of

yr/ anonYmouse kurryspondink.

49   *EP to Fang (TL-1)*

[St Elizabeths Hospital]
[Washington, DC]
[24 December 1951]

O FANG
and the tribe of FANG
for the new year.

Does Fang think there is a way of getting STONE edition to the councilor or ex-councilor Tcheou (or however he spells it now)? After all it was Tcheou who, when I took him the italian Ta S'eu, asked if I had read Pivot.

I have no address book of those days / I am not sure whether Tcheou's son has been put in charge of the Oriental Institute in Roma /

or that the delicacies of politics wd/ encourage him to communicate with Washington address. BUT the dignity of Harvard, possibly on official stationary, addressed to the Istituto Studi Orientali, Roma, Italy by the hnbl / Fang might elicit an answer or an address. Of course the frowsy ole Insteroot <u>ought</u> to buy a copy / after all their one time geographer and head under the deplorato regime, told me about Karlgren (wotever F's opinion of that tongue blocking Sweede). I mean Tuci HAD heard of a sweedish organization.

My "son-in-row" has sent on a hieroglyphic vocabulary, which designs, according to local hellenist "are as good as animal crackers."

Benedictions

anon Y mouse

Tcheou: Tchu (Zhu); see Letter 9 n.
Karlgren: see Glossary on Karlgren, Bernhard.
Tuci: see Glossary on Tucci, Giuseppe.
My "son-in-row": see Glossary on De Rachewiltz, Boris.

50   *Fang to EP (TLS-1; Lilly)*

[Cambridge, Mass.]
Dec. 29, 1951

Dear Mr Pound,

During the late twenties and early thirties there used to be a 朱 英 in the Chinese Legation at Rome. But he could not have spelt his name as <u>Tcheou</u>, which would stand for 周.

My colleague here, former ex-consul (Boston) Wang, has written to his N.Y. friends. If this source fails, I shall write to Tucci.

Yesterday I mailed you my Chronicle of Three Kingdoms; but it is so dull. Vol. 2, which will contain the facts about

Lieou-Tchin died in hall of the forebears—

   when his father wd/ not die fighting—

by suicide, slaying his children and consort [54/281]

is to appear next summer.

Jas. Laughlin was here sometime ago. He is going to turn over your Ode MSS to me so that I may sort out the seal-script text for you. J.L. told me that old Kimbal seems to be losing his mind.

With best wishes for the New Year,

Respectfully

[signed] Achilles Fang

朱 英: in a letter to EP of 4 January 1952 (Lilly), Fang forwards the address of 朱 英 (EP's Sig. Tcheou). See Letters 12 and 23.

my Chronicle of Three Kingdoms: see Letter 43 n.

Jas. Laughlin: see Glossary on Laughlin, James.

old Kimbal: see Glossary on Kimball, Dudley.

51   *EP to Fang (TL-1; Beinecke)*

[St Elizabeths Hospital]

[Washington, DC]

[4 January 1952]

O FANG

Thanks re/ Tsheou, who did NOT spell it like the dynasty/either in ideogram or in wop [Italian].

O, FANG, godddDAMMIT

ALL that odes ms/ is measured out to a milligram, so that the ENGLISH and the romanj can be set page by page, so as to SHOW the strophic form of the original.

WHEN the english strophes etc/ are COMposed, as pages then one can cut up the seal text so that a strip of SEAL would face and correspond, with and to the translation.

ALL of which the Kimball SWORE he understood/and made sample page of english and romanj/and SAID he wd/ then cut the metal plates for the seal, AS I should indicate by cutting up the fotos/

benediction

and WHOOF.

[In DP's hand:] Private P.S.

I do wish this could be got under way- - -

EP wants it for his own use . . . & the delay makes him furious.

This was all two years ago.

a very pretty page, after several tries.

52   *EP to Fang (TL-2; Beinecke)*

[St Elizabeths Hospital]

[Washington, DC]

[14 January 1952]

O FANG

Gloria enjoying yr/ history, wants [to] know if yu hv/ published anything else (apart from note on Stones). I dont dare tell her she took the bk/ by mistake before I had read it, as she is already too much overawed, and wd/ be too distressed at having done so.

Than' Q. for the volume. In mean time the ignote but admirable Schmidt has sent in 8 vols/ southern anthol/ plus 5 or 6 of Chu Hsi's commentary. <楚 辭 箋 註>

How many characters are going into yr/ new Dictionary? I note that Mathews seems to hv/ omitted 弗 埖

a lot of combines seem to keep und fu, which wd/ here be fu fu??? 2–5 as with 拂 which makes sense as it applies to dust, line preceding has whirl-wind.

As to cultural discipline, young Pablos charged in yester with 6 or 7 copies Stone Edtn/ 4 or 5 bought for his friends and 2 for Valle. He sd/ Bob NEEDED it and that I wd/ prob/ get writers cramp signing the lot.

The impertinence on back of cover is, as I trust you have recognized, a whim of the producer and pub/r, and was not submitted for my approval.

Another I cant find in our beloved Mathews is earth under hemp/ 塺 rad[ical] 32/ under rad 200. Fog like hemp plantation? underbrush, or dirty cloth?

whoever this moralizing bloke is, his continual êrh pu, is VURRY NOT music.

檕 this is ridiKUlus, must hv/seen it dozen times, but cant find in M/ ?having to do with jou² 3133/ or wott'ell? often meaning not important. but want some indication of approx sound.

yeh³ 埜?

Gloria: Gloria French, wife of the American poet and musician William French.
Schmidt: unidentified.
southern anthol...<楚 辭 箋 註>: *Chuci*, an anthology of poems by Qu Yuan and other ancient Chinese poets annotated by Zhu Xi.
Valle: retired lieutenant general Pedro A. del Valle, a defender of EP, is listed in Canto 105/771.

53   *Fang to EP* (TLS-1; Lilly)

[Cambridge, Mass.]
Jan 15, 1952

Dear Mr Pound,

Exceedingly glad to hear that you've got Ch'u-tz'u [Southern Anthology], for you will meet again a number of familiar faces. 屈 原 is Ch'ü Yüan (*kiuət ngiɔn <*6th cent. sounds; we are not certain of earlier sounds>): you have AFTER CH'Ü YUAN, which seems to be based on Giles' History (text 九 歌, 山 鬼: 若 有 人 兮 山 之 阿...) and SONG OF THE BOWMEN OF SHU, which in 1915 Cathay was attributed to KUTSUGEN (which is Jap. pronunciation of our poet).

宋 玉 is Sō-Gioku of Canto 4, sinicê Sung Yü (*Suong° ngiwok) but the text of "This wind, sire, is the king's wind, ... " (a fu poem on Wind 風 賦) is not in Ch'u-tz'u.

You will find HIGHTOWER's Topics (chapter 4) quite informative in this connexion.

The poet who affects erh-pu 而 不 (*ˏńźi piuət) is Liu Hsiang (Hightower p. 22).

坲 fou (*biuətˏ), "dusty"

塺 mo (*muâ°) & mei (*ˏmuâi), "dust, dirt"

壄 (more correctly 壄) = 埜 = 野.

I really don't know how many characters our dictionary is going to contain. Certainly more than Mathews. I think of putting all the ideograms in 辭 海 in ours.

Very flattered to hear Gloria (?) "enjoying" my dull book. (By the way, if you need another copy, I can manage to send you one.) This is my first book (oh, yes, I wrote a German grammar in Chinese some years ago.) In the Monumenta Serica (published in Peking by Catholic fathers, I am neither Cath. nor Christian), a sinological quarterly I used to be an editor of, contains some dozen or more articles, all pretty dull. Besides the 3 pieces in Harv. Journ. of Asiatic Studies, there is going to be another in the coming issue (6 weeks more): translation of Wen-fu. Perhaps you've looked through The Art of Letters by Reverend E. R. Hughes, M.A. (first class FOOL) published by Bollingen. My translation is, as I hope, quite accurate and not unreadable (MacLeish has gone through it). Then, there's a 24-page review of ex-missionary H[ughes]'s fool book. Both of these I shall send to you.

Yours respectfully
[signed] Achilles Fang

Ch'ü Yüan: see Glossary on Qu Yuan.
SONG OF THE BOWMEN OF SHU: *Cathay* opening poem, "Song of the Bowmen of Shu," a variant on Ode 167.
Sō-Gioku . . . Sung Yü: EP alludes to "The Wind" by Song Yu (Sō-Gyoku in Japanese, 3rd century BC) in Canto 4.
HIGHTOWER's Topics: James Robert Hightower, *Topics in Chinese Literature: Outlines and Bibliographies* (Cambridge, Mass.: Harvard University Press, 1950).
Liu Hsiang: Liu Xiang (*c.*77–6 BC). His "Nine Laments" is collected in *Southern Anthology*.
辭 海: *Cihai* dictionary. See Letter 38 n.
German grammar in Chinese: *Te-wen chin-liang* or *Gesprochenes Deutsch* (1941).
translation of Wen-fu: "Rhymeprose on Literature: *The Wên-fu* of Lu Chi (A.D. 261–303) 陸 機: 文 賦," *Harvard Journal of Asiatic Studies*, 14/3 & 4 (1951).
The Art of Letters: see Fang, "Review: E. Hughes, *The Art of Letters*, Lu Chi's 'Wen Fu,' A.D. 302," *Harvard Journal of Asiatic Studies*, 14/3 & 4 (1951).

54   *EP to Fang* (TL-2; Beinecke)

[St Elizabeths Hospital]
[Washington, DC]
25 Jan [1952]

FANG fuss

isn't yü² 余 [I, me] rather like the dative??
seems to fit a number of examples.

Erinnerung deutsches GrammatiKKKK [memory of German grammar]
(NO I am NOT going to look up hun spellink)
if not why Mat/ 7606 [7605] AND 7601
go to/out got
Gornoze wotthe choinilists [sinologists] do with 'em NOW.
enclose exercise/got to find some means of fixing approx sound in remains of disjecta mente [scattered mind].

Any arguments for Hawley, who seems to think ideograms are mere hieroglyphics/i.e. just pictures without concepts tied into 'em? (this prob/an exaggeration de ma parte <but I dont believe they just procede [proceed] on mere basis of melting differences down into sames.>

When F/ has nothing better to do/cd/he spare a few words re/the transformation from old seal to modern forms? when done, by whom? how long it took to do it?

F/seen a poor rag called "Philosophy of East and West." Hawaii Univ/ unreadable save for grain of sense from Santayana.

聞	成	使	敬
顯	至	周	花
先	在	栽	忠
仙	止	采	見

1. does this make sense
2. does it scan, according to an accepted chinese ear?
3. wd/ 4th line be considered bad taste, stunt merely changing tone?
nacherly SOURCE of different sounds, and prob/ earlier differences in total FOG.
grampaw find berry dif'kult merember noise appertaining pixchoor abbrev/
if F/objects to final character we can change it/cant fall into Foe and Lao

---

"Philosophy of East and West": *Essays in East-West Philosophy: An Attempt at World Philosophical Synthesis*, ed. Charles A. Moore (1951).
Santayana: see Glossary on Santayana, George.
敬 花 忠 見 . . . 聞 顯 先 仙: a poem of EP's own composition. See also Letters 55 and 66.
Lao: see Glossary on Laozi.

55 *Fang to EP (TLS-1; Lilly)*

[Cambridge, Mass.]
Feb. 5 [1952]

Dear Mr Pound,

Excuse me this delay; have been a bit unwell, weather. 令 = 令 ling. 皇 = 皇 huang.

The four lines

閒	成	使	敬
‚kan	‚ʑi̯äng	°si	ki̯ong°
顯	至	周	花
°χien	t͡si°	‚t͡si̯əu	‚χwa
先	在	栽	忠
‚sien	°t͡si	‚tsậi	‚t̯i̯ung
仙	止	釆	見
‚si̯än	dz'âi°	‚mjie	γien°

(= 現, to appear)

kien° (to look at)

cannot mean what you intend (granted that I do understand you). As for the
sounds, there are too many gutturals and too many of what the vorchristlicher
Christ called snake sounds; one labial does not seem to relieve the overwrought
alliteration. And rhyme? The fourth line sounds like a jeu d'esprit. Sorry to
disappoint you.

Yes I saw Philosophy of East and West; the people in Hawaii seem to be a
strange lot, I am sure.

Of course I have time to write on the transformation from great seal to little
seal (which is the script conventionalised from the reform script of Li Ssu, Li-ssé in
Canto LIV; cf. 今天下 ... 書同文 <Some critics think this sentence to be an
interpolation.> in Pivot 28), but I should like to know what you exactly want
me to write: history? comparison of the two? (The so-called great seal scripts are
not all too numerous, whereas the Shuo-wen is entirely based on the lesser seal.)

Yours respectfully

[signed] Achilles Fang

Li Ssu: Li Si (*c.*280–208 BC)., prime minister to the First Emperor of Qin (r. 246–210 BC), made the
"lesser seal" a standard Chinese script.
Shuo-wen: see Glossary on Xu Shen.

56   *EP to Fang (TL-3; Beinecke)*

[St Elizabeths Hospital]
[Washington, DC]
[February 1952]

O Fang

Mat/ 1848 fei⁴/廢 I take it variants alle sameee
?intensification of 奸
much more interesting kai ts'o 改錯/I take it coin?
METATHEMENON [currency fraud] even if the knife 刀 isn't in text.

bit dull, if it ain't. <may be author was just dumb.>
- - - - - - - - - -

Certain points shd/ be deferred until possible to talk/ what I am after re/ shift from seal/is the cutting down from the 500 or whatever radicals to 214/ How much actual reorganization of the whole system of concepts occurred.

So far hv/ seen no printed emphasis on great difference between a mere abbreviated picture/ hieroglyph, and that graph/ coupled with a more general concept/such as change or magic/

one hwa [華] being mere picture/what Mat/ calls LATER hwa [花] man / spoon/ under the growing leaves.

Total impossibility to form any idea of REAL sound of any language save by HEARING it spoken/ eRRRe eRRRe AOOW (spanish in Madrid streets)

I suspected four of Mat's hsin in a row was overdoing it.

Gloria says: but it dont sing. Referring to the T'ang anthol/ to my mind the K'ung anthol/ and almost ANY chinese verse I have looked at "sings"/ AND gives a measure (musical bar) <times the sound>

BUT I have not the slightest idea whether there is ANY similarity between the noise I make when "singing" the syllables.

(EVEN supposing I had some faint concept of what the difference between tones 1, 2, 3, 4 are.) <re the chinese sounds.>

Which I have NOT. and am unlikely to obtain from ANY printed statement about it. unless illustrated by musical notes

♫ ♪♩

For years I never made ANY attempt to hitch ANY sound to the ideograms/ content with the meaning and the visual form.

Whomever I have got to in South anth/ 13/15 seems to be linking up a lot of horse radicals/and (now) bow radicals/

?? as voulu as the four hsin

kan/ Xien, sien. acc/ A.F.

and as to what the Hnbl/ F/ means by gutturals ??? dunno. snakes/ sibilants. 40 years ago a hen on the North Am/ Rev told me Mr Tennyson objected to 'em.

(quite irrelevant to case before her/ which was consonants in ang/ sax/ alliteration . . . but still schnakes/ schnakes/ no bon.

Have managed to remember six sounds in a row in one line which Mat/ represents as K'ung fan chi erh kan hui

By which alphabetic etc/ he conveys NOTHING whatsoDAM to grampaw. the sense is O.K. but no real idea of the sound. What I (egomet ipse [myself alone]) was after, as to meaning in first effort was to intensify sense of respect or vegetable intelligence (vide Agassiz) and to blast all Mesopotamian flabbiness and going off into the indefinite. Focus damn well gittin down and taking hold of ROOT/ grabbing terram firmam./

whoosis' comment of Guido's Donna mi prega/ kussing them as "prende occhio per la mente [take the eye for the mind]." visual faculty augmented by attentive examination of floral (or any vegetative) metamorphoses.

How MANY words of modern chinese wd/ be required?

/ / / /

judging by F's consonants/ there was an awful slurring and same-ing of earlier <u>different</u> sounds/ such is as now obliterating english, in murkn polyglot

am unconvinced that whoever changed a spirit swirl into a bent elbow THOUGHT he was merely making a copy of the wiggle even in an attempt to improve its plastic (shape)

δ   厶   鬼

as to representation that ANY beholder can understand, the Egyptians "lay it open to the meanest capacity."

and SO forth/ dont hurry to reply if you are ill or busy.

廢 . . . 奸 . . . 改 錯: see Letter 57.

METATHEMENON [*currency fraud*]: the term from Aristotle, *Politics* 1275b16, occurs in Cantos 53, 74, 77, and 97.

Tennyson objected to 'em: EP states in "Patria Mia": "I sent them a real poem, a modern poem, containing the word 'uxorious', and they wrote back that I used the letter 'r' three times in the first line . . . and that I might not remember that Tennyson had once condemned the use of four 's's' in a certain line of a different metre" (*SP*, 113–14).

Agassiz: see Glossary on Agassiz, Louis.

Guido's Donna mi prega: "Donna mi prega" ("Because a Lady Asks Me") by the Florentine poet Guido Cavalcanti (*c.*1255–1300). See EP's version in *Dial*, 85/1 (1928); rpt. *LE*, 155–7.

鬼: cf. *Confucius* 23: "鬼 This ideogram for a spirit contains two elements to be watched."

57   *Fang to EP (TLS-2; Lilly)*

[Cambridge, Mass.]
Feb. 11 [1952]

Dear Mr Pound,

廢 is the standard form; the one with 矢 in place of 殳 is calligraphic affectation. The ideogram is composed of 广 (hill-slope, on which (cave-)dwellings were dug out) and 發 <u>fa</u>, which also gives the sound to the composite form.

姦 ˎkan was the original form. (There are a number of triplets, e.g. 犇 = 奔 <u>fen</u>, 麤 = 粗 <u>ts'u</u>). It seems that some clever and officious fellow wanted to help the tyro (possibly his own son) pronounce the 3-women ideogram [姦]; he eliminated one female and put 干 ˎkân in her place. 奸 Eventually people got lazy and liquidated one more woman, and we have 奸 as a variant of 姦. Originally 奸 meant the same thing as 干 in the sense of "to come into contact with some one with the intention of getting something out of him", i.e. "to touch someone".

As for 改 錯, it has nothing to do with monetary reform. 錯 刀 was a kind of coin put into circulation by Wang Mang 王 莽, who once usurped the Han throne. (By the way, Canto LIV: " . . . HAN PING/ simple at table, gave tael to the poor" refers to Wang Mang, i.e. "HAN PING" (P'ing-ti 平 帝 of Han) is to be read "WANG MANG.") This line

固 時 俗 之 工 巧 兮, 滅 規 榘 而 改 錯

in your Southern Anthology 13 <by Tung-fang Suo 東 方 朔, 2nd cent. B.C.>, and

何 / / / / / /, 背 繩 墨 / / /

in 8 are both imitated from Ch'ü Yüan's (roll 1)

固 / / / / / /, 偭 規 矩 而 改 錯

in which 改 = 更, 錯 (= 措) = 置. That is 改 錯 means "to alter, to change for the worse." I think Ch'ü Yüan's whining merely means:

Truly the world is clever & smart; they depart from the norm path to bring about chaos.

By the way, in the current language 改 錯 has a classroom vocable: to correct mistakes in composition, taking 錯 in the sense of 錯 誤 [mistake].

- - - - - - - - - -

Hope to send you musical notation for the tones soon. Meanwhile a superficial note on radicals:

Shuo-wen 說 文 (end of Han)	540 radicals.		by 許 慎 [Xu Shen]
Yü-p'ien 玉 篇 (Liang dy.)	542	"	by 顧 野 王 [Gu Yewang]
五 經 文 字 (T'ang)	160	"	
字 通 (Sung)	89	"	
六 書 本 義 (Ming)	360	"	
合 并 字 學 集 篇	200	"	
類 纂 古 文 字 考	314	"	
[Zihui] 字 彙	214	"	by 梅 鼎 祚 Mei Ting-tso

The last is adopted in 正 字 通 and K'ang-hsi's Dict. (I am sure you will want more details, which I hope to give you after some study myself. Frankly the classification into radicals does not seem to have any more value than the captions in Roget's Thesa[u]rus.)

Yours respectfully
[signed] Achilles Fang

固 / / / / / /, 偭 規 矩 而 改 錯: quoted from Qu Yuan's *Li sao* in volume i of *Southern Anthology.* See Glossary on Qu Yuan.
Shuo-wen: see Glossary on Xu Shen.

58 *EP to Fang* (TL-4; Beinecke)

[St Elizabeths Hospital]
[Washington, DC]
[20 February 1952]

FANG/

Invocation to patience/

re/ Four tuan/ any idea WHAT specific ideograms Mathews had in mind?
6541.8

Is M/ dead? or only at Harvard? or why do they print his dic/?

some bloke in that AWFUL east west HawaiLosophy wanted to trans/仁 as love
?? embrace?

The one word of sense among those dead leaves was ole Jarge Santayana
against having icecream and soup in same plate simultaneously.

Vague recollection that you mentioned a passage in Mencius BUT it didn't fit
which is not to say that Mat/ mayn't have thought it did.

A cold in the head fills one with benevolence // UGH ///

Perhaps one shd/ start thinking of how to trans/ a few english words into
Chinese so as to make sense in the more venerable language.

(this is not to transcurar' vr/recd/response re "decadence of the empire"
愛 <or 好 too limited> MANG/ iv, 2, xxviii/3 AI[4]

?宜? sheep that going to be DUTY

    me   UGH/

禮 li[2]

知 chih[1]?

智 has this enough weight?

    guess it's O.K.

Mencius II, i. vi 4/5 has got tuans/ but they cant POSSSSibly be translated
love, DUTY, propriety, wisdom. propriety, wisdom/ O.K. BUT the other 2/ cd/
even Mat/ think so? besides they are TUANs OF these things, at that point, not
postulating the four as the tuan/s ipse.

the TUANs are the commiseration/ shame/ modesty/ ap/and disap-proving.
as bases OF jen/i/li/chih

we cant fall back into the vanW/ Brooks era/ or the sewers of Babylon.
  ★★★

incidentally we hv/ a new prospective student on the west coast Miss Glory
produces-wheat-ear [Angela Chih-ying Jung]. (not to be confused with the local
Gloria [French])
  ★★★

What about prospect of PRINTING some more stimulae to oriental studies?

達

Legge fusses round with TA (Mat 5956) and interpolates duties/ duties etc. 5.
but nothing in Mat/ to indicate that TA means duty.

If only someone wd/ display a little sense of the meaning of words.

Obviously there IS a chinese word for duty??

---

east west HawaiLosophy: see Letter 54 n.

Jarge Santayana: see Glossary on Santayana, George.

愛...AI⁴: 愛 (love) is taken from *Mencius*, 4.2.28.2: "仁 者 愛 人 The benevolent man **loves**
others" and 4.2.28.3: "愛 人 者 人 恒 愛 之 He who **loves** others is constantly **loved** by them"
(Legge, ii. 333).

? 宜?: 宜 taken from *Mencius*, 4.2.28.4 (Legge, ii. 333) is a homophone (not a synonym) of 義, the
second *tuan*.

jen/i/li/chih: on 仁 義 禮 智, the four tuan, see Letter 42 n.

vanW/Brooks era: in *America's Coming-of-Age* (1915) Van Wyck Brooks (1886–1963) portrays an era
that values not cosmopolitanism but a native self-consciousness.

59   Fang to EP *(TLS-2; Lilly)*

[Cambridge, Mass.]
March 7, 1952

Dear Mr Pound,

Not much information about REV. Robt Henry Mathews of China Inland
Mission. He certainly has nothing to do with Harvard.

The people here pirated his horrible dixionary during the last war—princi-
pally in order to make Yankee boys gabble in broken mandarin with the pretty
lasses of Cathay. Serge Elisseeff told me that sometime after he played the pirate
in the service of the Federal government, he was approached by a representative
of CIM [China Inland Mission], who had to acknowledge his impotence when
he was reminded that no books published in China had copyright outside China.
(You know, China has never joined the Bern[e] convention.)

By the way, Mathews published Kuoyü Primer, a text book for missionaries,
who would be foolish enough to convert the heathen Chinese in their national
language 國 語, i.e. Mandarin. Revised from Baller's book again.

As you must have noticed from the preface, Mathews produced his scandal-
ous dix. on the basis of Baller's (also a missionary). He should not be responsible
for all those stupidities. As far as learning Chinese goes, none of the Aryan
missionaries (like to believe that there isn't any semitic or crypto-aryan missionary in China) can ever do the feat. Halleluja

Of course, M is downright stupid to equate the four tuan with the four concepts.
But he did. Old Legge is also very idiotic when he states: tuan is explained by tuan-
hsü, "the end of a clue," that point outside, which may be laid hold of, and will
guide us to all within (p. 79 note). When Chu Hsi wrote 端, 端 緒 也 he only
meant that the ideogram tuan here is to be understood in the sense of term
tuan-hsü, "end of the thread," and <u>not</u> in the sense of other tuan-compounds.
This <u>end</u> is ἀρχή [beginning] and not τέλος [close]. In other words, the feeling of
commiseration is the fountainhead of HUMANITAS (I can see old Babbitt
turning in his grave at this equation of humanism with humanitarianism). L's
rendition of tuan as Principle is not satisfactory, of course; I am sure old Baller or
stupid Mathews was misled by "principle," thinking that principle is the thing
itself. So does the mind (if we may credit it to Xtians) of missionaries work.

Tuan-hsü [端 緒], as I understand it, means one end of the thread, by tracing its provenience we may come to the whole skein or even the whole cloth; it is also possible to interpret it as the component (and essential one at that) of a fabric.

As for the meaning of the four concepts, I am really at a loss to suggest any sensible translation. Perhaps it would be best to not to try to translate them; after all, how is the attempted translation of Οωφροδύνη [character or conduct of someone of sound, discreet, moderate, chaste, sober mind]?

Take the term i 義, usually rendered as justice. As far as I know, no Ch. writer has thought of the idea of an eye for an eye. As a Chinese I shall never feel smug when I have repaid your kindness or service to a T. No, I will hold myself to be an unwashed barbarian if I did not repay you to a T PLUS. Tit for tat is not Chinese conception of justice; it is rather two (or n) tits for one tat (in goodness, of course; vin[di]ctiveness is not even thought of). To be concrete, if I borrowed an egg from the people upstairs, I am ready to return them more than one egg. (Corollary: I hate to borrow anything from anybody.)

Mathews p. 148 we have 斤 斤 較 量, which is a term used to denote a barbarian. "Carefully compare it"? Lit. "to compare or check the measure your pound against my pound," to see it that nobody is the loser by a fraction of an ounce. (The entry before that and the one still before that have just the opposite meaning: to be perspicacious or to hold to one's principle very carefully, i.e. in dealing with one's own self, without any relation with other people involved.)

It would be easy to say that i sounds like generosity. As I understand, generosity is a virtue, perhaps because it is exceptional. But i is not, in spite of what people say, a virtue; it is part and parcel of Chinese ethical outlook. (I confess, I shall not be able to end this paragraph happily and hence abruptly leave the question here.)

Of course, i means thousand other things. In the last analysis, it seems to be Quixotic for me to try to write about these Protean senses of a concept.

At any rate, I am convinced that it is almost impossible to "sell" the sane ethico-political Anschauung of the Chinese <A Chinese is nothing if not a homo politicus.> to the semites or aryans. Wonder if you will succeed <doing so>.

Expecting to get challenged,
I stop here for this time.

Respectfully
[signed] Achilles Fang

Serge Elisseeff: Serge Elisseeff, director of Harvard-Yenching Institute from 1934 to 56.

Baller: F. W. Baller, *An Analytical Chinese–English Dictionary* (1900); *Sacred Edict* (1907); *A Mandarin Primer* (1933).

Babbitt: Irving Babbitt (1865–1933), Harvard professor and author of *Democracy and Leadership* (Boston: Houghton Mifflin, 1924).
Chu Hsi: see Glossary on Zhu Xi.

60 *Fang to EP (TLS-1; Lilly)*

[Cambridge, Mass.]
March 13, 1952

Dear Mr Pound,

Your DUTY does not exist in Chinese. Modern dix. renders it as pen-fen 本 分, which usually means "one's lot" (as in to be content with one's lot) and i-wu 義 務, which must have been coined by japs (gimu they say) and couldn't be intelligible to KUNG or MENG.

(As function, d[uty]. may be rendered with 職 or its combinations 職 分,/ 掌,/任,/责, etc).

The nearest I can think of for DUTY is 義, but then it means a quite different thing, as I wrote in my last.

- - - - - - - - - - -

As far as I can see, the Ch. have never thought of DUTY in abstracto. They have been plenty dutiful, without ever bothering about Categorical Imperative. Don't you think DUTY is a modern catchword in Indo-European thinking?

Thinking always in concreto and never bothering themselves with divine sanction, they must have acted as dutifully as any duty-conscious human beings.

The jewish-Xtian moralist teaches: honor thy parents if you will prosper (or something like that). The Ch. find this very cheap and revoltingly utilitarian.

I wonder if there isn't some organic relationship between JUSTICE and DUTY. The TIT-for-TAT obsession is primitive, and must have been shared by early Chinese. But already in Chou times justice is relegated to decorum, etiquette, good manners: Chou-li 周 禮 [Rites of Zhou] supposedly formulated by Duke of Chou, is a treatise on the institutional life of the homo politicus sinensis. The section on justice or jurisprudence is in the fourth book, while the 5th & last is on handicrafts and art.

Why then does the Ch. act loyally, filially, etc.? Tentative answer: only because it is sensible to act in those manners, as KUNG and MENG proved convincingly.

I believe, Ch. have lived without the abstract concepts of JUSTICE and DUTY. (God was thrown away by KUNG once for all.)

Yours respectfully
[signed] Achilles Fang

61   EP to Fang *(TL-2; Beinecke)*

[St Elizabeths Hospital]
[Washington, DC]
[18 March 1952]

Fang/ad interim/

will look up passages later/

duty/doveri dell'uomo/[man's duties] vs/Tom Paine's rights/

china not corrupted by greek glossing over <seldom acknowledged> slavery under Aristotelian Anschauung. duty/serve/serve prince/serve parents/seems to me all Kung has implicit sense of duty/

ceremonies being the HOW the duty arising from human affections, the insides of the ceremony/

this not what am writing about in hurry. will go seriously into A.F.'s last, at grtr/leisure. this started to say my son-in-row's kid bro. Igor

de Rachewiltz

Kleingemeinergasse 21, Salzburg, Austria

thanks me for A.F.'s pamphlets/and if I hv/any more will I please send them. ergo a fit recipient for your new ones.

also the young Ig/in worrying how he can pay his rent and study chinese simultaneously/

he OUGHT to do an italian trans/of Mencius or the Analects/knows a great deal more of the language than I do/

Fang got any idea where Igor cd/hook onto any of these wasteful foundations that are blowing millions on useless etc?

I believe Tucci, head (or was) Inst. Orient. Stud/Roma interested only in geography or something. ANYhow any practical suggestion might be useful (no need to tie it to grampaw...

more re/serve/and duty and yr/pamphlets as soon AZ I ketch my breath.

duty, or whatever I am driving at/the measure UP TO WHICH, the propor-tion of what if fitting, acc/the different degrees of respect or affection/and the beyond which NOT.

A. F.'s last: Fang's insight would be fitted into Canto 99/731:

But the four TUAN
                are from nature
        jen, i, li, chih

Not from descriptions in the school house;
They are the scholar's job,
                The gentleman's and the officer's.

Igor: see Glossary on De Rachewiltz, Igor.
Tucci: see Glossary on Tucci, Giuseppe.

62 *EP to Fang (TL-2; Beinecke)*

[St Elizabeths Hospital]
[Washington, DC]
[9 May 1952]

Achilles/

Long time no noise.   該

埃 KAI¹ (3188) seems to be idea boundary limit/3191/ought

Not sure what Achilles the hell thinks DUTY means/

admit/that limit and propriety might seem to make second and third TUAN pretty much the same/but <NOT> absobloodylootly the same.

//

O.K. very the spontaneity (hilaritas of the aarif) got to be there/but IS there in the first TUAN anyhow and Purpose of law: to prevent coercion either by force or by fraud/

hence dislike of Blackstone among them as only interested in "bunk, seeing what you can put over."

***

cultivation of "person"/?? self-discipline?

certainly NOT something defined by someone else.

1. decent impulse
2. limits to which
3. modus in which
4. horse sense acquired by action.

As to how far different ideograms WRITTEN (gorNoze what is now comprehensible by chinese noises when spoken)

how far ideogram can be ALL parts of speech simultaneously when taken in groups?

how inclusive the sense can be

mid-heart?? as verb?

**

"Wheatear" [Jung] deplores degeneration in education in present China . . . and so on/

KAI¹ (3188)...3191/ought: see Letter 63.
Blackstone: see Glossary on Blackstone, William.

63   Fang to EP *(TLS-1; Beinecke)*

[Cambridge, Mass.]
May 30, 1952

Dear Mr Pound,
　YOUR
　　1. decent impulse
　　2. limits to which
　　3. modus in which
　　4. horse sense acquired by action

is OK with me. Only that it is doubtful if Mong [Mencius] took 2 & 3 (& possibly 4 also) as aspects of 1. True, humanitas is a very important thing in Kung and possibly in Mong (a jap. has written a thick <book> on the study of jen), but Mong probably did not want to subordinate the three virtues to DECENT IMPULSE. I mean, he leaves the question ambiguous and there has been much polemic over the relationship of the four. I don't see anything objectionable to your schematisation, nor would Mong himself demur.

　The trouble with Mong is that he is often carried away by his eloquence and mental juggling so that attentive readers often cannot help sighing. Take jen 忍 in 不 忍 人 之 心 IIA.6 for instance: in earlier and subsequent usages it means TO PUT UP WITH or TO BEAR. In certain cases this jen is a virtue (patience, tolerance), in certain others its opposite (as with MONG) is a virtue. It all depends on whether the motivation is altruism or not.

　Mong illustrates this jen-hood with the case of a baby falling into the well. I am sure he could have illustrated the sense of shame; but I wish he had given us some concrete instance of modesty and moral sanction (3 & 4). Are human being instinctively modest and discriminatory?

　Your schematisation, then, seems to be a step forward; at least, the four points seem to be inter-related.

　kai 3183 [3188垓], as far as I can find out, is never used in any metaphorical sense. kai 3191 [該] in the sense of "ought to" is only colloquial; in written language it means rather "comprehensive, extensive."

　This week's New Yorker has a short notice of your PIVOT; quite decent for N.Y., I think.

Yours respectfully
[signed] Achilles Fang

不忍人之心: *Mencius*, 2.1.6.3: "謂人皆有不忍人之心者 all men have a mind which **cannot bear to** *see the sufferings of others*" (Legge, ii. 202).

64　*EP to Fang (TL-1; Beinecke)*

[St Elizabeths Hospital]
[Washington, DC]
[16 June 1952]

Achilles

There is a bloke named W. Yandell Elliott, Haaavud Summer School, said to be DIrecting Mr Kissinger to edit a flabby mug'sgaZoon named "Confluence."

Elliot a cheerful an' exuberant/BUT Achilles MIGHT get it into Yelliott'z head that it is asinine to mention philosophy or ethics without mentioning KUNG.

That the League of Nation[s], UN, unesco, etc. were fahrts in various bales of wind/BUT there is no use wasting time in going into that. Full bribes, fullB-lights [Fulbright] etc /

There ought to be chairs of sinology/not diminution of oriental studies. AND there ought to be METHOD, Kung, to Agassiz, and a drive against abstract blather, implied in any mention of Kung, Agassiz or Dante ... kussing out ...

quel che la cosa per nome

Apprende ben; ma la sua quiditate

Veder non puote,

BASIS/Kung

plus a revival of greek studies, Sophokles at the top.

Those blokes got a mag/but NO writers whatsobloody ever. all slop at Maritain-Matthiessen grade, or I dare say below if there is a lower.

Elliot COULD be useful/even to himself, if he wd/move ON not wait for more other kawlidges to insert Kung and Fenollosa BEFORE the Bastun beanery starts.

IF you don't yet know Elliott (W. Y.), you can say I asked you to save his soul, mind, or central correlation <??> point, depending on which term you consider most likely to convey a meaning and/or impulse.

W. Yandell Elliott ... Kissinger: William Yandell Elliott (1896–1979) founded Harvard Summer Institute in 1952. Former US Secretary of State Henry Kissinger (b. 1923), then a Ph.D. candidate, edited its journal *Confluence*.
Agassiz: see Glossary on Agassiz, Louis.
quel che ... Veder non puote: "one who well understands the thing by its name, but cannot see its true meaning (if no one points it out)" (Dante, *Paradiso*, 20. 91–3).
Maritain-Matthiessen: the Catholic philosopher Jacques Maritain (1882–1973) was then at Princeton. The literary critic Francis Otto Matthiessen (1902–50) was a Harvard professor.

5
Pound as Miss Jung's Dissertation Adviser
"One's opinions change"

Arriving at the University of Washington with a BA from Beijing's Catholic University, Angela Chih-ying Jung (Rong Zhiying 榮 之 穎, b. 1926) had to determine what direction her professional future should take (see Fig. 5.1). It didn't take her long to decide to pursue a Ph.D. in English and comparative literature. It was by coincidence, nevertheless, that she chose Ezra Pound as a subject. In a seminar she attended in spring 1952, she noticed a student drawing Chinese characters in a notebook. Before she was able to correct his mistakes, the young man showed her the book from which he was copying these characters, *The Cantos of Ezra Pound*. In the following weeks Jung immersed herself in *The Cantos*, "attracted to Pound's profuse use of Chinese themes" (Jung, "Ezra Pound and China," University of Washington dissertation, 1955).

From *The Cantos* Jung moved on to Pound's *Cathay* "For the most part from the Chinese of Rihaku [Li Po], from the notes of the late Ernest Fenollosa" (1915; rpt. *Personae*, 130) and his Confucian translations—*Ta Hio* (1928), *The Unwobbling Pivot* (1947), and *The Analects* (1951). As a student from China she could not resist digging into Pound's Chinese borrowings. It was not difficult to identify the Chinese treasures that yielded Pound *Cathay* via Fenollosa and Mori. Nor was it difficult to account for the figures and events chronicled in his Chinese History Cantos (Cantos 52–61). But what source books in English or French or Chinese did Pound use for the composition of these cantos? How much Chinese did he understand? Already Jung had a topic for her dissertation: "The Chinese Enigma of Ezra Pound" (Jung, "Ezra Pound and China").

Unless she contacted Pound, these puzzles would remain puzzles. In late February Jung plucked up enough courage to write to the poet, who was still incarcerated in Washington, DC's St Elizabeths Hospital. In that letter she told Pound how much she admired his China-related poems and how curious she was about the origin of his interest in Chinese culture. Just when Jung was giving up hope of hearing from Pound, a reply from him arrived. He would answer her questions when she got to St Elizabeths.

It must have occurred to Pound that Miss Jung would provide a unique perspective. Between February and March he wrote her four more letters. In one letter he copied out a little Chinese poem he had composed and asked if it made sense to her at all. The attempt anticipated a single-line Chinese poem within Canto 110: "yüeh$^{4.5}$ | ming^2 | mo$^{4.5}$ | hsien^1 | p'eng^{2}" (月 明 莫 顯 朋 or "moon bright not appear friends"). Earlier, Achilles Fang had told him that these lines could not mean what he intended. In another letter he tried to find out what Miss Jung and her fellow Chinese students thought of American education: "do they verbally object to the falsification of history (and of news)? do they object to having the husks and rubbish of the occident offered them in place of Dante (Paradiso) and Sophokles?" (Letter 67). None of Jung's replies has survived. But from Pound's side of the correspondence we can assume that Jung tried to interpret his little Chinese poem, which only led him to echo his habitual remarks about the character: "ideogram INCLUSIVE, sometime not the least ambiguous but ideogramic mind not always trying to split things into fragments" (Letter 68).

Jung's goal was to get from Pound as much insight as possible for a dissertation on his various Chinese projects. During her four-month stay in Washington (April to August 1952), she visited Pound no less than fifteen times. Two of those interviews—the first, and another on 21 June when T. S. Eliot was present—are described in vivid detail in her memoir of 1974, "Homage to a Confucian Poet" (*Paideuma*, 3/3. 301–2). On her first visit, according to Jung, Pound brought from his room two armfuls of China-related books. Handing her his copy of James Legge's bilingual *Four Books*, he stated: "This little book has been my bible for years, the only thing I could hang onto during those hellish days at Pisa . . . Had it not been for this book, from which I drew my strength, I would *really* have gone insane . . . so you see how I am indebted to Kung." Later, when Jung mentioned his little Chinese poem, Pound said: "If I wrote it in English it would probably fill a book. That is why I used the ideogram; each of them could embody what one must say in a hundred lines. Besides I like the sound." Jung reminded Pound that he had written in 1940 that "the great part of Chinese sound is (of) no use at all." To this he retorted: "If I did, I don't remember. At any rate one's opinions change as one progresses . . . He should not be held responsible for what he said or wrote decades earlier. I have never heard how Chinese poetry should be read, but I like to play with it my own way." As to Jung's account of the other visit, Eliot rather than Pound is the focus of attention.

By the end of July Miss Jung got word from her adviser at the University of Washington that Harvard University Press had granted her permission to inspect Pound's Confucian Odes manuscript. Pound was vexed to learn this from Dorothy, who learned it from Jung herself. Neither Jung nor Harvard University Press had asked him for permission. In annoyance Pound let Dorothy send a telegram to Achilles Fang: "Odes not open for inspection of traveling students" (Lilly). Jung was upset when a secretary at the press handed her this telegram instead of the manuscript she had expected to read.

Of course, Pound did not mean to embarrass Miss Jung. On her last visit to St Elizabeths, to her surprise, he handed her some notes he had prepared: "China and E.P." as a title for her dissertation, followed by private information about his Chinese undertakings: "the Fenollosa coincidence," "Cathay," "Canto XIII," "49th canto from ms in family," "The Chinese Cantos/sources LI KI, Histoire Generale de la Chine," and so on. They were of enormous help to Miss Jung's dissertation, "Ezra Pound and China," which was completed in 1955.

Fifteen years later, in 1966–7, Jung, as professor of Chinese at the University of Oregon, took a nine-month sabbatical leave in Florence, Italy, to work on a Pound book (the result being *Italian Images of Ezra Pound*, ed. and trans. Angela Jung and Guido Palandri, 1979). Her visit to Italy would be incomplete without meeting Pound. From his Milan publisher, Vanni Scheiwiller, Jung got the phone number of his daughter Mary de Rachewiltz. De Rachewiltz suggested over the phone that she write to Pound at Sant'Ambrogio above Rapallo. In her letter Jung expressed her wish for another interview. To her joy, she received a reply from his companion Olga Rudge (1895–1996), writing on behalf of him: "Mr. Pound thanks you for your letter and would be happy to see you again and meet your husband .... You could arrive here in time for lunch with us & get back to Florence the same day, leaving after tea" (AJP). On 21 March 1967 Jung alone took a train to Rapallo. With Olga Rudge's direction, she did not have any difficulty finding Sant'Ambrogio. The eloquent poet had now become taciturn. Olga Rudge, whom Jung first met at St Elizabeths, did most of the talking. After lunch the three of them took a walk. When reaching a high point overlooking Gulf of Tigullio, Jung asked Pound, "Can I take a picture of you?" Without a word Pound posed for a picture (see Fig. 5.2).

Fig. 5.1. Angela Jung, 1952. (Angela Jung Palandri)

Fig. 5.2. EP at Sant'Ambrogio, 1967. (Angela Jung Palandri)

65   *EP to Jung (ALS-2; AJP)*

S. Elizabeths Hospl.
Wash/ DC
29 Fb [1952]

Dear Miss Jung,

I will try to answer your questions when you get here in april.

I like to get letters, but can not do much in the way of reply.

if you have any spare texts, I mean chinese texts of good poetry—that you are not using, I should be glad to borrow one or two—not a lot all @ once as I still read very slowly.

@ any rate I shall hope to see you in April. visiting hours 2–4 P.M.

Cordially yours
[signed] Ezra Pound

66   *EP to Jung (ALS-3; AJP)*

St Elizabeths Hospl
Washington DC
4 March '52
or better 4650

Dear Miss Jung,

I have a friend who really knows, & who says my little poem <vide infra> can't possibly mean what he thinks I want it to mean.

If you really want to help me you might tell me what you think it means, if it makes sense @ all.

The 4th line is a trick line, that I did not expect a chinese to approve. but it helps me remember the sound belonging to the ideograms—very difficult if one has begun to read by eye only & never been for more than an hour or so with anyone who speaks chinese.

—AND then: people who speak a language are often incapable of either reading or singing a poem.

The other problem would be: how many more ideograms would I have to add to make my meaning clear if it is possible to get @ it.

Cordially yours
[signed] Ezra Pound

聞	成	使	敬
顯	至	周	花
先	在	栽	忠
仙	止	采	見

or better 4650: dating from the reign of "Hoang Ti" of Canto 53, *c*.2698 BC.

67   *EP to Jung (TL-1; AJP)*

[St Elizabeths Hospital]
[Washington, DC]
[18 March 1952]

Further queries:

Do Miss J. c-y and her friends write down what they think (apart from writing verses)?

do they verbally object to the falsification of history (and of news)?

do they object to having the husks and rubbish of the occident offered them in place of Dante (Paradiso) and Sophokles?

Any of them want to translate the Seafarer into ideogram? Years ago one compatriot of Miss J. got through 6 or 8 lines, but apparently with crushing endeavour. He worked at my little table in London for an hour and half, but NEVER returned.

68   *EP to Jung (TL-2; AJP)*

[St Elizabeths Hospital]
[Washington, DC]
[24 March 1952]

notes from an anonymous correspondent w[h]ose identity
Miss Chih-ying Jung may guess at.

ideogram INCLUSIVE, sometime not the least ambiguous

but ideogramic mind not always trying to split things into fragments (syntacticly etc.)

sometimes VERY clear (at others impenetrable, at least to occidental and unskilled reader).

seems very important to distinguish the merely pictorial ideograms, such as old huah /, from the "newer" where the idea of flower (vegetation) is joined with idea of change / metamorphoses continuing in nature/

meant in first line to drive in the "respect for kind of intelligence that enables cherry-stone to make cherries" as emphasized in big scrawl preceding translation of "Analects."

I have the usual classics/finished a translation of the Shih [Odes] three years ago/but the powers of darkness and the enthusiastic but NON-functioning printers have, so far as I know, got no further than they were TWO years ago/ microscopic measurements of the format/to get the proportion of the page/keep the strophe divisions AND give the first seal text/that is to say to provide what we have not, a text in seal character for american students /

to go back to line one/ what I was trying to get across was respect for the changing power in florescence.

outside the classics available in Legge's series and those in Fenollosa's notes, I am very ignorant/ have been able to get two anthologies, one of which is lent to your more or less homophone Gloria French, Mrs. W[illiam]. French

1702 De Witt Ave. Alexandria. Va.

who hopes to meet you when you get to Washington. She is working hard, but of course none of us have the FAINTEST idea what chinese poetry really SOUNDS like.

and I will now try to get a more specific notion of the lines that say something about wind, horse and water.

anonymously yours, and hoping to see you next month.

old huah /, from the "newer": hua 華 is archaic for 花, a character in EP's Chinese poem. For Jung's "line by line prose interpretation" of the poem, see Angela Jung Palandri, "Homage to a Confucian Poet," *Paideuma*, 3/3 (Winter 1974), 303.
first line: first line of EP's Chinese poem: 敬 花 忠 見.
big scrawl: 敬 in EP's hand in *Confucius*, 193.

69   *EP to Jung* (ALS-1; AJP)

[St Elizabeths Hospital]
[Washington, DC]
24 march [1952]

Honbl glory produces wheat-ear?

No, I do not know the Shuo Wen C. T. & would be very grateful if you can bring a borrowed copy with you.

Very truly yours
[signed] Ezra Pound

glory produces wheat-ear: 榮 之 穎. Jung 榮 means "glory" and the left side of ying 穎 depicts a wheat stalk beneath a head.
Shuo Wen C. T.: see Glossary on Xu Shen.

6

Pound and Carsun Chang
"Confucianism as Confucius had it"

By 1953 Pound was once more moving ahead with his Paradiso. The first five cantos he composed at St Elizabeths Hospital, Cantos 85–9 of *Section Rock-Drill* (1955), again centered on Chinese history.

> LING²   靁靈
> Our dynasty came in because of a great sensibility.
>
>   (Canto 85/563)

Digging into Couvreur's trilingual and Legge's bilingual *Shu jing*, Pound had another Chinese scholar to turn to for insights. The new Chinese friend, Carsun Chang, was taken to St Elizabeths by William McNaughton, a student at Georgetown University and a regular visitor.

Carsun Chang (Zhang Junmai 張 君 勱, 1886–1969) was known in China as a third force in politics in opposition to Chiang Kai-shek and Mao Zedong and in the West as China's delegate to the 1945 United Nations Conference on International Organization, signing the "Charter of the United Nations." After studying at Japan's Waseda University (1906–10) and Germany's Berlin University (1913–15), Chang served as the editor-in-chief of the Shanghai newspaper *China Times* (1916–17) and as a professor of philosophy at Beijing University (1918–22). His early essay "On the National Constitution" earned him recognition as a leading constitutionist and political scientist. Consequently, he was appointed president of Shanghai's National Institute of Political Science in 1924 and commissioned to draft the Republic of China's constitution in 1946 (Roger B. Jeans, *Democracy and Socialism in Republican China: The Politics of Zhang Junmai [Carsun Chang] 1906–1941* (Oxford: Rowman & Littlefield, 1997)).

Chang used to describe his career as "vacillating between the worlds of scholarship and practical politics." For three decades he lectured and wrote on democratic socialism and Confucianism while keeping abreast of domestic political events. In 1953, when McNaughton first took him to St Elizabeths, he was in exile in Washington, DC, at work on a study in English (*The Development of Neo-Confucian Thought*, 2 vols. (New York: Bookman Associates, 1957, 1962)) (see Figs. 6.1 and 6.2). Not surprisingly, he was as enthusiastic as Pound about their meetings and their exchange of ideas.

Of the Pound–Chang correspondence only three letters and a postcard from Chang to Pound have survived. Among Pound's *Rock-Drill* typescripts at the Beinecke Library, nevertheless, is a leaf bearing both Pound's and Chang's autographs (see Fig. 6.3). What Pound wrote were the characters 止 ("the hitching post"), 靈 ("sensibility"), and 誠 ("sincerity"), and what Chang put down were his Chinese and English names. Evidently the two men discussed the three Confucian terms, two of which, 止 and 靈, were to recur in *Rock-Drill*.

Two letters to Pound from Chang's friend C. H. Kwock (see Fig. 6.4), and especially William McNaughton's memoir, "What Pound and Carsun Chang Talked about at St Elizabeths," can teach us something more about the Pound–Chang exchange. Chang was opposed to a "hackneyed exposition of the basic thought of Confucius," what he called a "museum approach" to a living tradition (*The Development of Neo-Confucian Thought*, i. 7). Pound, by contrast, was for "Confucianism as Confucius had it." Ironically, in their conversations the neo-Confucian Chang proved to be the more orthodox Confucian. McNaughton's memoir written for this volume also sheds light on the sources of some obscure *Rock-Drill* passages and the circumstances of their composition. Lines such as "亦／尚／一／人／it may depend on one man" in Canto 86/583 and "To know the histories 書／經 to know good from evil／And know whom to trust" in Canto 89/610 come alive when read together with this material.

Fig. 6.1. Carsun Chang in Washington, DC, 1953. (Diana Chang and June Chang Tung)

Fig. 6.2. Carsun Chang in San Francisco, 1957. (Diana Chang and Jung Chang Tung)

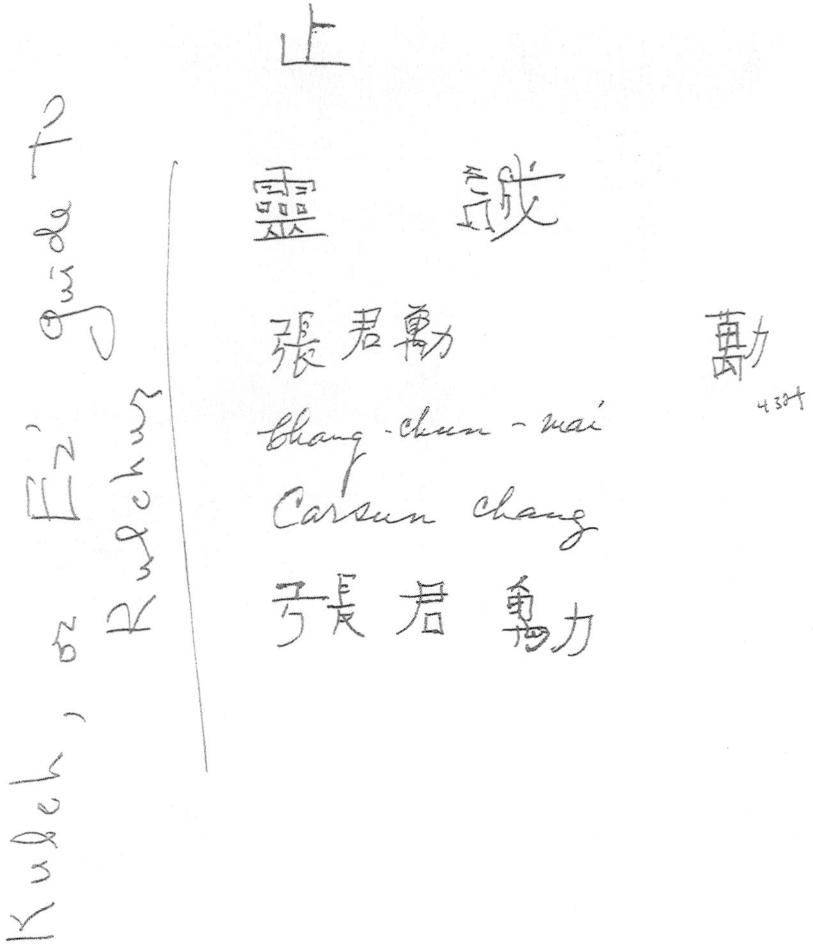

Fig. 6.3. Autographs of EP and Chang, 1953. (Beinecke)

Fig. 6.4. C. H. Kwock interviewing jazz musician Louis Armstrong in San Francisco, 1958. (C. H. Kwock)

70   *Chang to EP (ALS-3; Beinecke)*

502 third st. S.E.
Washington, D.C.
14 November 1953

Dear E. Pound,

It was a great pleasure to have a talk with you.

The Chinese scholars since World War I tried to make Confucius discredited. Dr. Hu Shih, the former Chinese ambassador to Washington, started a movement: pulling down the house of Confucius. Now it is much worse on the mainland of China; the Communists are trying to uproot the Chinese tradition of Confucius.

It gives me great pleasure to know that you are making the proposal that Confucius be included in the university curriculum.

After reading your books on Confucius I shall write an article in which your opinions on Confucius will be made known to the Chinese. I hope that you will give me a note to show how and for what reason you appreciate Confucius. This will encourage the Chinese to respect their own tradition and to fight against Communism.

I submitted my article to you: Wang Shou-jen or Wang Yang-ming. He brought the Chinese philosophical thought to a climax.

Please tell me the lines which you wrote on Confucius, which should be included in my article on your work in the country.

My work: Neo-Confucianism, the philosophy of Sung period, will be published in the next year. I shall send you a copy in showing my gratitude for your work on Confucius.

yours sincerely
Carsun Chang

Hu Shih: see Glossary on Hu Shi.
Wang Shou-jen: see Glossary on Wang Shouren.
My work: *The Development of Neo-Confucian Thought* (1957, 1961).

71   *Chang to EP (ALS-1; Beinecke)*

113 4th st. S.E.
Washington, D.C.
15 March 1955

Dear Mr. Pound:

I have not come to see you for a long time, because I went to the Pacific coast to attend my son's wedding & to give ten lectures in San Francisco.

I suppose you received all the translated texts of my lectures from Mr. Kwock, editor of the Chinese World. I tried to arouse the Chinese for a moral revival.

Mr. Bill MacNaughton [McNaughton] has moved away from the A street, so I lost contact with him. He must come often to see you. Please tell him to come to the Library of Congress, so we can come to you together.

Enclosed is a list of your friends, who are living in San Francisco. They are looking forward for [to] a change of the present moral atmosphere.

With my best regards to you & your wife.

> yours sincerely
> Carsun Chang

Kwock: see Glossary on Kwock, C. H.

72   *Chang to EP (ALS-2; Beinecke)*

> 826 Baker st.
> San Francisco
> 30 March 1957

Dear Mr. Pound,

Thank you very much for telling me to approach Mr. March D'Arcy through Mr. T. C. Chao.

The first volume of my book "Neo-Confucianism" will be released within one or two months. The second volume is also ready, but I must try to find a publisher. This is a half of the whole book so I am not sure whether he will like to include in his collection.

Last year I worked as a research fellow in Stanford University. The article on your work, which I promised to Mr. Bill McNaughton to do, has not begun, but I will certainly do it. The Chinese owe you a great deal for spreading the Confucian ideas in the West.

Hoping that you & your wife are going on well. In China there is a saying that a great man cannot avoid the fate of being kept in prison. King Wen was in prison, when he wrote the Book of Change[s]; Confucius came back to the Kingdom of Lu to edit the classics after he had been treated as a foe in the Kingdoms of Chen and Tsai. Ssu Ma Chien wrote his 史 記, after he was sentenced and put into prison. From these lessons you know that your present position is a sign of your greatness. Keep your peace of mind and your health! This is my hope.

> yours sincerely
> Carsun Chang

March D'Arcy: perhaps Martin D'Arcy, author of *The Mind and Heart of Love* (1945). See *Pound/ Theobald*, 59 (10 July 1957): "Father D'Arcy sd/to have purrsuaded N. Car. to be about to print it."
Ssu Ma Chien: see Glossary on Sima Qian.

73   *Kwock to EP* (ALS-2; Beinecke)

736 Grant, S. F.
12/18/54

My dear Ezra—

Met your Washington new friend Carsun Chang several days ago/spoken highly of you & your philosophy/said he'll write "The Philosophy of E. P."/ he'll be back in S. F. next month to deliver a series of lectures on Confucianism/ and to help revive the local Confucian Society which has been closed the past several years due to the lack of real leadership/will you like us to reprint your Analects in a bilingual edition/we are ordering some new Chinese types from Japan/Regards to Dorothy & Dennis O'Donovan.

日 新 又 日 新 [Day by day make it new]
with highest regards,
C. H. Kwock
The Chinese World

Dennis O'Donovan: unidentified.

74   *Kwock to EP* (ALS-1; Beinecke)

[736 Grant Avenue]
[San Francisco]
2/5/55

My esteemed 新—

Thank you for your excellent suggestion/have been thinking along that line too/Dr Carsun Chang also likes the idea/he'll leave here for Seattle by bus Feb. 17/and then enplane for the Capital about Feb. 22/so he'll see you on Feb 25 or 26 or 27/and explain why he has to use the James Legge translation/because that's the available one here!

C. H. Kwock

新: *xin* meaning "make it new," used as a salutation.
James Legge translation: in his lectures Chang cited Confucian ideas in Legge's translation. Kwock had sent EP English translations of these lectures.

William McNaughton's Memoir:
"What Pound and Carsun Chang Talked About at St Elizabeths"

I met Dr Chang through mutual friends in the intellectual Chinese community in Washington, DC. Chang then had a private cubicle at the Library of Congress, where he was working on his book on neo-Confucian philosophy. When he heard that I was acquainted with Pound, he asked if it would be possible for me to introduce him to Pound. Having received Pound's permission to do so, I took Dr Chang with me the next time I went to St Elizabeths. It was almost certainly the second or third Tuesday in November 1953. Over the next eighteen months Dr Chang went to see Pound many times. I would judge that there were a total of about ten interviews between the two men, all taking place not later than May 1955.

During their first meeting Pound told Chang—rather frankly, I thought, in view of Chang's absorption at that time in his work on neo-Confucianism—that he (Pound) wanted Confucianism as Confucius had it and that he "found little of interest in later dilatations." Among "late dilutations" it was clear that Pound intended to include neo-Confucianism.

Pound and Dr Chang talked about Pound's work; about Leopoldine reforms; and about Thomas Jefferson. Chang knew a good deal about Jefferson. He told Pound how he had come to draft a constitution for China on Jeffersonian principles. The draft later became the basis of the Constitution which was adopted and which is still supposed to be in effect in Taiwan.

On one of my visits to St Elizabeths with Carsun Chang, Pound said to him, "If there were only four Confucians in China who would get together and work with each other, they could save China." "Four?" Dr Chang laughed. "One is enough." In the exchange Chang showed himself, perhaps, to be the more orthodox Confucian. But into the *Rock-Drill* cantos, Pound did write from the Canonic Book of History the idea that "亦/ 尚/ 一/ 人/ it may depend on one man" (86/583). Before Dr Chang and I left that day, Pound said to me, "Bring him out again. He is somebody you can talk to. He is interested in the definition of words." Mrs Pound also asked me to bring Chang out again. "Eppy," she said, "is very hungry for adult company out here."

Later on Chang asked Pound to write an introduction for his book on Chinese philosophy. Pound wrote one page in which he said he thought that the reader would be delighted with a book about a thinker who once clapped his hands with joy at the sight of a leaf. Chang decided not to use the introduction. He had wanted something more scholarly, and Pound had written the introduction "like a poet." (In addition to his formal Chinese education, Dr Chang had been a postgraduate student in Germany, and his attitude perhaps had been colored by Germanic ideas of scholarship.) From Chang's manuscript Pound got the "rules for a man in government" which appear at the beginning of Canto 89:

To know the histories 書
　　　　　　　　經 to know good from evil

And know whom to trust.

Sometime during one afternoon Chang made the usual objections to Fenollosa's treatment of the Chinese written character. The talk then turned to James Legge and Arthur Waley, Pound remarked: "The trouble with Legge's versions is, whenever Confucius disagrees with St Paul, Legge puts in a footnote to say that Confucius must be wrong."

Chang quoted the Analects occasionally in Chinese (in his Jiangsu dialect), and then he would translate the passage into very good English. When Pound and Dr Chang took their leave of each other, Pound bowed to Dr Chang over his hands, Chinese-style, and Dr Chang reciprocated.

Chang admired the "remarkable genius" of Pound's translations of many paragraphs in the Analects, but he felt that sometimes Pound "went too far." As a specific example of Pound's "going too far," Dr Chang cited Pound's version of Analects 8.2.2: "Gentlemen 'bamboo-horse' to their relatives [*The bamboo is both hard on the surface and pliant*] and the people will rise to manhood." (Legge has: "When those who are in high stations perform well all their duties to their relations, the people are aroused to virtue.") Chang could not accept the "bamboo-horse" translation for tu^3 篤, "ideogrammic" as it was. Smiling, Pound said he understood the criticism but did not accept it.

I have a note from Pound, dated "23 Maggio," but not postmarked because it was delivered by hand. I believe that it was written 23 May 1954 The note says: "About time to see Chang again/ get him onto some real occidental writers/ Ric/S/V, as just a bit later than that his neo-Kungists. ETC." "Ric/S/V" is, of course, Richard St Victor; and the "neo-Kungists" are the neo-Confucian philosophers on whom Chang was writing at the time. Pound never did get Chang back to "essential Confucianism" and off the "neo-Kungists."

As important as the "subjects of conversation" between two men are the emotional tone and the intellectual spark that plays between the conversants. Between Dr Chang and Pound, for what I could see, there was a genuine affection; and if during their talks it was clear that Chang excited Pound intellectually, it was apparent afterward, as we rode in our taxi back to Capitol Hill, that Pound excited Dr Chang as well. For Pound, working as he was to get some of the "wisdom of China" into his Paradise, the friendship perhaps matched his ideas about "the laying on of hands," as one astute scholar has called it.

7
Achilles Fang and Pound's *Classic Anthology*
"The barbarians need the ODES"

Much of the Pound–Achilles Fang correspondence during 1953–8 deals with the Confucian Odes project. For Pound the 305 odes handed down from Confucius were both songs to be sung and characters to be deciphered. Accordingly, his edition of the Odes would have to include a singing key and a Chinese character text facing his English translation. In October 1948 Pound consulted Willis Hawley about typesetting the characters of the odes. Hawley sent Pound the photocopies of three Chinese texts, suggesting that it would be "practical to reproduce [one of these texts] instead of setting type" (Lilly). Of the three texts, the Tang script was ninth century, Song script was eleventh century, and the seal script alone was from Confucius' era. Naturally Pound chose the seal script text for his edition of the Odes.

In 1949–50 the Odes seal text supplied by Hawley passed from James Laughlin of New Directions to Laughlin's printer Dudley Kimball. Numerous letters concerning the layouts of the three-way Odes project were exchanged between Pound, Hawley, Laughlin, and Kimball. Laughlin working on the Stone-Classics edition of *The Great Digest & The Unwobbling Pivot* became increasingly reluctant to take on another complex project. By late 1951 Pound was losing patience. It was at that point that Achilles Fang came to his rescue (see Fig. 7.1). He approached the director of Harvard University Press, Thomas Wilson, and succeeded in stirring an interest.

The letters collected here provide a detailed record of Pound's and Harvard's conflicting desires, and of Fang's role as a mediator. Harvard's enthusiasm was for Pound's translation of the Odes. Pound, however, absolutely would not pull out from his manuscript the singing syllables and the characters (see Figs. 7.2 and 7.3). The negotiation of a contract broke down in late November 1952 after a letter from Wilson gave Pound the impression that Harvard did not value the sound key and the seal text. Pound began to think of other publishers. In January 1953 John Kasper, co-editor (with David Horton) of the Square Dollar series, reported to Pound Macmillan's and Twayne's interest in this project (Lilly). Meanwhile, Achilles Fang assured Pound that Harvard University Press would carry out his wishes. Right before Kasper was going to get the Odes manuscript from Fang, Pound changed his mind. With his energy almost exhausted he would have to rely on Fang to see the project through, and the logical place for the Harvard scholar to do his part of the job was Cambridge. By June 1953 Harvard Press offered Pound two contracts, first to publish a "trade edition" and then to bring out a three-way, "scholar's edition." In August Pound signed both contracts.

Pound experienced little excitement when the "trade edition" of the Odes, *The Classic Anthology Defined by Confucius,* came out in 1954. "WHEN the real edition is done," he grumbled, "there shd/alzo be a[n] index, or table of contents, or both" (Letter 112). He was pleased, though, with Fang's introduction, which includes a syllable-for-syllable transcription of Ode 1 and a footnote announcing a "forthcoming," three-way edition of the Odes. Fang's effort to affix a seal script 詩 (Odes) on the cover also won Pound's approval (see Fig. 7.4). Several other details of the production, nonetheless, made him paranoid. The typography of his name larger than that of Confucius on the cover especially irritated his eye. "It is the most BEEyewteeful anthology in the world," he told Fang, "and CONFUCIO had more to do with making it than had yr/anon/crspdt" (Letter 112). "Remember I want <to see> front matter of real EDITION when and/or/if" (Letter 115). However, the "real EDITION" never appeared.

Pound's correspondence with Fang of 1956–8 is characterized by impatience. Fang kept assuring Pound that Wilson had no intention to back out. Pound began to suspect whether the delay could have been caused by Fang's wasting time on the accuracy of his sound key. He wrote wryly to him on 4 February 1956: "if you are waiting to satisfy your letch for precision Gaw Damn it/there is NO alphabetic representation of chinese sound, let alone any fad of spelling it in amurkn alPHAbet" (Letter 123). By mid-June 1956, when there was still no movement, he wrote to Wilson, stating: "IF this means that Fang is bored with matter I wish you would return me the ms/and I myself prepare it for the press" (Beinecke).

In 1955–8 Achilles Fang busily corresponded with Pound's family (wife Dorothy, son Omar, and daughter Mary Rudge) and friends in efforts to get Pound released from St Elizabeths Hospital (see Fig. 7.5). In a letter of 10 August 1955 to Archibald MacLeish, for instance, he wrote: "I told [Mary] everything you told last winter—that the psychiatrists are willing to release him, that Dr Milton E[isenhower]. could be of some use, and that EP is the only obstacle" (Beinecke). Meanwhile, he was preparing his dissertation. In late 1956, perhaps as a result of Pound's chiding, he put aside all other projects to work on the sound key and the seal text. For nearly a year from January to October 1957, however, Fang neglected to inform Pound of the progress of the project. Pound grew restless and annoyed. He questioned Wilson on 14 October 1957 as to what was holding up the "proper edition of the Confucian Anthology." Wilson's reply was that the press did not yet have the complete manuscript: "To be just as frank as you are, we have no real desire to publish the complete text, but we are ready to do so when the complete manuscript is in our hands...We agreed, as the correspondence shows it very clearly, to publish the scholars' edition when Dr. Fang had completed his editorial work and the necessary introduction; not all of the material is yet in our hands; when it is, we will go ahead, unless you wish to withdraw the manuscript. If the latter is your wish, we should be very glad to fall in with it" (Beinecke).

Bewildered and furious, Pound turned to Fang for an explanation: "this puts ALL the blame on you for the delay in publication of the Odes in the ONLY form that interested me in the least" (Letter 126). Since January, according to Fang, everything essential had been held in the office of the Harvard Press editorial department. The only thing that he had not turned in was an introduction. To him it was unnecessary. Should Harvard Press insist on having it, he said, he would write it in a short while. Harvard's demand for an introduction was legitimate. For Pound, however, this was an excuse, betraying the US system of education's "hatred of the Chinese Classics" (Letter 126). His bitterness was not assuaged by Fang, who tried to take all the blame: "Let me take all the blame from each side if need be. Let's have the book at all costs. Barring accidents, we may see the book out next year" (Letter 127). This did not at all help close the rift between them. "Fang after years of patient fidelity," Pound warned, "in danger of losing the respect and friendship of illustrious translator because a cheap, super-market dirtShirt, fumbles and fusses, and IMPEDES" (Beinecke).

Pound's last letter to Achilles Fang is dated 18 May 1958, about ten days after his release from St Elizabeths Hospital: "The sabotage, the blocking of my work remains...The infinite vileness of the state of education under the rump of the present organisms for the suppression of mental life is not your fault" (Letter 128). In a reply Fang again assured Pound that Harvard University Press would start working on the project after summer vacation. By then Pound had lost confidence in Harvard. On 10 November 1958 he wrote to Wilson from Italy, requesting return of the manuscript and photographs of the complete edition of the Odes (Beinecke). With the termination of the contract regarding the scholar's edition of his Confucian Odes a decade-long correspondence with Achilles Fang also came to a close.

Fig. 7.1. Achilles Fang on his way to Washington, DC, 1953. (Ilse Fang)

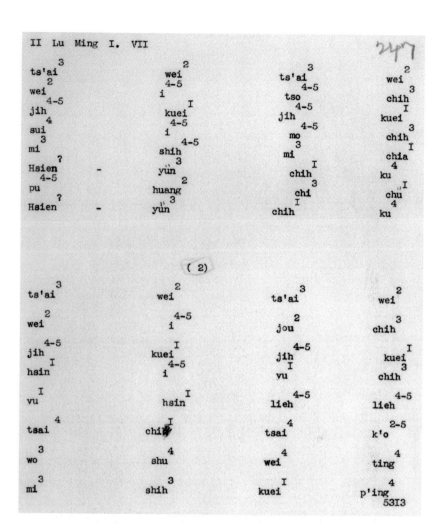

Fig. 7.2. EP's sound key to Ode 167. (Beinecke)

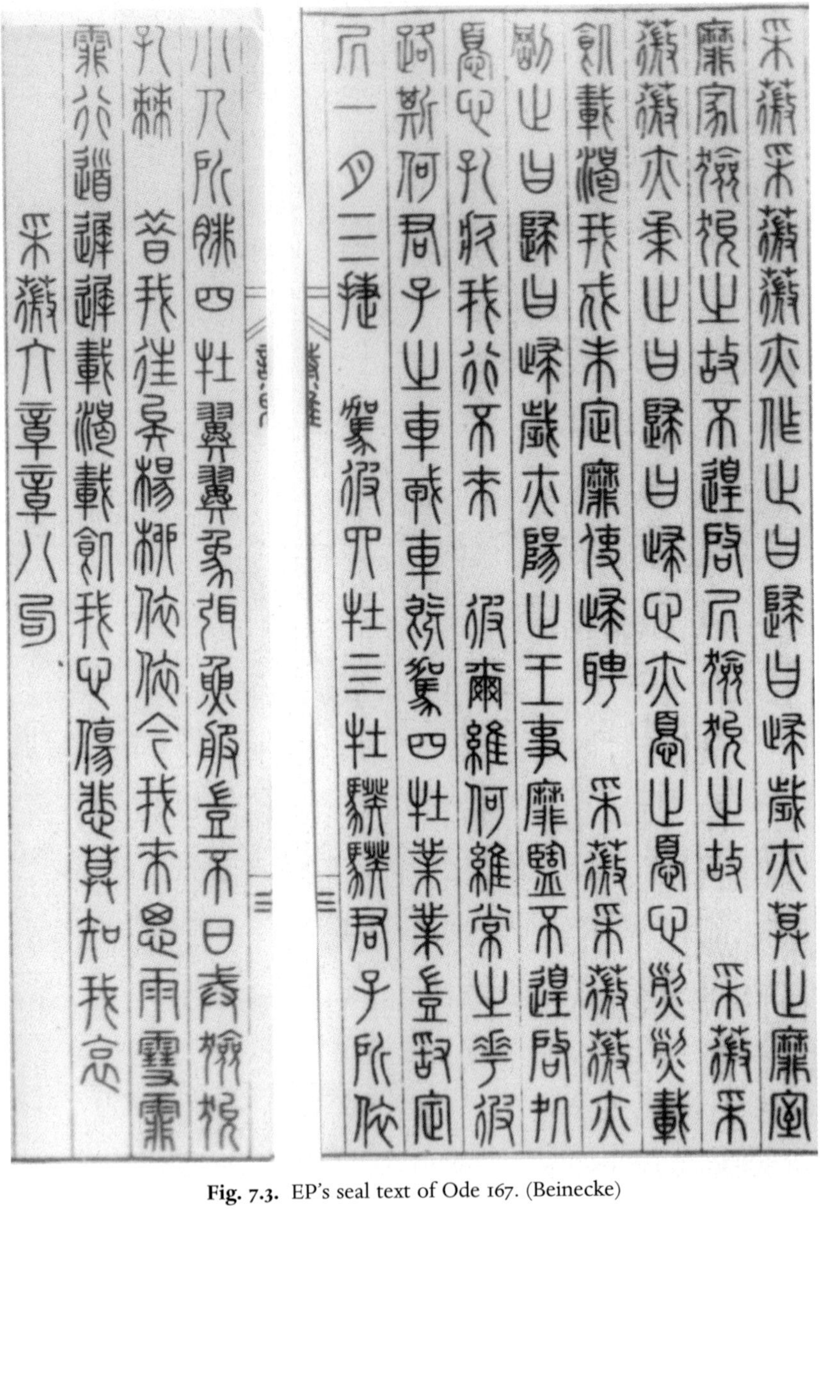

Fig. 7.3. EP's seal text of Ode 167. (Beinecke)

THE CLASSIC

ANTHOLOGY

DEFINED BY

CONFUCIUS

EZRA
POUND

Fig. 7.4. Cover of *Classic Anthology*. (Harvard University Press)

Fig. 7.5. Achilles and Ilse Fang, 1957. (Ilse Fang)

75 *Fang to EP* (TLS-1; Beinecke)

[Cambridge, Mass.]
July 25, 1952

Dear Mr Pound,

Thank you VERY much for A Visiting Card; and I like your Chinese script.

Just now John Hawkes (The Beetle Leg, N.D.), Harvard Press, Production Deptment, with your Odes, asking to know the best way of printing the phonetic part. He is trying to estimate production cost. Advised him to tell Wilson of the Press to communicate to you directly. More anon from La Drière, who comes tonight for a Bierkneipe [get-together at the pub]; J. H. will be there to tell him the details. (I've already dined with L. D.; a nice man.)

By the way do you want to have the sound-script printed as a separate volume?

Hope the price of the book will not be prohibitive—I am afraid it cannot be less than 10 at the least. Can every interested reader afford it???

All this is between us. Until you are officially "advised" by the Press.

Yours respectfully
[signed] Achilles Fang

A Visiting Card: EP's *Carta da Visita* (1942) translated into English by John Drummond (1952).
Wilson: see Glossary on Wilson, Thomas James.
La Drière: Craig La Drière (1910–78), professor of English at the Catholic University of America, hosted EP in his Washington home before EP left for Italy. He was a visiting professor at Harvard in 1952.

76 *EP to Fang* (TL-2; Beinecke)

[St Elizabeths Hospital]
[Washington, DC]
[31 July 1952]

Dear FANG   Kung Tzu shi [Confucian Odes]

I believe the ideogram [矰] is an ARROW/whether you follow it by five dashes or repeat 5 times, or whether its simple and primitive vigour expresses the plenum, I cannot say with authority.

UNLESS the phonetic symbols are visible (NOT as in that Princeton horror), VISIBLE simultaneously with the ideograms AND the translation/the phonetic transcript will NOT help the ignorant reader (like yr/friend here below unsigned) to SEE what sound belongs to what ideogram (seal or other)

therefore ten deaths, the execution with 34 cuts or some other ADEQUATE punishment shd/be held over the NECK of anyone who attempts to separate those phonetic (approximate etc.) expositions FROM the chinese text (which shd be on left hand page facing TRANSLATION into barbarian tongue, and highly imperfect but useful (it dont much matter if uniform) representation of the SOUND.)

AS was measured to a millimeter by the Kimball/<imperfect> sample page IF it with the ms/from Kimball's debacle or schivolation <enclosed>.

and god DAMN it the form of the chinese strophes is to be CLEAR to the eye/as it was in the case of Guido's Canzone Donna mi Prega.

The columns of the romanj shd/be spread as far from each other as the page permits. WHEN the space is crowded a black dash can indicate strophe ends. as inked in enclosed.

BUT this proof lacks 8 lines of final strophe, so smaller font must be used.

It was perfectly possible to get two twelve line strophes on a page/NO broken strophes.

AS to price/Eliot's specification IF Faber were to take sheets was that it must "LOOK LIKE" a two guinea book.

Obviously a cheap edition, even without chinese text can be issued in 30 years time. <After it is once done RIGHT.>

That FILTHY Princeton production was priced ten bucks.

I never heard of Tschumi, but certainly Geneva is NOT the place whence light has been accustomed to emerge/for at least six centuries, but with augmented vileness during the past 3 or 4 decades. However Calvin etc/etc/

AN INTERESTED reader can always afford ten bucks/depends on for WHAT. An uninterested reader sent me the Princeton horror out of his heart's kindness, and so on.

I hear the <or an> imperial nephew is in the vicinage, and hope to return his grandfathers, that is his gt/gt/gt or whateverth ancestor's benefit.

As to Li Ki/what is the etiquette governing intercourse between a confucian and the Dalai Lama?

after all one isn't a proselyting Xtian, but on the other hand one shd NOT put a pouch over the HSIEN[3] [light]

and salute John chü[1] [Hawkes]

or does his plural rate conjugal happiness (acc Mat) ChuChiu.

Princeton horror: Princeton's Bollingen edition of Richard Wilhelm's *I Ching* retranslated by Cary Baynes (1950).

Kimball: see Glossary on Kimball, Dudley.

Guido's Canzone Donna mi Prega: see Letter 56 n.

it must "LOOK LIKE" a two guinea book: see Letter 89 n.

Tschumi: Raymond Tschumi of University of Geneva authored *Thought in Twentieth-Century English Poetry* (1951).

Calvin: John (Jean) Calvin (1509–64), French theologian and reformer, founded University of Geneva in 1559.

Li Ki . . . the Dalai Lama: in a reply of 5 August 1952 Fang wrote: "There are any number of details governing intercourse between a Confucian and the Dalai Lama in Li Ki and esp. in I-li. I don't think that imperial nephew of yours will demand them" (Lilly). Dalai Lama is the title of the Tibetan Buddhist leader.

chü¹··· ChuChiu: Mathews, 1580 雎 鳩: A kind of fish-hawk, "a waterfowl, emblematical of conjugal harmony." Ju jiu 雎 鳩 occurs in Ode 1, line 1. See Letter 91 n.

77 *EP to Fang (TL-1)*

[St Elizabeths Hospital]
[Washington, DC]
[22 August 1952]

accuse reception one essay by
Hnble FANG
re short-comings of Hu [Shi], Amy [Lowell] etc/

sd Hu?? A Xrister? once in charge an university for importing the WRONG occidental works into Celestial ex Empire?? or wot?

whoZZZ eee mean by grammar?

Charm of classic chinese largely attributable to there being very little such?? exact degree, or even approx difficult fer barbarian to grasp. but wot ov it?

In present rage to destroy considerable chink Kulch Hu or anyUVum likely to be available to funnel in a little of occidental-NOT-rot?

Mild diversion of Hnbl/FANG might be found in Wyndham's Rotting Hill, and in bits of Writer and Absolute, tho latter not partic[ularly] necess/if have not wasted time on lower frog and brit/babblers.

Gawd bless Wyndham, chief delouser of dying Britain AND so on.

Hu [Shi], Amy [Lowell] etc: Fang, "Imagism & Chinese Renaissance." See Letter 86. EP and fellow American poet Amy Lowell (1874–1925) had not been on friendly terms ever since 1914, when, in his view, she reduced the Imagist movement he had started to "Amygism."
Hu: see Glossary on Hu Shi.
Rotting Hill . . . Writer and Absolute: Wyndham Lewis (see Glossary), *Rotting Hill* (London: Methuen, 1951); *The Writer and the Absolute* (London: Methuen, 1952).

78 *Fang to EP (TLS-1; Lilly)*

[Cambridge, Mass.]
September 1, 1952

Dear Mr Pound,

HU SHIH is now at Princeton. He appears in Boylston Hall now & then; I have somehow managed to miss him.

Your [Guide to] Kulchur will be read in China—in thirty years. The crowd in Formosa will never cast a glance at the book. (I have a pretty low opinion of them, not that I have any higher esteem of those on the mainland—at this moment.)

Someone gave me a book containing La Prima Decade dei Cantos di E.P. But who is Ennio Contini?

I am asked to write a review of PIVOT for New Mexico Quarterly. As it is not for me to mete out 褒 [pros] or 貶 [cons] I intend to write a compact essay on PIVOT's position in E.P.'s universe. I shall be grateful if you care to give me some hints—what points you would like to see emphasized, etc.

Hope to write that essay after my Colorado trip. The Sub-Committee on Chinese thought (subsidized by Ford Foundation) is holding a meeting at Aspen, Sept. 7–14. All expenses paid to the participants (about a dozen). Have sent them a paper on the difficulty of translating from the Chinese—some sixty pages, mainly about how one should become a good sinologist. I believe it is sheer waste. (Shall leave Cambridge on 4 and return on 17 Sept.)

Yours respectfully
[signed] Achilles Fang

HU SHIH: see Glossary on Hu Shi.

La Prima Decade dei Cantos di E.P.... Ennio Contini: L'Alleluja (1952) with ten poems by Ennio Contini and Mary de Rachewiltz's Italian versions of Cantos 1–9 and lines 1–55 of Canto 10 (Gallup D56).

on the difficulty of translating: Fang, "Some Reflections on the Difficulty of Translation," in Studies in Chinese Thought, ed. Arthur Wright (Chicago: University of Chicago Press, 1953).

79   EP to Fang (TL-2; Beinecke)

[St Elizabeths Hospital]
[Washington, DC]
[5 September 1952]

THIRTY years, O Fang, my phoenix!!!

what celerity, what almost indecent celerity/

it took Seymour 37 years to get Patria Mia into press.

it has taken 40 for Harriet's snot-rag to print a french poets, bilingual issue/ and now nacherly, as they tell me, it represents about the wust possbl SElection to illustrate whatever mental life is left in froggery.

WHY shd/ the heathen chinese git thaaar sooner than the goddam BARbarian??

pien³ [貶]/ given by mathews/

wot I spose means praise dont SEEM to be in Mr Mathews

PAO¹ [褒]/ I spose/ rad[ical] 145 (yes, Mat has it)

KEEP on, you'll drive me into eggspandin my VOcabulary.

PIVOT position: CHUNG [中], I spose, plumb in deh MIDDLE whaar it ought to be.

Contini, young wop [Italian] with nerve enough to annoy the woptalian Bloomsbury by printing what his connazionali do NOT want printed.

Pivot? emphasis? perhaps that it is better to be a Confucian than a sinologist/ not that the two categories are necessarily in opposition. Many of yr/race must have (at any rate are said to have) come to understand that the ANSWERS are ALL in the four books/at 25 one sees this re/some of them/and finds the rest of them later. Just read McNair Wilson's "Gipsy Queen." McN W/is a nice Xtian. Kung wd/have saved him several non sequiturs/

book worth Fang's attention. (1934 . . . I dont know why I hadn't seen it, as I cite McNW in Intro Tx Bk.

I take it F/g has already followed up lines Agassiz/Del Mar, Brooks Ad/ Blackstone/

Cant rember names of chineeee given in small wop/vol/generation after the "ten remnants" but most brilliant already dead in 1937.

Small trans/of Tuan Szetsun (very simple) Wu Yung/a couple of vols/in english seen in hell-hole/Catharine Karl//information re <contemporary> Celestial ex-Empire NOT very abundant.

IN FACT, (as printed), doubt if more than 80 people in Perikles' Athens.

tsai chien (WHY did that bitch pronounce it: chen?)

Patria Mia: in 1950 Ralph Fletcher Seymour issued EP's *Patria Mia* (*SP*, 99–141), which Seymour, Daughaday, and Co. (Chicago) failed to publish in 1913.

Harriet's snot-rag . . . bilingual issue: the *Poetry* magazine (Chicago) founded by Harriet Monroe (1860–1936) in 1912 presents ten contemporary French poets in its September 1952 issue.

pien³ . . . PAO¹: 貶 . . . 襃. See Letter 78.

McNair Wilson's "Gipsy Queen": EP owned a copy of *The Gipsy-Queen of Paris* by Robert McNair Wilson (1934).

Agassiz . . . Blackstone: see Glossary on Agassiz, Louis; Del Mar, Alexander; Adams, Brooks; and Blackstone, William.

Tuan Szetsun . . . Wu Yung: EP owned copies of *Exposition of Confucian Cosmopolitanism* by Tuan Szetsun (1936) and *The Flight of an Empress* by Wu Yung (1937).

Catharine Karl: unidentified.

tsai chien: see Letter 84.

80 *EP to Fang (TL-2; Beinecke)*

[St Elizabeths Hospital]
[Washington, DC]
[13 October 1952]

Achilles

[Fang's notation: "EP's reaction to my Aspen paper."]

I HOPE that'll set 'em down on their WUMPZ and keep 'em down.

as to heresy/there wd/seem to be basic agreement at least to effect that some emphasis is placed on the idea POLitica of "gittin it over"/

as to what Kung WD/have said had he had 2500 MORE years of human imbecility in consideration/gorNOZE

I suspect about FOUR of them ejaculatory arrow signs.

human imbecility (qui donne une idee de/l infini" etc. 2500 of LaoZe aestheticism/and horrible translations from ** into waleeze [Waley] ***

As doctrinaire propagandist/might hold that WHEN K/said it it wasn't a cliché/

and therefore shd NOT be represented by the drool that passes fer langqitch in the Slimes whether of Limeyburg or Jork/
   **

now when yu git to grammar/there I retain curiosity/but having suggested something like agglutinative element in Aeschylus/re/whose lingo I know even less than that of the dark-haired children of the fatherland///

wotterELL do I kare/

and if/poisoned by low grade western infiltrations the WRTTEN symbols of Chink thought have become no better that [than] those of Sulzberger and Matthiessen **

what has that to do with WAN/with kulch/ellegunce or whatsodam/whatso JEN [humanity] or other occupations of the ChunTz' [Zhuangzi]

I wish I did know a bit more about how much a bunch of IDS/CAN interact/ backword forward/as do radicals when conjuncted in one ID/

as from mere hieroglyph in hwa [華] the representation and 花 hwa/with whole poesia of metamorphoses conjuncted/an IDEA-gram tho/or whole poem on paper phonetikly incomplete

nice guy in this P. M. who really likes his Li Po (as befits his tender years) and does NOT swallow bloomsbury bugwash/

do yu do any teaching at haaaVud? or merely talk to half-masted profs/in hours of idleness/I mean where were yu to ram a li'l sense into Locke?

I can't tell these kids much till yr/abysmal employer prints out them INcorrect, but possibly useful graphs of the SHIH [Odes] sound/not that they LOOK much like any grunts and wheezes any celestial, darkhaired etc/has ever made in my presence/

what did I hear the other day, when I said: Mei jin pu hao [Beautiful people not good]. something sounding like: Mei kuo rin pu hao [Americans not good].

Very hard for senile ignoramus to attain vocal fluidity. what does Ni hao ma? [How are you?] sound like in the North Kepertl [Beijing]? A rose of Shanghai pronounces: "manchu," in way almost impos/disting/fr/"damn yankee."

ANYhow/without centuries of damXristers/no freud possible/doubt if even Lao Tse is as obscene as the english alledged version by wa-lee 哇 or 窪 阞 [Waley].

Sulzberger: Arthur Hays Sulzberger (1891–1968), publisher of *New York Times* (1935–61).
Matthiessen: Francis Otto Matthiessen (1902–50), Harvard professor of literature and history.
Li Po: see Glossary on Li Bo.

Locke: Fred Locke. See Letter 81.
A rose of Shanghai: Veronica Huilan Sun (see Glossary).
version by wa-lee: Arthur Waley (1889–1966), *The Way and Its Power: A Study of the Tao Te Ching and Its Place in Chinese Thought* (1949; rpt. New York: Grove, 1958).

81   *Fang to EP (TLS-1; Beinecke)*

[Cambridge, Mass.]
Oct. 27, 1952

Dear Mr Pound,

Completely knocked out for three full weeks—flu. The heavy shoulders wouldn't allow the fingers touch the typewriter keys. Hence this delay in writing.

I am not teaching, nor do I care to play the slave who leads on idiot boys—pedagogue. Sorry Fred Locke was such a disappointment to you. He was not known for his brilliance while he was here. Essentially a philologist or grammarian, and Catholic at that.

Met J. Hawkes a few days ago; the printing project going fine. Mei jin pu hao is too literary, mei jin usually standing for a beauty. Hence Mei-kuo-jin pu hao [Americans not good]. More idiomatically, Mei kuo [美] 國 [America] pu hao [not good]. (Traditionally Chinese did not distinguish the native of a land from the land itself.) Jin 人 is pronounced ren around the northern capital, but elsewhere yin. Ni hao ma sounds really melodious in the mould of a northern girl. The intonation is more or less similar to the phrase Muss es sein? in Beethoven's last string quartet, in F. But the voice is not raised in the last syllable. You know, there is not stress in Chinese. When a word is to be emphasized, it is pronounced in full TONE. The enclitic ma being practically atonal, the whole phrase sounds rather like es and sein transposed: Muss seine es? (One reason why the jap. language sounds so horrible is that the important word—verb—ends a sentence and stress is put on the SUFFIX to the verb and not on the root of the verb itself. Me no savee: wakarimaSENG [I don't know].

I have already made it clear that Waley is too obsessed with sex (v. Harvard Journal of Asiatic Studies, p. 558, note to §122). I am inclined to think that Ta[o]-te-ching can be used as a metaphysical foundation for Jeffersonian democracy. It is the later Taozers who misinterpreted him. Lao-tzu was no more Taoistic than you are.

Thank you very much for your comment on NMQ Lu Ki. I still think you should do MONG.

If Guggenheim is willing to be useful, I shall try to translate Wen-hsin tiao-lung next year.

文 質 彬 彬 is from the Stone-Classic (we have also T'ang stone-classics here): Analects VI xvi. (Lash should not have put 文 質 at the beginning. I gave him choice, but he took both.) The second ideogram is 5257 Mathews.

Respectfully
[signed] Achilles Fang

Wen-hsin tiao-lung: Liu Xie (c.465–c.532), Wenxin diaolong (Literary Mind and the Carving of Dragons). See Fang, review of V. Y. Shih's translation of the book in *Times Literary Supplement*, 4 December 1959.

文 質 彬 彬: EP renders the phrase as "accomplishment and solidity as two trees growing side by side and together with leafage" (*Confucius*, 216).

Lash: Kenneth Lush, editor of *New Mexico Quarterly.*

82   EP to Fang *(TL-1; Beinecke)*

[St Elizabeths Hospital]
[Washington, DC]
[4 November 1952]

and az to strange doctrines
ACHILLES
Mr W[aley]'s alledged translation of Lao/being OF the most obscene bks/ printed even in the Perfidious Isle the question of the alledged source might be reduced to enquiry
    Does Lao contain ANYTHING useful that is NOT in the Four Books (and their preludes, the Shih [Book of Odes] and the Shu [Book of History]) [?]
an nif not why bother wiff deh superfluous.
    The bamboo grove and so on/cant eggspect the young to eschew all dalliance or rise presto presto to senile calm. we grant THAT.

83   Fang to EP *(TLS-1; Lilly)*

[Cambridge, Mass.]
Nov 14, 1952

Dear Mr Pound,
    Your latest, on Lao and the bamboo grove boys, was forwarded to me in Mass. General Hospital. Lao certainly is ambiguous to have much value for sensible beings—at any rate he cannot be rendered sexually. BUT Chuang Chou, generally misunderstood to be a Taoist (but he is more Confucian than Taoist), should be of great importance to sensible Confucians.

On Nov. 3 I lost balance and fell down 7 steps. Left foot sprained and the heelbone shattered. Went to the above mentioned hospital on the 6th, had the bone set aright, and the foot and ankle in cast. Came home on the 12th.

Yesterday was invited to Faculty Club: lunch with MacLeish, Hawkes, and Wilson (host).

The boss of the press showed me a sample sheet of your Odes. Both the Syndics (or is it Syndicate) and Wilson have come to decision: they will publish.

Only that they are figuring out how to reduce the production cost.

Gathered that the press is toying with the idea of publishing a de-luxe ed. of text-cum-ideogram-cum-sound and another ed. of text solus simultaneously.

Wilson wants to communicate to you directly—I encouraged him. By the way, Wilson used to teach frog lit.

W is a nice chap: wants to have the Odes out as soon as possible. Old Mac joined in, of course.

(The preceding paragraph is strictly between us. You will hear from W soon, I think.)

This compulsory vacation is exasperating.

Oh yes, e. e. cummings asked me to come and see him. Wrote him that when I get a bit agile with the crutches I shall come. Thanks.

With respect
[signed] Achilles Fang

Chuang Chou: see Glossary on Zhuang Zhou.
MacLeish: see Glossary on MacLeish, Archibald.
Wilson: see Glossary on Wilson, Thomas James.
e. e. cummings: see Glossary on Cummings, Edward Estlin.

84   *EP to Fang* (TL-1 + ALS-2; Beinecke)

[St Elizabeths Hospital]
[Washington, DC]
19 Nv [1952]

yes, my Achilles

(doing it thoroughly) I got hit on the heel over 50 years ago by a base ball/and there being v. litl circulation in that part of the corpus, I know it takes d/n/long time to git over soreness.

★★★

offset is a printing METHOD, at low cost, once the kumperzishn is did.

★★★

O.K. re Chuang Chou/but I still want [to] know WHAT he ADDED.

It is my hypothesis, based on NO data (that is no extraneous data) whatsodam, that every intelligent chinYman fer 1000 years has meditated the Four bks/
trying to see wot he cd/leave out, or add/result being dam little.

Before that they spent 1400 years deciding Mencius cd/be added to the
THREE bks/

**puzzled by the one about wot he (K) ate and his night gown/of course
quite simple. IF one consider that it had to get affirmed that Kung was not a
solar myth or the incarnation of hindoo djinn procreated by a fish swallowing
the etc/(wot them hindoos wont think of?/?) !!!

as per Voltaire: the first man who did NOT.

Regnery has reprinted Wyndham L[ewis]'s "Revenge fer Luvv" mebbe that
wd/beguile yr enforced ex-deskness/

the kumrad kumminkz [Cummings] is abl/bodied/tell him to come to YU
with my kumplimentZ.

- - - - - - - - -

    Condolences
    ye compleat
    Achilles.
    a heel fer
    a heel
                Ez P
    incidentally
    young Chien
    recognized yr
    friends calligraphy
    on the wall.
    Thank
    Kuanon
    arrows are
    out of
    date
    or unobtainable
    in Boston

as per Voltaire: in *Ancient and Modern History* Voltaire (1694–1778) refers to Confucius as a philoso-
    pher who "does not pretend to inspiration, or the gift of prophecy," one who "places all his
    merit in a constant endeavor to gain the mastery over his passions, and … writes only as a
    philosopher" (*The Works of Voltaire*, trans. William Fleming (New York: St Hubert Guild, 1901),
    xv/2.173). Cf. *Confucius*, 191.
"Revenge fer Luvv": Wyndham Lewis (see Glossary), *The Revenge for Love* (1937).
Chien: T'sai Chien. See Letter 79.
yr friends calligraphy: see Letter 36 n.
Kuanon: Kuanon (Guanyin), Goddess of Compassion, is honored in Cantos 74, 77, 81, 90, 97, 101,
    and 110.

85   *EP to Fang* (TL-1; Beinecke)

[St Elizabeths Hospital]
[Washington, DC]
[November 1952]

No, my Fang
    D.P. has just recd/a thoroughly DIRTY letter from yr/friend Wilson.
                    NO soap.

letter from . . . Wilson: this letter is lost or discarded.

86   *Fang to EP* (TLS-1; Beinecke)

[Cambridge, Mass.]
Nov. 25, 1952

Dear Mr Pound,
    Thank you very much for the condolences. The damaged heel will be repaired in 3 more weeks. Cast meanwhile.
    Am sorry to hear that Wilson has disappointed you. I didn't expect him to do so, for he was very willing to do whatever you wanted. I still think he can be made reasonable.
    A few days ago John H. Randall, JR (Columbia), editor of Journal of the History of Ideas, wrote me a two-page insulting letter together with the MS (Imagism & Ch. Renaissance). I don't mind the rejection, but the letter was too much. It was so stinking, that I doubt if it could have been written by anyone but a Yankee or a Britisher. Well, I did not deem it worth even answering. <So, the MS lies in the drawer.>
    What's matter with homo americanus academiensis? A chronic campus-follower that I am, I am sometimes nonplussed.
    As for the Ode-Wilson mix-up, can I do anything for you?

Respectfully
[signed] Achilles

87   *EP to Fang* (TL-1; Beinecke)

[St Elizabeths Hospital]
[Washington, DC]
15 Jan 16 Jan [1953]

O FANG
    moderation is the thief of time (perhaps).
    anyhow have telegraphed Kasper to WAIT, bloody WAIT

But whether he will hv/left N. Pork [New York] and be howling at yr/door, having missed telegram, I dont know.

At any rate I shd/like clarification before chucking the Odes at some other publisher. AS Cairns whispered an incomprehensible message, re decent intentions at Haaavud/

AND I suppose it wd/be more convenient fer Fang to do his part of the Herculean, in Cambridge.

BUT no harm to know that the impulsive Kasp/has two other publishers interested.

The contrast between K[asper]/going off half cocked/and C[airns]/thinking two weeks absence is NOT a delay. Oh yes, he was coming back with two holy doves of Picassian peace etc.

Any how Kasper's instructions are to WAIT, whether he has recd/'em in N. York or gets 'em from yu when he produces a tommy-gun.

anyhow the KasPER is NOT to have the ms/until I know quite a lot more about who, whom, wherefore etc.

Kasper: see Glossary on Kasper, John.
Cairns: see Glossary on Cairns, Huntington.
two other publishers: in letters to EP of 31 December 1952 and 14 January 1953 (Lilly) Kasper reports
    Macmillan's and Twayne's interest in the Odes project.

88   *Fang to EP (TLS-1; Lilly)*

[Cambridge, Mass.]
Jan. 19, Monday, 1953

Dear Mr Pound,

Your telegram at 5 Friday afternoon. Checked with Hawkes if impulsive Kasper had appeared. Apparently he also got your wire in time: he did not turn up on Saturday morning, as he said he would, per his letter received Sat. morning.

I am really glad that you've changed your mind: I think the Odes should be printed here at Harvard. The people here are not so bad: Wilson gave me the impression that he has the best of all intentions toward the book. It takes time, of course, to handle the Syndics. I am sure everything will turn out as you wish.

Two weeks ago a fellow here in Boston announced (N.Y. Times Book Review) that he was about to write a biography of E.P. Authorized?

Again, some two weeks ago I read in the same paper that Aaron Copland's record (Vienna) of your Lustra poem, An Immorality, is in market.

Social Crediter is not in our storehouse. Re/Yale & Xtianity, I hope to get some information soon.

Poor old Lash (New Mexico Q.) has sent me his last appeal: shall have to sit down and write a "review" of your Confucius this evening.

The foot, still limping. Carrying the cane.

Yours respectfully
[signed] Achilles Fang

a fellow here: Charles Norman, whose *Ezra Pound: A Biography* was published in 1960 (New York: Macmillan).

Aaron Copland: American composer Aaron Copland's record of "An Immorality" was released in 1926 (Gallup E4j).

89   *EP to Fang* (TL-2; Beinecke)

[St Elizabeths Hospital]
[Washington, DC]
[24 January 1953]

O FANG

IF the hawk [John Hawkes] has wings, he might save a little time by doing a sample page/UNLESS a final sample by Kimball is with the ms/

I thought K[imball]/HAD solved the problem, but the sheets I still have do NOT show the result.

It does NOT take a Copernicus to conceive a page I forget if it was 9½ or 10¼ (but in either case, as page that wd take on left side the SEAL in present size and on the right side 24 lines english/i.e. maximum of TWO unbroken 12 line strophes AND 24 lines romanj, spaced out as might be musical bars (if no Kimball sample has this, I can send something to show how the romanj shd/go/ IF same is not laid open to the meanest capacity by MY typewritten pages.

This should save such idiocy as that shown by Wilson's letter the photos to be cut up AFTER the page proofs of the translation and romanj have been achieved/

PAGE proofs, not galleys/then the photos can be cut to correspond.

ALZO a sample page might serve to satisfy the Rev. Elephant [Eliot] who SAID Faber wd/take it on condition it shd/LOOK like a two guinea book.

Of course our eminent contemporary is a damn Xrister/and NOT keen on Oriental wisdom (or much else) BUT he is not wholly responsible for the goddam delay/the pusillanimous and blithering Bubblegum wasted a year/ apparently from sheer stincgking vigliaccherian What happened to Kimball, god knows, he was all enthusiasm and had measured out the pages. May be black mail, gorNOZE/

the egregio Sig. H. C[airns]. murmured something incomprehensible but seems incapable of measuring TIME. These people to whom a fortnight is as nothing //

in short UNtergang des goddam
Abendland/
mania for gathering last year's peaches

AND the unclean desire of most of my friends, pubrs/etc. that all further edtns/shall be posthumous.

The impulsiFFFF kaspeRRRR had two pubrs/"lined up" BUTT until Cairns makes coherent communication either in writ/or verbattt/

let us remain in suspense.

All heal to the heel, and the quicker the sooner. BUT I dun tell yu that part of the anaTOMY is slow to recover.

Kimball: see Glossary on Kimball, Dudley.

Wilson's letter: in a letter of 25 November 1952, Wilson proposed to hold off the "desire for immediate publication of the *Odes* with complete apparatus" (Beinecke).

two guinea book: T. S. Eliot (1888–1965) visited his career-long friend EP on every trip to Washington in 1946–58. Probably on one of those visits he agreed to print EP's Odes on the condition that it be like "a two guinea book." During that period Eliot corresponded also with DP, Omar Pound, Olga Rudge, Archibald MacLeish, and others in efforts to help EP. The EP/Eliot relation is treated in Robert Langbaum's "Pound and Eliot" in *Ezra Pound among the Poets*, ed. George Bornstein (Chicago: University of Chicago Press, 1985).

kaspeRRRR had two pubrs/"lined up": see Letter 87 n.

Cairns: see Glossary on Cairns, Huntington.

90   *Fang to EP (TLS-1; Beinecke)*

[Cambridge, Mass.]
Jan. 31 1953

Dear Mr Pound,

Ignorant as I am of the profound thinking of American professors of literature, I like to believe that Leary is quite 誠 [sincere].

Obviously nothing much can be said in 40 minutes. But the discussion period, participated by some hundred professors and sub-professors (so I was told by someone here), can be quite fruitful. Instead of wasting time by answering inane questions, I plan to give them a lecture on EP as Confucian (things which I have left unsaid in my "review" of your CONFUCIUS for New Mexico Quarterly)/or try to overwhelm them by making a line-after-line exegesis of Pisan Cantos (I shall write Leary that I wish all the participants to bring their copies of the Cantos or, at least, the Pisan volume—this will make Laughlin happy, I hope). Either way, their mouths will be shut.

As for Leary's postscriptum, it would be a fine thing if you would (and could) meet his request. If "message" is abhorrent to you, I personally will be very grateful if you could read the first 3 passages of Pisan (ending with the Wanjina passage), which I like to make an exegesis of. If even that is unfeasible, I wonder if you would let me tape-record a poem (or a canto) from Harvard Library. Of course, any recording you make should be used for the nonce, if you so request.

I am looking for a competent violinist to play the music of the second Pisan canto—a few dollars and a nice exhibit for my paper. I may also show round a picture of Cafe Dante and that of Isotta's tomb with tempus tacendi and tempus loquendi, etc. etc.

At any rate I haven't answered Leary's second yet.

- - - - - - - -

I have not contacted Hawkes yet. I am trying to find a way to <breaking> the irrational mentality of Wilson and company. A bit of active interference would be in order.

I still have Kimball's sample page with me. Wilson showed me his sample page; I suppose you have seen it too.

Would it be advisable for me to tell Hawkes or Wilson that Faber & Faber would take the two guinea book to-be?

As it stands, someone with a bit of worldly prestige (Cairns or perhaps e. e. cummings) must preachify to Wilson before he gets over his pusillanimity. (May I speak to cummings on my own?)

Respectfully
[signed] Achilles Fang

Leary: enclosed are copies of two letters from Lewis Leary, requesting a paper on EP for the English
     Institute meeting in September 1953.
Cafe Dante: Café Dante in Verona is referred to in Canto 78/501.
Isotta's tomb: EP's 1922 visit to Tempio Malatestiano with the tomb of Malatesta's third wife, Isotta
     degli Atti, (*c*.1433–74) inspired Cantos 8–11.
Cairns: see Glossary on Cairns, Huntington.

91   *EP to Fang* (TL-2; Beinecke)

[St Elizabeths Hospital]
[Washington, DC]
4 Fb [1953]

OUAN SOUIIIIIIII [Cheers]

O.K. my Fang

Didn't I record a canto from the Chinese hunk when I was in N. England in '39.

I have told 'em to keep the stuff on ice, but will gladly release it for performance IF in connections with Fang's exposition.

As for message/there is a stright tradition. Kung, Mencius, Dante, Agassiz.

And that shd/be stressed sometime.

The answers are all in the Four Books/

BUT the barbarians need the ODES. K. collected 'em to prevent anyone from trying to reduce wisdom to abstract formulae or from putting across, or trying to put over any general statement whatsodam without root and branches, and life.

***Item, Monsieur Emery has sent in two gr/hulking vols/of typescript re/ 84 Cantos/

This is an aside. But indicates care.

Can't LEARY be hurled at the Wilson, ALSO?

What is the Eng/Inst/? seems to be in Cambridge??

Mons. Cairns HAS writ to Wilson very briefly.

By all means provide the kumrad KUMMINKZ [Cummings] with hydrogen, atoms, and whatever, and let him explode after all its HIS country and he shares the disgrace of the ODES being unprinted, and held up for trivial reasons/

ALSO for having stayed alive and out of jail during the era of infamy/ excuse being that was IN JAIL during the other one/prematurely.

No hv/NOT seen Hawkes' foot print on the trial page/and shd/like to/

and MOST certainly tell 'em that T.S.E[liot]. SAID in years before the deluge that Faber wd/take it, on condition that it "LOOK like a two guineaaaa book."

Owen and Russell both clamouring/English distribution certainly obtainable once the thing is printed.

As to cost, I suggested that the difficulty of composing with tone numerals/ which Cairns SAID they SAID wd/treble cost

kuan¹ kuan¹ etcetera/<cd be solved> if they wd/set kuan kuan, then have the numerals inked in kuan¹ kuan¹ and the thing offset. perfectly simple once Pallas Athena has descended and kicked someone's ear.

Emery: Clark Emery, professor of English at University of Miami, was a signatory with others to EP's 1953 Manifesto (*Paideuma*, 6/1 (Spring 1977), 114).
Owen and Russell: Peter Owen reprinted *The Great Digest & The Unwobbling Pivot* (1952). Peter Russell reissued *Six Money Pamphlets* (1951–2) and *ABC of Economics* (1953).
kuan¹ kuan¹: *Ode 1, line 1*: "Guan¹ guan¹ ju¹ jiu¹ 關 關 雎 鳩" or " 'Hid! Hid!' the fish-hawk saith" (*Classic Anthology*, 2).

92   *Fang to EP (TLS-1; Beinecke)*

[Cambridge, Mass.]
Feb. 11, 1953

Dear Mr Pound,

Here's the sample page made a long time ago. As you will see from the enclosed Hawkes letter, the Press is going to follow your wishes when they print the book. The sample was a try-out, made with the sole purpose of calculating the production costs. My intention in obtaining and forwarding it is quite simple: to convince you that Wilson and company are seriously interested in the Odes.

I have taken the liberty of black-pencilling the sound key. With your permission I hope to make the key invulnerable.

Here are also two clippings of yours. Thank you very much.

Haven't had a chance to contact Cumrad Cummings; perhaps next week, when he delivers his first lecture of the term. After which he might have some free time.

Respectfully
[signed] Achilles Fang

93   *EP to Fang (TL-2; Beinecke)*

[St Elizabeths Hospital]
[Washington, DC]
[17 February 1953]
<OUR Valentine>

Respected FANG

Sono matti per légare [They are lunatics]/or as the churmun prof/saidt of hiss vife, a poor sailor: if she dont lie she schwindels.

   //

A truly horrible page/of a book no one cd/carry/made for buggars in bibteks.

The whole BLOODY thing was measured to millimetre/the SEAL/on left page/

exact and full size of photos/

on the right page/space for 24 lines (i.e. 2 12 line strophes maximum in eng/ trans/

and below/the romanj to match.

This cd/be a bit crowded on the exceptional pages that needed the full 24 lines/mostly there wd/be lee-way to space prettily.

REMind the blighters that Possum [Eliot] said "LOOK Like a 2 guinea book."

   ///

the wife's complaint makes TWO pages.

AND the characters will be easier to find by the STEWdent as is the case with PIVOT/

This is nearly as bad (no its NOT, not nearly as bad, as the Princeton potawatamie)

AS the good HAWK [Hawkes] admits/O.KAY.

any tinkering (i.e. correcting yu find time and patience to use) on the romanj, will be with gratitude WELLcomed.

my theory/cant be tested till one has the stuff on the page to work on, is that the variations in pronunciation occur in a dimention that does not greatly bitch the prosody

ONLY point I am fanatik on is putting in the ARCHAIC sound pwt pwt (or however it's spelled) for the flap of the fish tails on the stone quai/

As to Peter Pan and the wild life of Cambridge/you will consider him (and in some degree her) as if about to set down a drawing of one thrush hesitant on blueberry bush, NOT as components to be employed in ORGANIZATIONING the kulch of this dummysphere/

my view of which enhanced by the
MOST flubloodyGOdDAmenzaaaaaaa

had better be left to an imagination schooled in the hell sections of chink-mythology.

Thank for letting me see the HORROR.

A truly horrible page: on 7 Feb. 1953 Fang wrote: "Next week I shall mail you a sample page the Harvard Press made months ago. It was just a trial or try-out" (Lilly).
Princeton potawatamie: see Letter 76 n.

94   Fang to EP *(TLS-2; Lilly)*

[Cambridge, Mass.]
Feb. 21, 1953

Dear Mr Pound,

Very glad that you are going to let me go through the sound key—it shall be sound even to pedants (and all sinologists and asinologists are nothing if not pedantic). Am sure the work can be done in no time.

Going to have a five-o'clock with kumrad kumminkz & frau [Mr and Mrs Cummings] next Wednesday.

Last monday Feb. 16 e.e.c[ummings]. gave his first of the 3 lectures of the term. He read little prose pieces he wrote these many years. Before he came to the piece he wrote for Charles Norman, PM symposium on EP, he dropped a remark, which sounded like "the greatest and most generous poet of the world Ezra Pound." Though no visible effect was noticeable, like to think that the audience (Sanders theatre, full house, ca. 1200?) caught the words distinctly.

Recently come across Sergei Eisenstein's The Cinematographic Principle and the Ideogram (in FILM FORM), first publ. in transition 1930 (The C. P. and the Japanese culture). Why doesn't he acknowledge that he owes much if not all to Fenollosa-Pound?

Here's a comic braying:

In Ezra Pound it (i.e. the endless preoccupation with new artificial techniques by purely intellectual poets) took the form of the exotic, the exoteric, a constant search for Ultima Thule rarities. He was strongly drawn to Old French, Chinese, Japanese, all sorts of out-of-the-way erudition, and it often looks like the pundit's desire to impress. Here is his complete poem "Papyrus"—I think the number of dots is correct:

Spring...
Too long...
Gongula...

In an unknown minor poet that snippet would be considered a folly to write and an impertinence to publish. Does anyone know why the title, or what Gongula may be?

The ass's name: James Devaney / Poetry in Our Time
a review of contemporary verse
Melbourne University Press, 1952

Respectfully
[signed] Achilles Fang

Charles Norman: see Letter 88 n.
Sergei Eisenstein: (1898–1948), Russian film theorist.

95   EP to Fang (TL-2; Beinecke)

[St Elizabeths Hospital]
[Washington, DC]

Hnbl ACHILLES   [8 May 1953]

Hell No/Faber and TSE [Eliot] wd/be perfectly INcapable of getting the Odes set up. They shd/be damn glad of the chance of getting sheets from Haavud/If that beanery still exists.

Eliot HEARD of the Translation years ago/and said O.K. re/taking copies for England "but it must LOOK like a 2 guinea book."

His skull so full of mouldy christianity he has apparently forgotten the incident. Tell HIM the book should be printed and be properly printed/and get him to kick Harvard in the pants and START doing it. four years late but what is that in a cloaca? <As to the exact moment when one shd/lose patience with ones friends/re/initial item in this communiqué/gorNOZE/still I think it wd/be in order fer FANG to appeal to Eliot's intellectual honour in assisting the said Fang to get something done.>

I trust you will NOT go to Cambridge eng[land]/UNTIL this job has been done/great drawback is that yu could probably never get your money OUT of England if they paid you more than you now get.

Between one hell and another/as it used to read on Jastrow's door "there is small choice in rotten apples."

You wd/be nearer Europe but equally far from the altar of Heaven. I shd/ prefer you in Eng/IF I were Europe/but I damn AINT.

fer the honour of Haaavud/now known as Weenie's beanery/and associated with 20 years of american degradation.

The USE, i.e. the possible of TSE wd/be to blast yr/local tyrants and stick-in-the-muds into action/NOW, not post mortem.

The Confucian concept of "in season"/TSE is NOT Confucian/the timely moment was 4 years ago/BUT Eliot expected someone in the U.S. to get started. so he is not criminal/merely excessively patient/and NOT given to extra exertion/God DAMN it.

my lively friends <of my own generation and before it> are under the sod/ save Wyndham [Lewis] who is blind.

putt down a row of them arrow ideograms with emphatic and that special significance/gawDDDAMMMit.

Cambridge eng[land]/: a possible job at Cambridge, UK.

Jastrow: Morris Jastrow (1861–1921), Penn professor at the turn of the last century, authored *The Study of Religion* (1901).

96   *EP to Fang (TL-1; Beinecke)*

[St Elizabeths Hospital]
[Washington, DC]
[June 1953]

孝 [filial piety]
Sagetrieb, as I see it, ties in with verse re/son, the bloke that carries on with father's job. tradition
    renewal idea, and also 敬 [respect]
- - - - - - - - -

[DP's postscript] I can hardly tell you how happy we were with your visit [see Fig. 7.1].

Believe me
Sincerely
Dorothy Pound.

孝 *Sagetrieb*: Sagetrieb plays a role in *Thrones* (1959).

97   *EP to Fang* (TL-1; Beinecke)

[St Elizabeths Hospital]
[Washington, DC]
[22 June 1953]

Achilles/himself/see what you can do without busting the whole negotiation.
15% royalties are not unusual on sales over 1000 copies.

Anyhow the H[arvard]. Univ Press can sell sheets to Faber or [Peter] Owen
and leave question of paying the ten% on retail price of copies sold. BLAST this
ribbon.

In fact probably just as comfortable for the Press.

Isn't the title

the CLASSIC ANTHOLOGY

compiled by Confucius.

The fact that that buzzard Eliot has bitched the title on my Essays, is no
reason for letting everyone ruin other titles.

arranged, compiled, cant remember but there was the right word on the ms/
NOT Confucian Book of Odes.

and to arise from the slums for a moment

Couvreur S. J. translates in Régle de Iao

庸

as exsequi [carry out]

which confirms something I may hv/sd or even writ on that K-raKter

of course you know why Iao gave TWO daughters not one, but is it written
down anywhere?

negotiation: on 17 June 1953 Thomas Wilson sent EP two contracts to cover a trade edition and a
  scholar's edition of the *Odes* (Beinecke). EP asked Fang to negotiate certain points.
Owen: see Letter 91 n.
Couvreur S. J.: Séraphin Couvreur (1835–1919), *Chou King* (1950). See Letter 29 n.
Iao: see Glossary on Yao.
庸 *as exsequi*: Couvreur 10–11: 汝 能 庸 命 as "Si tu possis exsequi mandata (mea). . . ."

98   *Fang to EP* (TLS-1; Beinecke)

[Cambridge, Mass.]
June 24, Thursday, noon [1953]

Dear Mr Pound,

Just now the signed contract, which I shall keep here with me; shall return it
to you together with the new ones.

All your letters (and Mrs Pound's) as well as telegram received earlier.

Your provisos can be negotiated; hope to get most of the points, if not all of them (and why not?), accepted by good old Wilson (he's a good fellow, let me assure you). Shall make appointment immediately.

Yes, Yao gave Shun his two daughters—attested in Shu, 2nd chapter. If you still have the worm-bitten text of 書 經 [Book of History] I brought to you two years ago, you will find the story there.

Thanks for the information about Henry M, père et fils. Have a bunch of doubtful things; shall bother you after the contract is settled.

Always thought Harriet stood for Harriet Wilson, who had affair with Wellington. Today saw a copy of Pagany, in which EP refers to her. After all, EP is not so "obscure."

University of Philadelphia [Pennsylvania] wants me to participate in a discussion on Ch. poetry with Cleanth Brooks (Nov.) and give a lecture on Walt Whitman in the light of Lu Ch'i's Wen-fu (Feb. 54), paid. Columbia paper will not earn a penny; on the contrary, I have to pay my expenses and $7 ticket.

Yours

[signed] Achilles Fang

attested in Shu: Yao (see Glossary) married both his daughters to his successor Shun (see Glossary) because he wanted to "try him" and "see his behaviour" (Legge, iii. 26–7).

Henry M: Henry Morgenthau (1856–1946), American banker and diplomat, and his son Henry Morgenhau, Jr., US Treasury Secretary (1934–5), targets of EP's animosity. Cf. Canto 74/459: "That old H. . . . / . . . /and young H/"

Harriet Wilson: in her Memoirs (1825) Harriet Wilson (1789–1846) records a conversation about sex with Wellington. Cf. Canto 78/502: "Harriet's spirited heir | (the honours twice with his boots on, | that was Wellington)."

Pagany: in "The First Year of 'Pagany' and the Possibility of Criteria," Pagany 2/1 (1931), EP writes: "Some day I shall perhaps do a monograph of the British woman of letters from Harriet Wilson to Harriet Weaver" (110).

Cleanth Brooks: Cleanth Brooks (1906–94) professor of English at Yale, 1947–75, was the author of The Well Wrought Urn (1942) and co-editor with Robert Penn Warren of The Southern Review, 1935–42.

Lu Ch'i's Wen-fu: see Letter 53 n.

99   EP to Fang (TL-1; Beinecke)

[St Elizabeths Hospital]

[Washington, DC]

[13 July 1953]

良

FANG

got any bright ideas re/this KER/akter? Mencius VII, 1, 15

I don't recall it in KEY position in Odes, Shu, or 3 Kungs/cd/be mere definition of term in the Mang/

on other hand he not much given to definitions Kung style.

question whether the liang [良] occurs in INTeresting contexts elsewhere/

FANG not go thru a whole reading course in obscure CHINK authors to gratify this idle fantasy.

In text before me the typography dont suggest what it sometimes looks like. i.e. bloke seated looking at his food in lap or x/d/legs

and i am too lazy to look up seal/alzo the top isn't an eye ANYhow.

In fact, an idle question re/usage.

Mang and Orage concur re/compassion.

Legge OBvious BUTTT mebbe all that is there.

LATER

CONsiderin' the use of ~~that~~ radical <138> in various characters on next 3 or 4 pages/wdn't it be livelier to translate that liang: NUTRITIVE? Nutritive knowledge, nutritive ability?

良: Legge renders 良 能 and 良 知 in *Mencius*, 7.1.15.1 as "intuitive ability" and "intuitive knowledge" (ii. 456).

Orage: Alfred Richard Orage (1873–1934) edited the *New Age* (1907–22). In a letter to John Drummond of 1934, EP praises Orage for having done "more to feed me than anyone else in England" (*Selected Letters 1907–1941*, ed. D. D. Paige (1950; rpt. New York: New Directions, 1971), 259).

100   *EP to Fang* (TL-1; Beinecke)

[St Elizabeths Hospital]
[Washington, DC]
27 Ag [1953]

YES,
my Achilles,

Mathews (R. H.) is doubtless an occidental GOrillaaah. Nevertheless I pray you, do NOT omit any <u>any</u> <u>vide infra</u> of the nasty little ref/numbers in my romanj/

they refer to points at which the sd/Mat is NOT being a GOrillaaaa.

AND, as I remarked with perhaps too light a tone, they DO save the helluVAlot of commentary, and a whale of a lot of printing eggspentz/and they are calculated to NOT distract from the initial perusal, as the goddam notes to annotated edns/of Dante often do.

AND they, as against the ubiquitous s.o.b., protect ME from charges of impressionism, or to some eggstent justify certain interpretations/

and a stewd-dent who brot in a[n] attempt at 4 lines (of I suppose Li Po) deMONstrates how bloody much need the yankstew/has of PARticular eeel-ucidation.

Kenner seems in his intro to have shot ONE good pinch of insecticide at a notorious nuisance and vulgarisateur (in the wust sense of the term vul)
★★★★★★★★★★★★★★

INFRA

I mean I can damn well see how yr/revulsion from M/wd/spur yr/conscience to WANT to omit 'em. BUT nondimeno [nevertheless], leave in them damn numerals. s.v.p.

OBviously a stewed-dent who RELIED on Mat/wd/NEVER get to the finer nuance of various passages/one of which has just been drawn neath my iggurunt eye. must beat the young into analyzing separate components of compounds.

Kenner: in *The Poetry of Ezra Pound* (London: Faber and Faber, 1951), Hugh Kenner argues, "what the reader of the *Cantos* should try to grasp is not where the components came from but how they go together" (13–14).

101   *Fang to EP* (TLS-1; Beinecke)

[New York]
Sept. 9, 1953

Dear Mr Pound,

Gracias for the helpful notes. I have been a dolt to overread.

As for your wishes about the Mathew[s] reference, I shall retain them: when-ever I have some problem, I shall duly consult you. Please set your mind at ease.

Getting a free ride to N.Y. this morning; in fact, a few minutes from now.

(My paper, finished last night, will provoke some anger among the audience. Like a Xtian preacher, I took courage in my hand and hinted that the 170 professors are all, or mostly sinners.)

Yours in haste,
[signed] Achilles Fang

102   *EP to Fang* (TL-1; Beinecke)

[St Elizabeths Hospital]
[Washington, DC]
[25 November 1953]

HAS
An item labled

IN CIRCUIT
yet reached Achilles?
nif not/WHY not.

103   *Fang to EP (ALS-1; Beinecke)*

[Cambridge, Mass.]
Nov. 30, '53

Dear Mr Pound,

In Circuit is, apparently, still in circulation. Is it "subversive"? Shall I ask the postmaster about it?

The Odes are now in order—the printer is taking care of them by this time.

Sat. morning, young Morton Lebeck (Yale) came to inquire about Ch. studies here. Told him to concentrate on Greek & French—Ch. (o leider Gott [unfortunately] Jap) he can study on the graduate level.

Best regards
& yours
Achilles Fang

104   *Fang to EP (TLS-1; Beinecke)*

[Cambridge, Mass.]
Jan. 26, 1954

Dear Mr Pound,

After three weeks of sampling, Jack Hawkes and Mrs Chase Duffy (very sympathisch, 30ish, copy-reader of the Odes) have made the enclosed; this afternoon I was with them studying this and that samples.

I hope you find it satisfactory. If you have any suggestion to make, the Press people are willing to accept. But I can see that they have done their best.

In case you have no objection—as I piously hope—will you kindly inform me of your OK and keep the sample (if you care to)—the printing will start immediately. If you wish some alteration, your wishes will be complied with, of course.

I shall be at Univ. of Panna. [Pennsylvania] on Feb. 9, to talk on (Heaven help me) on Whitman vs Lu Chi. If you are NOT otherwise engaged, I like to come to visit you on the 10th P.M.

The Pound Newsletter is quite interesting. Hope something good could come out of it.

Yours
[signed] Achilles Fang

Pound Newsletter: *Pound Newsletter* edited by John Edwards and William Vasse ran for ten issues from January 1954 to April 1956.

105   *EP to Fang (ALS-1; Beinecke)*

[St Elizabeths Hospital]
[Washington, DC]
[30 January 1954]

Be de-
    -lighted
   see
Achilles.
   3 Nod.
   EP

106   *Fang to EP (TLS-1; Beinecke)*

[Cambridge, Mass.]
Feb. 2, 1954

Dear Mr Pound,

Yours with sample this noon. Went to see Jack Hawkes and Chase Duffy (further information: a southern lady, prob. Virginian). Showed them Cavalcanti & Faber ed. Cantos. J. H. thought the former was more or less Caslon and the latter pt 10 on 12 of Bodoni bold face. And I am told that the Ode sample I sent you was Bodoni 8 on 10 bold.

J. H. is completely agreeable to your wishes. Why shouldn't he, for your points are well taken. He is going to try out a completely new sample (by the way he has sampled 6 or seven), perhaps Gramont 11. If the new sample is ready before I leave for Philadelphia and Washington, I shall bring it to you. If not, through mail. The delay wouldn't be very much. Hawkes, who thought (innocently) that the sample could have pleased you, is willing to make another try. He also knows full well that your heart's desire is the ideographic ed., and is sorry that the sample was wide of the mark. The same is shared by Chase Duffy and the entire production department.

Wrote to Overholser for permission.

With anticipated pleasure

Yours
[signed] Achilles Fang

Received NOIGANDRES yesterday; very excellent. (Wish knew some Prota-goose [Portuguese], instead of trying to make out on the strength of Ital. and Span.) Pound Newsletter is quite interesting too.

Cavalcanti: *Sonnets and Ballate of Guido Cavalcanti* (1912).

Overholser: Dr Winfred Overholser, superintendent of St Elizabeths Hospital.

NOIGANDRES: a magazine started in 1952 by Brazilian concrete poets Haroldo de Campos, Augusto de Campos, and Décio Pignatari, the Noigandres group, of Sao Paulo, who took the disputed word in the Provençal poet Arnaut Daniel (*c*.1180–1220) from Canto 20.

107 *EP to Fang (TL-1; Beinecke)*

[St Elizabeths Hospital]
[Washington, DC]
[11 March 1954]

10 Mx/NOW see possibility of acceding to precedent and at the time apparently TOTALLY impract/request of ACHILLES.

IF he can get news of what happen[e]d in Pekin at Imp/Ct/when Mr Caleb Cushing arruv with treaty proposals in 1844/5.

something concrete/and VISIBLE, i.e. the event as seen NOT from Hong Kong or wherever, Goa/or whatso but in view of the Temple of Heaven.

- - - - - - - - - -

[in DP's hand:] It is quite a thrill to be correcting galleys of Odes! D.P.

Caleb Cushing: see Letter 109.

108 *EP to Fang (TL-2; Beinecke)*

[St Elizabeths Hospital]
[Washington, DC]
[15 March 1954]

NO!

No, my very dear ACHILLES, almost sole comfort to my declining years. The PENalty for altering a VOWEL in verse is DEATH.

You are reprieved because of yr/love of exactitude, but don't do it again.

I am trying to teach these buzzards PROSODY, as well as respect for a few civilized chinese.

Naturally the dichotomy, splitting, ERH etc. makes the edtn/annoying.

I shall prob/try to elevate Hawk[es] when he has finished the job.

***

alZO/the noises made by yr/compatriots have almost NO relation to sounds represented by barbarian alphabets.

and the changing from one fad to another adds nowt to the poeTIKKK values.

I meant you to have carte blanche in the romanj/which, incidentally, can serve as datum for my conjecture re/what wobbles and what does not during the flow of time, from the original onomatopoeia.

BUTTT FURST, the ODES were SUNG.

Secondly a FEW (very few) chinese place names are known to yanks/brits/etc. and have a poetic association. Ergo a poetic value.

DON'T go Nipponic, or feel downcast. We learn by living. And apart from one Wan/no partic/damage has been done/it all depends on relation to vowels in the context.

Dont let 'em waste time trying to re-consult my orig/text. I have putt back the three necessary spellings/Wan once, Hsin once, Kiang once.

OUAN SUI [Cheers].

When Wang Yang-ming is pronounced by purr-light chinkessa as Wei-ya-min . . . etc.

phonograms are NOT revealing.

Though you are dead right to stick to what you think the best system IN PROSE and philologic displays.

Dont despair/Wen is even better in some places than Wan was.
***

B.B.C. says they are to broadcast TRAXINIAI on Apr/25, now someone can hear what funny noises the brits/make when dealing with a MURKN text. Thank GAWD ONE intelligent actor at least will be in it. The Hyllos part, which needs more understanding than most of the others.

BUT gornoze wot he will SOUND like.

A few gents/survive EVEN in britain, one turned up last week. Race and not goulash.

In case it may have escaped yr/aquiline eye/study of Spanish 40 years ago/was useful in Odes/Odes useful in TRAX/

AND I suppose some mainland composer preceded Hokusai on the length of apprentissage. Brancusi said he had finished his 30 years ago. But it is doubtful if that was more than momentary optimism on his part.

I don't know off hand whether the altering of a consonant is fatal. YOU had some definite feelings about THAT. I shd/have to consider particular cases. Certainly the dropping of the pwt pwt, wd/be a defect/in fact HAS been a defect.

The simple dropping of consonants with no compensation is presumably evil (low morals).

I trust yr/consort and descendants are flourishing and beginning to appreciate Kung as well as Bach.

dev/mo

Wang Yang-ming: see Glossary on Wang Shouren.
TRAXINIAI: EP, "Sophokles: Women of Trachis," Hudson Review 6.4 (Winter [1953/]1954).

one turned up: probably the BBC radio actor Denis Goacher (b. 1925), who wrote the Foreword to
  Sophokles: Women of Trachis (1956).
Hokusai: Hokusai Katsushika (1760–1849), Japanese artist noted for his wood-block prints of
  landscape.
Brancusi: EP met the Romanian sculptor Constantin Brancusi (1876–1957) in Paris *c*.1922.

109   *Fang to EP (TLS-1; Beinecke)*

[Cambridge, Mass.]
March 17, 1954

Dear Mr Pound,

So far little success with Caleb Cushing, 1800–19[8]79, US Commissioner to
China 1843–1845. When he negotiated the socalled peace treaty, he was rather
unfortunate in that he had to handle the matter along with the French, and all
this a short while after the ignominious Nanking treaty of 1842, when the British
drove a rapacious bargain on the strength of the Opium War. (You know, the
British forced Indian opium on the Ch.; when the Ch. burned the drug, the
British blasted right and left). The Ch. thought Yanks and frogs were trying to
share the spoils of the British. If you can wait a while, I shall look into
contemporary diaries etc. to see if anything visible can be dug out.

As for Wan, Hsin, Ching, etc. I confess I overdid it. Mea culpa, mea maxima
culpa [my fault, my utmost fault]. The proofs are arranged as you desire. In my
extenuation I like to observe that in

Wan's line
and clan

Wan and clan should rhyme. But the trouble is: when Legge wrote Wăn he meant it
to [be] pronounced either wɛn or wən (WEN, now)/文 is never pronounced wæn in
any dialect or at any time. I was afraid that some pedants might charge you with not
knowing Legge's sound key. Hence changed all your wan to wen.

At any rate, I have changed wen there back to wăn. (Put the extra circumflex
to show that it is sounded like English wan, as in "Why so pale and wan, fond
lover?" and not as wɔn.) Sin would not be behovely, ergo Hsin. (Shin is
tempting, then it is an English word.)

荆 is altered to Ching. Thought Khing might be pronounced as English king
(sinicê, k'ing).

All in all, please set your mind at east: I have looked through the galley sheets
and have restored your corrections as you wished. Your reproof meekly and
ruefully accepted.

Hawkes brought me the 3rd batch of galley, up to Ode 256 today. Your
instructions duely [duly] carried out.

Hope you like the seal-script for SHIH, to appear on the title page. (Keep the
cut please, if you like.)

Am now writing a few words on the nature and history of the Anthology. Wilson insists that I should do so.

Cordially
[signed] Achilles Fang

110   *EP to Fang* (*TL-2; Beinecke*)

[St Elizabeths Hospital]
[Washington, DC]
[March 1954]

REPine not, oh my Achilles/

le'ZOpe you haven't gone back and recorrected too much/In some places Wen improves.

AND there were only the three places where one needed to restore my original barbarisms.

***

Of course I shd/be glad to see Archie [MacLeish]/CAN you get it into his head that I am perhaps the only other member of our rabbit-headed generation of yokels and amateurs who might sympathize with him/to extent of approving his taking office, or seeing that a man might get more DONE in a govt/office than in a night-clubb or an arte-shoppe???

You might even tip him off that as Mon/Wed/Fri are NOT visiting days, he might by saying he is in Wash/fer limited time, get in on one of those days, and so have uninterrupted CONverSaySHun.

***

Thanks for debunking the English treaty/'1843/Quite possible that the Emperor did NOT bother to make ANY note re/Caleb [Cussing]/

Benton properly lambastes him (C.C.)

However Bent/dont mention the hop/A brief Spring and Autumn to the effect

another s.o.b., this time from the land of the Cherokees, has got to Goa, and probably wants to put in MORE opium, presumably of inferior quality.

Benton said: "200 years of trade, no trouble, why treaty?" Caleb went over, in some fancy clothes, and after hanging round for some time, the Emperor said: "200 years trade no trouble, why treaty."

"HAW!" sez T[homas]. B[enton]. "an they burnt up a frigate in doing it."

Thanks for SHIH, seal script, does the tree over one hand, occur regularly for earth over inch/in a lot of cases, or is this PEculiarrr? ANYhow, vurry in'erestin'.

WHEN I git the REAL edtn/I shall start investigatin SEAL.

fer yr intro/do HAMMER that the anthol. is a WHOLE not scattered jems/ and that the bhloody translator does NOT consider translation complete without the accompaniment of ideograms and sound-graph.

No need to pretend that I know anything about it except what KUNG himself says/re/ORDER, and the final summary

"no twisty thoughts."

fer the rest je m'en conbougrement FOUTRE [I couldn't give a damn fuck]. any literation with a ' (such as K'ing') is O.K. Kiang is READ by common people with a NICE sonority. S'in, would also do/it is the INITIAL impression that matters in getting the feel of the passage TO the reader.

GIT the MEANING across.

///note recent Kenner/not question of whether I omit Soph[ocles]'s WORDS. DO I omit any of his meaning?

Hell, NO. or let us whope knot.

Apparently some flylosophic periodical has discovered that I may have philosophic intentions. (nooZitem, note the date.)

recent wop (Tempo, Roma) to effect that all Ez did was to say at sbagliato [wrong] time, on sbagliato [wrong] microphone wot all murkns are now saying. (the bloomin HOPtimist, wop tendency to overestimate murkn mind). Vanni's li'l books putt a few dots on some iiii s.

benedictions

Archie: see Glossary on MacLeish, Archibald.
debunking the English treaty... Caleb: see Letter 109.
Benton: see Glossary on Benton, Thomas Hart.
recent Kenner: Hugh Kenner, Introduction to EP's *The Translations* (1953).
Vanni: see Glossary on Scheiwiller, Vanni.

111   *Fang to EP (TLS-1; Beinecke)*

[Cambridge, Mass.]
March 27, 1954

Dear Mr Pound,

Archie MacLeish is very happy to learn that you like the idea of his visiting you. (I should have told him so long ago.) However, he finds that he can't come to Washington in the near future. Presumably he will be in D.C. this summer.

The proof sheets are all back in the Press; Soon to have page proofs.

Glad to know that you like 蓁. For 思 無 邪 I am using the Stone-Classic text of Analects.

By the way the upper-right part of <u>shy</u> stands for 之, originally picture of bud φ or ψ out of the ground _; hence defined (in Shuo-wen) as 出. And ψ = inch 寸.

B.t.w. again, 詩 was originally written 𧥳 = 訨 (there's no <such> ideogram now) = 誌, which is analysed into 言 志, hence the phrase 詩 言 志 in <u>Shu</u> [Book of History], ch. 2. Directio voluntatis.

Hope to finish the introduction next week and submit a carbon copy to you.

Cordially

[signed] Achilles Fang

思 無 邪: 思 無 邪 [No twisty thoughts] from *Analects*, 2.2 at the end of *Classic Anthology*. Cf. *Confucius*, 197: "He said: The anthology of 300 poems can be gathered into the one sentence: Have no twisty thoughts."

Shuo-wen: see Glossary on Xu Shen.

112   *EP to Fang (TL-2; Beinecke)*

[St Elizabeths Hospital]

[Washington, DC]

18 Giugn [June]/[1954]

yes, my Achilles,

ber' nice introduction.

VERY glad the photo is on destructable jacket not in volume itself.

WHEN the real edition is done, there shd/alzo be a[n] index, or table of contents, or both, of the poEMZ.

Now the jacket is VERY interesting, AND on some future occasion when the Hnbl FANG is present, coram, IN person, his anonymous correspondent will attempt to explain moeurs [customs] of the utter barbarians to banished celestial LAMPRA SUMBAINAI [symbolic light] perhaps. We await the real edition.

~~Van der Loon/Leiden E. J. Brill 1943/did an index which cd/be offset/or rather one wd/offset his first and second colums, and then give first lines as in my version. no need of alphabetical chinese romanj.~~

In fact I reckon the simple list of contents with first lines of the english wd/be sufficient.

some stewdent might be given a pass mark for tabulating

Hid, hid

Shade o' the vine

She: Curl grass

In the South be drooping trees.

Locusts a-wing

O omen tree/ in fact if nobuddy wants to do, I might even have a go at it myself.

It is the most BEEyewteeful anthology in the world, and CONFUCIO had more to do with making it than had yr/anon/crspdt perhaps the hnbl F/g shd hv/enc/for his file the buzzard who sent it did not, if I recall say what smear sheet conveyed the item of infamy.

In any case they putt the portrait on the BACK cover and the hnbl Kuan's finger on the FRONT cover is O.K. since/or even not since/THAT is good emphasis/GOOD, yes, grampa pleased with that. IF however the hnbl FANG will consult Marsano edtn Guido, he will encounter a different Anschauung.

Salute the member of his family.

Not knowing IF or what goDDAMMbrit is dealing with what/, I limit addition to the addresses of (review copies) ABC, co/Boris de Rachewiltz

33 via Quattro Fontane

Il Caffè

co/G.B. Vicari via Salaria 334

Roma Italy.

(I am putting men, with names of papers where they will see that a review gets printed.

Camillo Pellizzi 12 via d Villa Albani, Roma

Carlo Scarfoglio

(haven't address of paper where he writes; send him co/O. R. Agresti, 36 via Ciro Monotti. <Largo Pon chielli 4 Roma> He has just done large blurb in Paese Sera/havn't that address, issue for June 16th/

The Caffè splurges are in March and April issues. Absence is making the EyeTalYan heart grow fonder.

Mark the above/"review copies."

Ask the Mercure de France, 26 rue de Condé, Paris V, IF they desire copy for review? dont send it until they say YES.

AND you can transfer the personal names in yester letter to the ADVERTIS-ING column. and add

Stanislas de Yankowski/co Mrs Demant 540 East Ab 28

Los Angeles 31

Pinkafornia (which yu be'r spell Cal on the henvelope.

he is now on TRAXINIAI

Old Yarp has been asked to state that SOPHOKLES wrote the play. similar ideogramic or sense of permanence wd/become.

---

the utter barbarians: the reference is to the typography of EP's name larger than that of Confucius.

F/g shd hv/enc/: an enclosed clipping of news from Tokyo: "Peking Working on an Alphabet."

Kuan's finger: in a letter to EP of 14 June 1954, Fang explains: "As for the picture of the five fingers on the front cover, it is that of Kuan P'ing-hu . . . [my wife] Ilse's lute (k'in) teacher in Peking—one of the foremost masters of the ancient instrument" (Beinecke).

Boris de Rachewiltz: see Glossary on De Rachewiltz, Boris.

G.B. Vicari: Giambattista Vicari (1909–78), publisher of EP's *Carta da Visita* (1942), founded the review *Il Caffè* in 1945.

Carlo Scarfoglio: in 1964 journalist Carlo Scarfoglio (1887–1964) published an Italian version of EP's *Classic Anthology* (Gallup, D81b).

113   *EP to Fang* (TL-1; Beinecke)

[St Elizabeths Hospital]
[Washington, DC]
21 Jun/[1954]

O my Achilles   新

have yu a Kalligraphist who can make a hsin [new or make it new] sign without arogance?

They have been using a plain bit of print font/I asked x for a proper one made with brush, but La Sibille says it shows arogance.

I had not looked at it carefully/neither the tree [木] grows as tree, nor does the piled wood have weight, and the axe [斤] is flighty.

Now there are feelings to be considered. Those of the olblging wielder of the brush and black ink/

BUT there is also the higher aim/

I forget if yu hv/old Legge's 4 bks/pirated edtn/in which the tree is a TREE (title page)

None of the vanity of the RAYS/in the Jap hand, used for the Fenollosa.

Know anything about a buzzard named Chang Kuangchi acc/Morgan itz a nuthr of 'em, not Carson [Chang].

新: 新 ['make it new'] appears in Cantos 87, 93, and 94.
La Sibille: Veronica Huilan Sun (see Glossary).
Chang Kuangchi: K. C. Chang (1931–2001), author of *The Archaeology of Ancient China* (1968) and numerous other books.
Morgan: Frederick Morgan (1922–2004), editor of the *Hudson Review.*

114   *Fang to EP* (TLS-1; Beinecke)

[Cambridge, Mass.]
June 24, 1954

Dear Mr Pound,

Mrs Duffy told me that she had the 8 review copies and 5 advertising copies all mailed to the addresses you gave me. She further told me that she had your 9 copies mailed to DP.

As I wrote in my last, the Press is out to kill: they sent out quite a number of review and advertising copies themselves, so much so that the stock of their free copies is practically exhausted. I wonder if I can ask them to give a couple of free copies to me. (May I impose on you to the extent of requesting you to honor me with a copy of (out of) your lot, —with appropriate <u>inscription</u>. If you don't have any to spare, I shall not feel unhappy either.)

Am enclosing SIN [新]. Are you planning to re-issue any of your books?

Yours

[signed] Achilles Fang

115   *EP to Fang (TL-1; Beinecke)*

[St Elizabeths Hospital]

[Washington, DC]

27 Jun [1954]

O FANG

yu are certainly welcome to two copies or whatso yu can bone out of the LOCAL powers/

and D.P. <[in DP's hand:] with pleasure> will probably consent to carry a signed copy to the post/at any rate a signature is at yr/hnrb disposal.

Now as to character showing in brush strokes/Hui Lan gave a feathery axe etc. The YOUNG using that hsin sign as basis, point out the solidity of the plain damn print block.

queery [:] DOES the tree grow and STAND/has the wood pile weight, will the AXE cut, or at any rate strike hard [?] The young said re/my clumsy attempts in ANALECTS/frontpiece yes, they were clumsy but humble

AS to PLANNING//dirty word/I am ever blasting at pubrs/to get on with JOB/

However, the Sq/$/and possibly Scheiwiller are BUILDIING basic kulch/fer wops [Italians] and yanks/

The author is not the person to be pestered/clean men should blast kick DAMN and push pubrs/Mc hoRRse has velleity/The fringe has DELAYity.

Jobs are TOLD 'em/then time meanders.

Remember I want <to see> front matter of real EDITION when and/or/if. Cause there is something more to print in that front. In fact I think something was missed out, this time, but it don't matter.

Hui Lan: see Glossary on Sun, Veronica Huilan.
Sq/$: the Square Dollar series copublished by John Kasper and David Horton reissued EP's favorite works in booklets that sold for a dollar.
Scheiwiller: see Glossary on Scheiwiller, Vanni.
Mc hoRRse: New Directions managing editor Bob MacGregor.

116   *EP to Fang (AL-1; Beinecke)*

[St Elizabeths Hospital]

[Washington, DC]

[3 September 1954]

eye suppose.

平 opposite p. 155 stone classics, or rather <u>is</u> it a way of writing p'ing 苹 [just, equal, peaceful]

    mathews 5303.
    <u>& if</u> not what?
- - - - - - - - - - -

near to benevolence but the strokes sure do seem to be put on differently.

平: in *Unwobbling Pivot* EP renders 力 行 近 乎 仁 as "energy is near **to** benevolence" (*Confucius*, 155). See also Canto 93/648–9:

力 li⁴
行 hsing²
近 chin⁴
乎 hu¹ 2154
仁 jên²

    holding that energy is near to benevolence.

117   *Fang to EP (TLS-1; Beinecke)*

[Cambridge, Mass.]
9/12/54

Dear Mr Pound,

    Under the date of Dec. 6, I wrote to Farrar as follows:

Harvard University Press has forwarded to me your letter of inquiry about The Classic Anthology of Ezra Pound. I am sorry to disappoint you but I have no information as to when and under what circumstances Mr Pound produced the work you admire so much. All that I know is that Mr Pound executed the translation all by himself and that he spent much effort on the scholarly apparatus to be published soon in the second edition of the book.

    Once more I apologize for my inability to offer you any information.

"All by himself," because a number of people have asked me, just because I wrote the introduction, if I had helped with translation.

"The second edition"—loose language, of course.

Abstained from entering into the matter concerning Bollingen. Since I were not to quote you, I can't take the matter into my hand.

    The Press is mailing a copy of the book to Mr Moore as you desire.

Yours
[signed] Achilles

Farrar: Robert Farrar and Stanley Rinehart in New York issued the first American editions of *A Draft of XXX Cantos* (1933) and *The Fifth Decad* (1937).
Mr Moore: The American poet and psychiatrist Merrill Moore (1903–57) visited EP in 1952 and 1954.

118   *EP to Fang* *(TL-1; Beinecke)*

[St Elizabeths Hospital]
[Washington, DC]
[29 January 1955]

ages before the year of the sheep [1955]/Herr [Mr] Fang sent a work in krautisch/nippisch und chink/by KUNZE. given my imperfect knowledge of krautisch, HAS Mr Fang ANY idea what bloodysodam Herr Kunze thought he was up to?

A totally unreliable source told me Weenie's [Harvard] were GOING to print a decent edtn/of the ODES.

a man of probably very bad character enquires IF?

I gather Mr Personal-violence (or Force-of-Nature) [Tze-chiang] Chao is unknown to you. He has an admiration, most respectable, for Tu Fu.

whether any celestial [Chinese] can be mentioned in presence of, or in letter to, any OTHER celestial (any more than with a damWOpp [Italian]) I do not know.

Li Ki may have some light on subject but it has not reached me. Neither has current Hudson YET, tho I hear that blue ink has been employed.

- - - - - - - - - -

29 Jan/and will be posted I spose domani [tomorrow] o lunedi [Monday]

this day recd/one dried tortoise shell with remarks in probably hindoostani, possibly sanscrit, and arabic. Any demand for this ware among the high intelligentsia?

KUNZE: Reiner Kunze, *Praktisches Zeichenlexikon chinesisch-deautsch-japanisch: 6000 Zeichen etymolo-gisch erklart mit neum praktischen Schlasse* (1938). See Letter 119.
current Hudson: *Hudson Review*, 7/4 ([1954/]1955) with Canto 85.

119   *Fang to EP* *(TLS-1; Beinecke)*

[Cambridge, Mass.]
3/II/55

Dear Mr Pound,

I haven't heard that Herr Kunze passed sinological aptitude test, nor does his Zeichenlexikon indicate its author as possessing high sinological I.Q.

I forced the book upon you imprimis [firstly] because I (or rather meine Gattin [my wife]) thought (at that time she did not know that you had thumbed through Mathews more than she had done) the book with numerous clear-type ideograms might be of some use to you, secundo [secondly]—I (not Ilse) thought you might take kindly (not that you weren't kind) to the unfortunates in S. Liz's, who seemed to me saner than Herr Kunze.

Who's this Chao? Not Chao Yuen-ren. (Half of Chinese verse-mongers are for Li Po, and the other half for Tu Fu.) A certain William Hung, D.D. (here at Harvard), native missionary, in 1952 published an unreadable book (Harvard Press) entitled TU FU, China's Greatest Poet. (Preface: Bible and Tu Fu are the two greatest books to Hung pater filiusque [father and son].)

Please enlighten me on Weenie's project. Haven't heard anything about the Odes project.

As for the scratched tortoise-shell, I am really interested. I always thought that Chinks were the only ones who had socalled oracle-bones. It would be very interesting to see what the East Indians scratched on crustacean. I know no Sanskrit, but there are people here who read it without much trouble (I hope). It may turn out to be a real Ch. specimen (Hsia Dynasty). Grateful if DP could consign the shell to mail when she goes to the PO next time.

Notice a short prose-piece in japonaise by Reck (on VOU) in that egregious "Poetlore."

Yours

[signed] Achilles

Chao Yuen-ren: mathematician, linguist, and composer Zhao Yuanren compiled *Concise Dictionary of Spoken Chinese* (1947).

William Hung: William Hung, *Tu Fu, China's Greatest Poet and Notes for Tu Fu, China's Greatest Poet*, 2 vols. (1952).

Reck: Michael Reck traveled to Japan in 1953. In a letter Katue Kitasono, of the avant-garde poetry journal *VOU*, reports: "I was surprised to see him speak Japanese so fluently" (*Pound/Japan*, 125).

120   *EP to Fang (TL-1)*

[St Elizabeths Hospital]

[Washington, DC]

7 Feb [1955]

0 ACHilles/estimated age of turtle (shell) about 80 years/age of animal at date of demise, uncertain.

Inscription presumably made by friend of Gege, as I don't spose SHE knows enuf snskrt or even aRABik to have done it herself.

The term WEENIE, diminutive of one of the minor poets of the Spewsfeld era/both of 'em Harvard men of the WORST variety hence application of term to institution for degradation of learning which feeds yu

自 弓??

mr Chao Tse-Chiang ("personal violence" or "force of nature," as yu choose to select from Mathews' list of whichwhats. He LIKES his Tu Fu. AT any rate brot in several Tu Fu that I did not know and was glad to read.

- - - - - - - - - -

"Gege" is I take it diminutive for "Virginia," whether blonde or brunet, I do not know. I LIKE to get letters and even oddities from the enthusiastic (presumably) young.

As Stock is sailing from Orstraliaaa to Napoli, I am telling Igor to see him/ and asking Boris to certify nature of his kid broth.

Gege: "Gege" corresponded with EP from 1955 to 1956 (Lilly).
Stock: see Glossary on Stock, Noel.
Igor: see Glossary on De Rachewiltz, Igor.
Boris: see Glossary on De Rachewitz, Boris.

121   *Fang to EP (TLS-3; Beinecke)*

[Cambridge, Mass.]
4/III/55

Dear Mr Pound,
   Here are errata for [Canto] 85 489:
   i   ǐ
   moaǒ   /read/   mouǎ
   pǒu
   gnîng
(last line). palatiam/read/palatium
492: cymba et remis/read/cymba et remus
      Praecognita/read/Praecogita
494: tá houéi Meng tsīn/read/Méng
Heōu Tsi/read/Heóu Tsǐ
Ping/read/Pin
Ts'oung tàn ming/read/Ts'ōung tàn mîng 聰 亶 明
   Don't you want to write
                    Tàn ts'ōung mîng 亶 聰 明
                    (as in Couvreur)?
tsǒ iuên heôu / read / heóu
495: chèu t'sì / read / tchèu ts'î
nài tcheù t'sì / read / nài tchèu ts'î
極 Shouldn't it be 血? For 血 is Pt IV, Ch. III while both 極 and 偏
血   極 are in pt. IV, Ch.IV.
偏   偏
496: 戻/read 民 (the first is li⁴, M3854)
配 p'ei/read p'éi
497: (t'ien⁴)/read/t'ien¹ (presuming that it is 天).
498: T'SOU KIA/read/TSOU KIA

OU' TING/read/OU TING

wei tcheng tcheu/read/wêi tchéng tchēu/or/wei tcheng tcheu.

499: kiaó, chiao [1–4]   胥

      hsü, in the first tone Shouldn't the lines be inverted?   教

Hiŏ kòu jōu kouàn/read/Hiŏ kóu jŏu koūan (學 古 入 官)

500: Halloran/read/Holohan (assuming that it refers to Major William V. Holohan)

Houng Ieo/read? Houng Iao

501: 胃 read 冒 (the first doesn't exist). M 4373.

- - - - - -Query

487: Galileo's Dialogo sopra i due massimi Sistemi del Mondo Tolemaico e Copernicano (finished in 1630 and published in 1632) was put on the Index per Decr. 23 Aug. 1634 (cf. Index, ed. 1758).

    Copernicus' De Revolutionibus orbium coelestium was indexed March 5, 1616, with the priviso usque corrigetur (Encyclopedia Br. s.v. Galileo). 1758 Index lists this book with the priviso nisi fuerint correcti juxta emendationem editam anno 1620, Decr. 15 Maii 1620 (this refers to the fact that Cardinal Gaetani completed his revision of the book in 1620).

    Now, in 1616 G had to recant his heliocentric theory. Perhaps by "indexed" you are referring to this.

Failed to discover anywhere that Cleopatra wrote of the currency.

    May I have the source?

And the sources of

    1. che funge (500) (Mussolini? If so, ubi?)
    2. e canta la gallina (495) 牡 雞 之 晨 (Courveur p. 185)
    3. "Liking some, disliking others, doing injustice to no man"(495)
    4. the sheltered grass hopes, chueh, cohere (488) ? 厥?
    5. Hulled rice and silk at easter

            (with the bachi held under their aprons
      From T'ang's time until now)
    6. UBI JUS VAGUM (does it refer to UBI JUS INCERTUM, IBI JUS NULLUM?)
    7. "cui ditta è dentro" (does it refer to Purg. 24.53–54: ed a quel modo che ditta dentro, . . . ?)
    8. SAGETRIEB (bis) 教 (Frobenius? ubinam?)

Otherwise 85 is perlucid to me. Shall be very happy to have my mind cleared about the 8 hard nuts.

Yours

[signed] Achilles Fang

By the way, Couvreur's tone system is:

ī â 3̣ 4́ 5̆

490–491

獲　perhaps better　匹 ?
自　　　　　　　　夫
盡　　　　　　　　匹
匹　　　　　　　　婦
夫　　　　　　　　獲
匹　　　　　　　　自
婦　　　　　　　　盡

errata for 85: in the first Italian and American editions of *Rock-Drill* (September 1955, March 1956) "moaŏ" becomes "moua," "Meng" becomes "Méng," and 旬 (not 天) is inserted to justify "tien⁴."

Frobenius: see Glossary on Frobenius, Leo.

122 *Fang to EP (TLS-1; Beinecke)*

[Cambridge, Mass.]
May 3, 1955

Dear Mr Pound,

Jack Hawkes, to whom I forwarded your letter, has expressed his apology and promises to please you when he takes care of the major edition. (I met him weeks ago, but have been too busy to convey his message to you.)

Have been educating myself by taking the Cantos as my sextant: gone through Jefferson, Adamses, Van Buren, as well as Zobi, Mengozzi (Monte dei Paschi), Monumenta del Palazzo Ducale di Venezia, Muratori (Antichità Estense), Sanudo (Vite), etc. Am grateful for the Cantos and like to express my wonder at the immense reading you have made.

Mary de Rachewiltz has sent me a copy of *Confucio*, a neat production. (Since the publisher has also sent me two copies, I shall deposit one in the Harvard Library).

In what stage are the two Cantos announced for the next issue of the Hudson? If they contain Chinese items, I offer myself as a proof-reader, if you are willing.

Yours
[signed] Achilles Fang

Zobi: Antonio Zobi, *Storia civile della Toscana dal MDCCXXXVII al MDCCCXLVIII*, 5 vols.(1850–2), source of Cantos 42–5, 50 (Terrell, 170, 192).

Mengozzi: Narciso Mengozzi, ed., *Il Monte dei Paschi di Siena e le Aziende in Esso Riunite*, 9 vols. (1891–1925), source of Cantos 35, 42–5, 50 (Terrell, 139, 170, 192).

Monumenta . . . Venezia: Giambattista Lorenzi, *Monumenti per servire alla storia del Palazzo Ducale di Venezia* (1868), source of Canto 25 (Terrell, 99).

Muratori: L. A. Muratori, *Rerum Italicarum Scriptores*, xxii (1733), source of Canto 26 (Terrell, 103).

Confucio: *Confucio* (1955) with Mary de Rachewiltz's Italian translation of Fang's "A Note on the Stone-Classics."

the two Cantos: Cantos 88–9 in *Hudson Review*, 8/2 (Summer 1955).

123   *EP to Fang (TL-1; Beinecke)*

[St Elizabeths Hospital]
[Washington, DC]
4 Feb [1956]

Pleasant to find Ch. El Norton in Santayana Letters
saving what a lousy hole is Haaavud.

IF Wilson has grounds for puttin the blame on yu/ <if you are waiting to
satisfy your letch for precision> Gaw Damn it/there is NO alphabetic representation of chinese sound, let alone any fad of spelling it in amurkn alPHAbet
that will fit 27 different kinds of chinkese thru 3000 years/

You can identify Hou Chi with fertility hoocheyKoochey if yu spell it CHI
but as they pronounce it JE/

it takes ten years if you dont HEAR sombuddy SAY it find a nice li'l JE-tzu in
his presepio [crib] long before the defilements of kikery.

and HOW the HELL do yu expect me to improve the translations UNTIL I
have some approx sound AND the seal text opposite the present version/[?]

which is intended as where to go ON From / not that the dambastids ever do
go ON.

I give 'em frog [French] in 1918 / nobuddy took the chance / left fer grampaw
to tidy up NOW, etc.

Am I to start quoting Walter Scott and the serpent's tooth . . . . . .

Rustichello da Pisa has just done a beaut to beat LaPira etc.

Norton: Charles Eliot Norton (1827–1908), Harvard's first professor of fine arts (1873–97).
Santayana: see Glossary on Santayana, George.
Hou Chi: "Hou Tsi" of Ode 245 (*Classic Anthology*, 161–3), ancestor of King Wen of Zhou (Chou).
Walter Scott: Scottish poet and novelist Walter Scott (1771–1832).
Rustichello da Pisa: Italian romance writer to whom Marco Polo (1254–1324) dictated *The Travels of
Marco Polo*.

124   *EP to Fang (TL-1; Beinecke)*

[St Elizabeths Hospital]
[Washington, DC]
2 March [1956]

Dear Fang

Wilson on his own showing did NOT discuss english edition with D.P.
however.

He now says he can not do the proper decent and complete edition because
you haven't given him the manuscript.

ever yrs.

125   *EP to Fang* (TLS-1; Beinecke)

[St Elizabeths Hospital]
[Washington, DC]
18 Jan 57

Dear Fang

Hawley said Harvard had wanted some pages of seal text replaced.
He seems to think this means publication. If it takes place I trust the
enclosed note as to how we got the fotos will appear, giving due credit to
W. H[awley].

Best for '57
Ez P

seal text: in a letter to EP of 11 January 1957, Hawley writes, "I see Harv'd is finally coming across
   with seal ed!"(Beinecke).

126   *EP to Fang* (TLS-1; Beinecke)

St Elizabeths Hospital
Washington D. C.
[October 1957]

Dear Dr. Fang

I have just recd/a letter from Wilson, of which he indicates that you have a
copy.

As I read it, this puts ALL the blame on you for the delay in publication of the
Odes in the ONLY form that interested me in the least. <I naturally wait for
your side of the story before accepting it.>

As I recall it there was NO mention of added materials. All that was asked of
you was to correct the obvious errors in typing the syllab[l]es which were
intended MORE as a graph of the metric than as a phonetic equivalent of the
MUCH disputed chinese sound, re/which no two sections of China are agreed,
let alone re/the original phonetics that Kung would have, conjecturally, heard.

You professed some interest in the subject. And I thought you agreed that the
lack of any ~~seal text~~ <text in seal character> for students should be remedied.

I should be glad if you can tell me when in YOUR opinion the necessary
matter will have been presented to Mr Wilson, so as to come to a decision
re/withdrawing the whole thing, which would of course imply complete freedom
to use it where I liked along with the <matter of my own> truncated popular
edition which he now says he wormed out of me by promising to do a proper text
from which I could myself more conveniently work toward improving the english.

sincerely yours
[signed] Ezra Pound

P.S.
Your editing was not supposed to <u>commit</u> you to agreeing with my interpret-
ations. There was no intention of implicating you in an agreement, which you
could have disavowed in a single sentence.

At a time when I was physically too exhausted to correct the proofs and when
anyone familiar as you are with your own language could have caught errors in the
alphabetic representation which wd/have needed verification one by one, by me.

The hatred of the Chinese Classics boils thru most of our Universities.
Whether it rages more corruptly at Yale than elsewhere I don't know. They
print handsome text book to guide their victims to newspapers printed in
ideogram, and at least one of their degraded stooges and brain-washers has
plainly said that they are NOT trying to interest pupils in the great literature.

127   *Fang to EP (TLS-2; Beinecke)*

[Cambridge, Mass.]
24/X/1957

Dear Mr Pound
Last Saturday (19/X) I happened to make one of my angelic visits to my former
office (the dictionary project is now thrown out of the window since January,
when the new director of the Harvard-Yenching Institute took office; I stay home
now, but shall continue to get my salary until next June) where a copy of Wilson's
letter to you was waiting for me. This week I managed to contact Mrs Kewer of
the Editorial Department (Wilson was busy and the Production Manager Burton
Stratton was not in his office) and found out Wilson is waiting for my "introduction," insisting that he must have everything together once for all.

The fact is, Mrs Kewer has almost everything in her office: the complete seal-
script text (I am told that Hawley has supplied her with the missing sheets) and
the sound-key.

As for the sound-key I followed your wishes and did the minimum to it. I did
not adopt the pronunciation of Kung's time (Archaic Chinese), nor that of every
scholar (Ancient Chinese), nor even that of what I call orthophony (which
resembles the system employed by Couvreur and Karlgren). In fact, all I did
was to revise errors and supply lacunae, all in accordance with Mathews.

The sound-key was veri-typed and delivered to Mrs Kewer last January, when
we had a conference (Mrs Kewer, B. Stratton, and myself) in order to speed up
the matter. At that time I asked the Press to go ahead and print (or rather
photograph) the whole (ideograms, sound-key, and translation) immediately.

For the past 10 months I have been waiting to hear that the work was all done. (When Omar [Pound] came to see me in June, or was it May?, I could assure him that the book will be out by if not before Xmas.)

As for the "introduction" I insisted at the afore-mentioned January conference that there is no necessity, except the one written by E.P. himself. However, I told the people that if Wilson insists on having a short note on the seal-script text and the phonetic system you have employed, it could be done in a short while as soon as the photographing is done.

For some reason Wilson and the Syndics of Harvard University Press seem to set value on that introduction.

All I have now to do to "expedite" is write the required introductory note (I shall ask Wilson to put it rather at the end of the book; after all, the book is yours).

If I promise to you that I shall write a dull matter-of-fact note, I hope you will not raise Cain with poor Wilson, who is a[n] honest and honorable man, about it.

We may see the book out next spring.

Between you and me, the cause of all this delay is David Livingston Duffy, so named in commemoration of the African trip the Duffys made. Ever since the boy was born, Chase Duffy has been playing the happy mother at home; she seems to be doing editorial job for the H.U.P. only occasionally. The whole process of coordinating seal-script, sound-key, translation, and restoring your notes cut from the first volume, can be completely done only by Mrs Duffy, who went through the said first volume. Wilson probably is waiting for her to find time to do the work.

Now, my advisement (not advice) at this moment is: Please forget what Wilson wrote to you, and have (sorry to use the word) patience. At any rate, leave everything to me to act in between. (It is unfortunate that the author and the publisher should irritate each other; but the main thing is to have the author's book published by the agreed publisher. Let me take all the blame from each side if need be. Let's have the book at all costs.) Barring accidents, we may see the book out next year.

- - - - - - - - -

I am now compiling An Anthology of Chinese Literature (2 vols.) for Grove Press, New York. This is meant to be a school book, about 300 pages each. If you could give me advice, as you have done so to so many others, I shall be very grateful.

- - - - - - - - -

Allow me to offer you my heartfelt congratulations on your birthday. I do hope that Bridson succeeds in making the promised BBC broadcast on that day.

Cordially yours,
[signed] Achilles Fang

Bridson . . . BBC broadcast: D. G. Bridson interviewed EP in 1956 and 1959. He presented edited tapes of the interviews on BBC in July 1959. See Poetry and Prose, ix. 293–309.

128   *EP to Fang* (TLS-1; Beinecke)

3514 Brothers Place
Washington s.e. D.C.
18 May [1958]

Dear Fang

The spring is advancing, but there is no sign that the nature of the Harvard Press is improving, or that your "friend" whats his name has ANY intention of publishing a decent edition of the ODES.

I am sorry to draw this matter to your attention again,

but curious as to whether you still retain ANY vestige of optimism.

The sabotage, the blocking of my work remains.

I cannot do any more toward improving the translations until I have a convenient edition to work FROM. I.E. the sound, the seal text in front of me.

The infinite vileness of the state of education under the rump of the present organisms for the suppression of mental life is not your fault.

etctera/

in fact et cetera is about all that CAN be said for the state of scholarship under the pestilence.

cordially yours
[signed] E. P.

129   *Fang to EP* (TLS-1; Beinecke)

[Cambridge, Mass.]
29/V/1958

Dear Mr Pound,

Thank you for your note on the Anthology. I shall see to it that the Press starts on the work after summer vacation. There is no reason to believe that Wilson et al. intend to back out.

Congratulations (excuse this banality). My wife and the two little ones are touring Germany this summer (parents and Geschwister [siblings] still there). I shall have to do a lot of work.

Actually I am compiling an Anthology of Chinese Literature (some 400 pages). It is not so much what should go into it as what is available in English and American.

Cordially
[signed] Achilles Fang

8

Pound's Discovery of an Ancient Economist
"Chao ought not to be wasted"

By 1954 Pound had attracted a not too small group of disciples to his discussion sessions on the St Elizabeths lawn (see Fig. 8.1). He was encouraging an increasing number of young poets and artists to publish on his favorite subjects. Among them were David Gordon, who translated Mencius under his tutelage for *Edge* (Melbourne) and *Agenda* (London), and William McNaughton, who edited *Strike* (1955–6) to which he contributed "China and 'Voice of America.'" The following year a Chinese translator, Tze-chiang Chao, was drawn into this circle (see Fig. 8.2).

Graduating from Sun Yat-sen University with a BA in English, Tze-chiang Chao (Zhao Ziqiang 趙自強, 1913–c.1985) worked for a time as a schoolteacher and as a journalist. In 1940 he began teaching economics at Lingnan University. Six years later he joined Shanghai Commercial Bank as a research officer. In 1949 he came to the US to take courses first at Harvard and then at New York University, where he earned an MBA in banking and finance (1951). While looking for a job he attended lectures in English at Columbia.

The Pound–Chao correspondence began after Chao wrote to New Directions, asking if Pound would be willing to review his proposed collection of translations of Du Fu (712–70) and write a preface. For Chao Du Fu deserved a place no less than Li Bo "because he [wrote] in the tradition of the Chinese Anthology Defined by Confucius" (Beinecke). At his urging, Pound began reading Du Fu both in translation and in the original. On 7 February 1955 Pound told Achilles Fang that "mr Chao Tse-Chiang . . . brot in several Tu Fu that I did not know and was glad to read" (Letter 120). With Pound's recommendation, Chao's translations of Du Fu appeared in Noel Stock's *Edge* and Peter Russell's *Nine* (London).

In order to help Chao find a teaching job, Pound put him in touch with Norman Holmes Pearson at Yale and Guy Davenport at Harvard. In June 1957 he even enlisted the aid of John Theobald, a young instructor at a California university, with whom he had just begun a correspondence: "if you cd/ get Chao you wd/ have a treasure . . . Chao ought not to be wasted/ more data if any chance of your getting him <a job>" (*Pound/Theobald*, 37). His attempts came to naught.

Chao proved his true worth when Pound began seeking an economic theme for *Thrones* (1959). He shared with Pound literary as well as economic interests. While teaching at Lingnan, Chao published an article on the monetary theory of Guan Zhong (Kuan Chung), a seventh-century BC economist. The subject struck a chord when mentioned to Pound in December 1956. Guan Zhong was not an unfamiliar name. In *The Analects*, it occurred to Pound, Confucius acknowledged his debt to this man: "Kwan Chung reciprocal'd, aided Duke Hwan as prime minister, overruling the princes; unified and rectified the empire, and people till today received the benefits. But for Kwan Chung we'd be wearing our hair loose and buttoning our coats to the left" (*Confucius*, 257).

Chao rendered the last statement as "Kung says that without benefitting from Kuan Tzu (or Kuan Chung) he might have been subjugated by a foreign race" (Letter 134), which becomes "But for Kuang Chung we should still dress as barbarians" in Canto 106.

The correspondence between Pound and Chao culminated in the summer of 1957. It is a pity that Pound's letters to Chao are all lost. From Chao's side of the correspondence we can tell that Pound was pressing for more information about Guan: How did Guan's work escape the burning of books under the First Emperor of Qin? What were his quintessential economic concerns? Pound's enthusiasm for this topic is evident in a letter to Theobald of 11 June 1957: "Chao…has just dug up Kuan Chung. MOST important economist recommended by Confucio/ I thought he had been lost in burning of books/ am awaiting further data from Chao" (Pound/Theobald, 37).

Guan Zhong plays a role in Canto 106: "The strength of men is in grain | NINE decrees, 8th essay, the Kuan | .... | How to govern is from the time of Kuan Chung." The elliptical references have been rightly attributed to *Economic Dialogues in Ancient China: Selections from The Kuan-tzu*, edited by Lewis Maverick (1954). However, it was Chao who introduced Pound to Maverick's book. Before Pound received a copy of *Economic Dialogues*, Chao had already copied out for Pound key passages from its first essay, "filling granaries." Further, Chao provided Pound with a biography of Guan and a chronology of the legalist tradition started with him, which combined to facilitate Pound's putting into perspective Guan's ideas. Only when he was certain of a connection between Guan's legalism and Confucianism did Pound list Guan in Canto 106.

In September 1957 Chao left the East Coast for San Francisco to take up a teaching job at the American Academy of Asian Studies, a school of the College of the Pacific. Their correspondence continued for eight more months till Pound got out of St Elizabeths Hospital and returned to Italy.

Chao lived a loner's life in the next two and a half decades. He died without a family or relatives in San Francisco around 1985.

Fig. 8.1. EP on the St Elizabeths lawn, 1957. (Beinecke)

Fig. 8.2. Tze-chiang Chao, 1935. (Sun Yat-sen University Alumni Directory, 1935)

130   *Chao to EP (ALS-1; Beinecke)*

[New York]
[1954]

Dear Poet Pound:

Enclosed please find my translation of Tu Fu's poems. Kindly read them in your leisure moments. If they are worthy of publication, I hope you will give me a letter of recommendation.

Martinelli has got out of the hospital. She is staying in her girl friend's home. With best wishes,

Yours respectfully,
Chao Tze-chiang

P.S. Please mail back my manuscript with the enclosed stamped, self-addressed envelope.

Tu Fu: see Glossary on Du Fu.
Martinelli: American artist Sheri Martinelli (1918–96) lived between New York City/Greenwich and DC in the 1950s. As a regular visitor she was adored by EP and DP. EP arranged to have her book of painting *La Martinelli* published in Milan in 1956.

131   *Chao to EP (ALS-1; Beinecke)*

205 Worth Street
New York 13, N.Y.
Jan. 26, 1955

My dear Mr. Pound:

Please accept my deep gratitude for encouraging me to translate Chinese poetry. The afternoon of Jan. 19, 1955 when we met is, to me, the most memorable afternoon, for you are the greatest poet I have ever talked to. On you I have two impressions: sensitivity (or quickness of mind) and sympathy which are, I suppose, the essential gifts of a born poet. Your sensitivity reminds me of Tu Fu's description of nature, while your sympathy reminds me of Tu Fu's attitude towards animals.

I received your notes with thanks. In a few days I shall contact Caedmon for recording my reading of Tu Fu's poems.

Sincerely I hope that you will get out of St Elizabeths very soon and be a free man again.

With all the best of luck to you. Remember me to Martinelli and McNaughton.

Very truly yours
Chao Tze-chiang

Caedmon: Caedmon Publishers in New York issued "Ezra Pound Reading His Poetry" in 1960 and
  1962 (Gallup, E5c, E5d).
McNaughton: see Glossary on McNaughton, William.

132   *Chao to EP (ALS-1; Beinecke)*

[New York]
March 19 [1956]

Dear Poet Pound:

Many thanks for your letter. I do not know whether Carsun Chang has got a
publisher for his History of Neo-Confucianism or not. But I have written to him
and told him about your suggestion for the publication of his book.

I have been trying to get the New York Art Club to organize a lecture on the
poetry of Ezra Pound. If I should be successful, I would like to have a pro-Pound
man, like Pearson, to deliver it.

With kindest regards to you and D.P.

Respectfully yours,
Chao Tze-chiang

Carsun Chang's address
2295 Hanover St.
Palo Alto, Calif.

Pearson: Norman Holmes Pearson (1909–75), Yale professor of American literature, served on the
  editorial board of the Square Dollar series.

133   *Chao to EP (ALS-2; Beinecke)*

[New York]
Sept. 11 [1956]

Dear Poet Pound:

I highly appreciate Pearson's 無 倦 [persistence]. You are also 無 倦 [persist-
ent]. Like a Chinese classical scholar of the older generations, you live up to 仁
[humanity]. It is very unfortunate that China under the bad influence of Europe
and America has had very few people who carry out this conception of Kung in
their actions. But in you I found an embodiment of the principles taught me by
my Confucian teachers in my childhood days.

Kung says: " 爲 人 謀 而 不 忠 乎 " ("to get to the middle of mind when
planning with men"—your own translation.) You got to the middle of your
mind when you wrote to Pearson and did other kind things for me.

About two months ago I sent to Prof. [George] Kennedy a letter of application for instructorship in Chinese literature, but have not heard from him. Perhaps he is on vacation. Of course I shall write to Pearson. When I get his reply I shall go to see him and Kennedy.

A few days ago I met [David] Wang. He was excited by your idea of Chinese heritage. The difficulty is that the people we want are scattered in this country, but we will contact some other people in the N.Y. area. We will start with people in nearby places and then write to Emery, Bynner, Espey & Kwock. We will use Carter's Shenandoah to publish a special issue on Chinese literature. McNaughton & Danton may write for us. It is good if you write to Fang about this idea.

I have sent my "Vegetable Roots" to Bynner & my two Tu Fu poems with an analysis on prosody to Stock. Stock has got my "Ode on War Chariots" by Tu Fu published in 20th Century (Australia).

With best wishes to you & Mrs. Pound

Respectfully,
Chao

無 倦: 無 倦 from *Analects*, 13.1 (*Confucius*, 248) surfaces in Canto 97: "not lie down │ 無 │ 倦" (703).
Kennedy: see Introduction, n. 23.
Emery: see Letter 91 n.
Bynner: see Glossary on Bynner, Witter.
Espey: John Espey, author of *Ezra Pound's Mauberley: A Study in Composition* (1955).
Kwock: see Glossary on Kwock, C. H.
Carter's Shenandoah: Thomas Carter (1931–63), a student at Washington & Lee University, edited the small magazine *Shenandoah* from 1951 to 1953.
Danton: Larry Danton, a young poet in EP's circle.
Tu Fu poems: "Poems of Tu Fu," *Edge*, 1 (October 1956).

134   *Chao to EP (ALS-4; Beinecke)*

[New York]
Dec. 24 [1956]

Dear Poet Pound:

Many, many thanks for your sympathy. Please send Pearson my thanks. Dignity of the individual is an empty talk unless he is given means by society. Every one deserves a job suitable to him, or there must be something wrong with the economic order.

I am also interested in economics. Ask some one to borrow for you from the Library of Congress a copy of Kuan-Tzu, the greatest economist China has ever produced. Kuan-Tzu was made prime minister by Emperor [Duke] Huan of Ch'i. He made Ch'i the strongest empire of the time.

In spite of the fact that China is rich in poetry, she lacks poems like Milton's Paradise Lost, Browning's dramatic monologues and Pound's Cantos. The Chinese have no poems of such grand scale. I always drove this point home to those Chinese who are interested in both Chinese and English literature. If I perfectly understand these poets, I may have something to contribute to Chinese literature from the Western point of view.

I have read Mullins' essay. She [He] should write a longer one.

In a few days I shall mail to you my <u>revised</u> version of Tu Fu.

With kindest regard to D.P & E.P.

Respectfully yours,

Chao

孔 子 曰 微 管 仲 吾 其 被 髮 左 衽 矣

Free translation: Kung says that without benefitting from Kuan Tzu (or Kuan Chung) he might have been subjugated by a foreign race.

管 子 (also known as管 仲)

Kuan Tzu in English translation

Show this to the librarian. I am sure there is such a book in English translation.

Pearson: see Letter 132 n.

Mullins' essay: Eustace Mullins (b. 1923), a regular visitor since 1949, authored *Mullins on the Federal Reserve* (1952).

135   *Chao to EP (ALS-1; Beinecke)*

[New York]

June 2, 1957

Dear Poet Pound:

Only recently I found The Kuan Tzu which is supposed to contain the writings of Kuan Tzu. Enclosed please find 13 pages of quotations from this ancient Chinese economist.

Kindly tell Marcella [Spann] to send me her address.

With kindest regards to you and D.P.

Respectfully yours,

Chao Tze-chiang

The Kuan Tzu: Lewis Maverick, ed., T'an Po-fu and Wen Kung-wen, trans., *Economic Dialogues in Ancient China: Selections from the Kuan-Tzu* (1954).

13 pages of quotations: quotations copied from ibid. 31, 287, 290–5.

Marcella: see Glossary on Spann, Marcella.

136   *Chao to EP (ALS-2; Beinecke)*

[New York]
June 16 [1957]

Dear Poet Pound:

I am very glad that you are pleased by the economic thought of Kuan Chung. To me Kuan is the greatest statesman and economist of China.

Enclosed please find a short biography of Kuan. It does not contain much information. It is very unfortunate that biographies in traditional Chinese style are very brief. I have translated the most reliable biography of Kuan Chung by Si-ma Chien [Sima Qian], the greatest Chinese historian who lived in the Han dynasty (about 2000 years ago). I like to keep that translation for a few days in order to revise it because I want to give you a very correct translation. I understand you are anxious to know more about Kuan's life. But I worked in daytime and have time to do my own things in the evenings and weekends. I hope that you will excuse my being slow.

With kindest regards for you and D.P.

Respectfully yours
Chao Tze-chiang

P.S. For Kung's praise of Kuan, read your translation of Analects (p. 67 verses XVI, XVII & XVIII, especially section 2 of XVIII.)

137   *Chao to EP (ALS-1; Beinecke)*

[New York]
Aug. 3 [1957]

Dear Poet Pound:

The bookseller in Hong Kong wrote to me that he had put The Kuan Tzu in registered mail. If not detained by the customs house, the book will arrive in about five weeks.

With kind regards to you and D.P.

Respectfully yours,
Chao Tze-chiang

138   *Chao to EP (ALS-1; Beinecke)*

[New York]
Aug. 20, 1957

Dear Poet Pound:

I shall join the staff of The American Academy of Asian Studies, a graduate school of the College of the Pacific, as an associate professor of Chinese language and literature. The school is in San Francisco. Before going there I shall come to see you in the middle of September in order to know more about your life and your poems.

Enclosed please find some excerpts in connection with Kuan Chung.

With kindest regards to you and Mrs. Pound.

Respectfully your,

Chao Tze-chiang

excerpts: "The Legalist Tradition which Kuan Chung is in" (one typed page); "Nine-Square Fields" (five typed pages), copied from J. J. L. Duyvendak, *The Book of Lord Shang: A Classic of the Chinese School of Law* (London: Probsthain, 1928), 41, 43–4, 48–9.

139   *Chao to EP (ALS-1; Beinecke)*

1326 Hyde St. Apt. 4

San Francisco 9, Calif.

Nov. 3, 1957

Dear Poet Pound:

I appreciate your kind advice very much. I must follow it very closely.

My friend in New York told me that he had re-directed to you a Chinese edition of the Kuan Tzu sent from Hong Kong. I imagine you have received it by now.

It is unfortunate that my stay in Los Angeles was too short for me to visit Maverick and Hawley. But I have very happy correspondence with Maverick. I wrote to Hawley and have not heard from him. Perhaps I did not write his right address on the envelope.

I sent you a Chinese bowl, a Chinese spoon and a pair of chopsticks as birthday gifts. But I am sorry to say that they are not authentic.

With best wishes to you and Mrs. Pound.

Respectfully yours

Chao Tze-chiang

Maverick: Lewis Maverick, professor and publisher, edited *Economic Dialogues in Ancient China: Selections from the Kuan-Tzu* (1954).

140   *Chao to EP (ALS-2; Beinecke)*

1326 Hyde St.

San Francisco 9, Calif.

May 6, 1958

Dear Poet Pound:

I am very grateful for your recent letter. Yesterday I sent you and Mrs. Pound a Chinese ivory ball with a dragon carved on it, together with a pedestal for it, as a gift to <u>celebrate</u> your regain of liberty. Don't value it highly. It is ordinary Chinatown stuff, though it was made in Hong Kong. It is difficult to get ancient Chinese things in this country.

Is Beauson [Pao Swen] Tseng the granddaughter of the so-called "one of the Confucian remnants"? I understand she is a Christian. How can a Chinese Christian understand poetry?

It is my earnest hope that you will organize poets and scholars to work for the integration of Chinese and Western cultures. With your reputation as a great poet and your translations of the Odes, Kung, etc., you are certainly the leader. I hope you will consider this suggestion.

I regret very much that when I was in New York, I did not go to visit you in Washington more frequently. I only wish that I could see you again and learn more about poetry from you. Some day I shall translate your Chinese Cantos into Chinese.

James Laughlin sounds like a careless publisher. I sent him my Tu Fu poems about one and half years ago, but he misplaced them somewhere.

I <u>CONGRATULATE</u> you again on your freedom. Carsun Chang asked me to extend you his congratulations.

With kindest regards to you & D.P.

Very respectfully yours
Chao Tze-chiang

If you don't receive the ivory ball by next Monday, please let me know so that I shall inquire at the San Francisco Post Office.

9
From Poetry to Politics
"Wang's middle name not in Mathews"

Among Pound's disciples of the St Elizabeths period was David Wang. Born in Hangzhou, China, David Hsin-fu Wang (Wang Shenfu 王 燊 甫, 1931–77) immigrated to the US in 1949, where he attended La Scuola Italiana of Middlebury and completed his BA degree in English at Dartmouth College in 1955 (see Figs. 9.1 and 9.2). He contacted Pound after writing poetry in his shadow for several years. In his first letter (July 1955) he claimed that Pound's wisdom had "surpassed that of Confucius" (Letter 141), which only prompted Pound to state: "Mencius had the sense to say there was only one Confucius" (Letter 142).

While Pound was not impressed by Wang's compliments, he was charmed by his middle name. The *shen* 燊 character was not in *Mathews' Chinese–English Dictionary*. He at once wrote to David Gordon, Tze-chiang Chao, and Willis Hawley, inquiring about that word. Chao was the first to respond: the *Shuowen* dictionary defined it as "flourishing or prosperous" and the *Guangyun* "flame (fire burning on a piece of wood)" (Beinecke). Thus on 13 July Pound was able to write back to Wang, addressing him as "Mr Flame-style King" (Letter 142).

The ideogram of Wang's middle name, fire burning on a piece of wood, came back to Pound when he opened *Thrones* with enlightened monarchs from Martel to Charlemagne. It was logical to insert in this context: "Wang's middle name not in Mathews 燊" (Canto 96/673).

The correspondence between Pound and Wang initially focused on literary interests. Wang sent Pound drafts of his poems and translations, which Pound returned with suggestions. Through Pound Wang got to know Noel Stock, who printed his "Tang & Sung Poems" in *Edge*, 3; Chao, who collaborated with him on a Chinese heritage project; and Marcella Spann, who shared with him the reading list of her college comparative literature course.

In early 1957 Pound was gathering material from F. W. Baller's edition of *Sacred Edict* (1907) for a new section of *The Cantos*. Slim though it appears, the volume contains two Chinese versions of Emperor Kangxi's "Sacred Edict," a literary version by Emperor Yongzheng and a colloquial version by Salt-Commissioner

Wang Youpu. Baller provides only a translation of the latter. Pound advised Wang to render into English Yongzheng's text "BOTH because I shd/ like it, and because Stock cd/ print it" (Letter 148). Wang obviously was not interested in the task. Although he kept saying that he was working on it, he never turned in his translation.

Their correspondence became more political than literary during 1957–8. As a refugee from China, Wang was anti-Communist. From enthusiasm for eugenics he moved on to regard some races higher than other races. His pride in his "high" breeding and his false sense of injury, combined with the influence of segregationists like John Kasper, fed his anti-Semitism. In exchanges with Pound he indulged in his master's unabashed, offensive rhetoric. Some of his statements are neo-fascist. In a letter of 12 July 1957, for instance, he said: "My impression of the French is that they are of all Europeans the closest to the kikes in spirit and nature . . . I am for a united Europe under the rule of either Germany or Italy. Adolf [Hitler] and Benito [Mussolini] were certainly close to saints" (Beinecke). Whether he was speaking his mind or aiming for shock value could only be conjectural.

In October 1957 Wang organized a club called "North American Citizens for the Constitution: An Affiliation of the Whib Party." There were no more than a dozen followers in the band. The name "Whib" or "Wheat in Bread" was taken from Pound. Wang was soon in trouble. A former classmate of his, David Rattray, after interviewing Pound, published an article in *The Nation* (16 November 1957), in which he accused Wang of protecting "white supremacy." Wang wrote to Pound on 14 January 1958, complaining that the accusation made him fear deportation "to RED China" (Letter 160).

A good service Pound rendered Wang was putting him in touch with William Carlos Williams. After a visit to the ailing poet in Rutherford, New Jersey, Wang began collaborating with him on some thirty-eight translations from Chinese poets, which eventually appeared in *New Directions*, 19 (1966). Williams proved a better influence on Wang. From the Williams–Wang correspondence (Beinecke and Dartmouth College Library) we see that Wang regretted to a degree his past doings. In one letter (30 June 1959), he expressed contempt for his former friend David Horton, referring to him as still "promoting the elimination of Jews, Negroes, and other 'inferior' people" (Beinecke). In another letter (27 January 1961), he told Williams that he had lent his name to get a place for an African American friend. "Maybe, someday," he wrote, "there will be a Jewish or a Chinese president who will do something for the Negroes" (Beinecke).

Wang took his MA at San Francisco State College in 1961 and his Ph.D. at the University of Southern California in 1972. In April 1977 Wang's body was found outside a hotel in New York City. He had stayed in that hotel for a meeting of the Modern Language Association's Commission on Minority Groups. That story, along with Wang's entire career, has been treated by Hugh Witemeyer in "The Strange Progress of David Hsin-fu Wand [Wang]" (*Paideuma* 15/2 & 3 (1986)).

Fig. 9.1. David Wang, c.1955. (Dartmouth College Library)

Fig. 9.2. David Wang, c.1955. (Dartmouth College Library)

141 *Wang to EP (TLS-2; Beinecke)*

3515 West Point
Dearborn, Michigan
July 10th, 1955

Dear Mr. Pound,

I sincerely hope that this letter will reach you without interference, for about two weeks ago, while I was in Hanover, New Hampshire, I mailed a little book of my verse, The Goblet Moon, to the following address:

Mr. Ezra Pound
Creator of World Literature
Washington D.C.
U.S.A.

and it was sent back to me a few days ago with a note that the directory service in Washington has been discontinued. To me, it seems that the post office in Washington is appallingly ignorant. For how on earth could they (the postmen) be totally uninformed about your whereabouts in Washington, while they have no difficulty in forwarding any letters to a congressman or a senator? Literature may not be important at all to the average person, but to be ignorant of a man of genius living in their midst is unforgivable.

Though I do not have the honor of ever meeting you in person, I have always been fascinated by your works as well as by your personality. I know some of your friends at Harvard, and have met Signorina Aida Mastrangelo, who promised to introduce me to you sometime. In my opinion, you are doubtless the greatest poet writing in the English language, in spite of some unkind attempts by trivial persons to bury your accomplishments under layers of smearing mud.

As one of the younger generation, I am most grateful to you for what you have done for English poetry as well as world literature in general. Americans may try to forget you and your contributions, but as a Chinese I feel myself forever in your debt. You open my eyes to a world which I shall never be able to envision without guidance and stimulate me to venture into regions of daring endeavors. I proclaim you the maestro [master] of modern Chinese literature and consider your wisdom to have surpassed that of Confucius.

I shall soon remail my booklet of verse to you, if I can be sure that it will reach you. It contains three translations from the Chinese and ten of my original poems. None of these poems has appeared in a professional poetry journal, though practically all of them were printed in the Dartmouth Quarterly. In fact, I have sent them to Mr. Richard Ashman's New Orleans Poetry Journal, but he declines to print any of them, saying that they reminded him too much of your writing. I hope I am not "plagiarizing" you. Of course, I cannot help being influenced by you to an extent, but to copy your style is, to say the least, a monstrous crime.

May I have the pleasure of hearing a word or two from you? I have never had any wish to get acquainted with any literary personages except you and the late Bernard Shaw. Although drama and poetry enrich my life, I am bound by financial limitations to a humdrum existence. My flights into fancy can never exceed the journey of the mythological bird, Peng (鵬).

With my best wishes to both you and Mrs. Pound—

Yours gratefully,

[signed] DR Wang   王

David Rafael Wang   燊

(Wang Hsin-Fu)   甫

The Goblet Moon: The Goblet Moon (Lunenburg, Vt.: Stinehour Press, 1955). An inscribed copy of this privately printed book is kept at HRHRC.
Aida Mastrangelo: Aida Juliett Mastrangelo corresponded with EP from 1950 to 1964 (Lilly).

142   EP to Wang (TL-2)

[St Elizabeths Hospital]
[Washington, DC]
13 July [1955]

Dear Mr Flame-style King

I can't find your admirable HSIN [燊] ideogram in "Mathews" so, please correct me if I am misled in interpretation.

BUT you can not have it both ways. I cannot be more intelligent [than] Confucius and less intelligent than Mencius, and Mencius had the sense to say there was only one Confucius. Without KUNG one would not see that it was "there" in the Shu [Book of History]. But the enemy is very active, cheap books about ISM confucianISM, to get the mind off lucidity and focus it on all the irrelevancies of all the idiots who have pullulated in China for 2500 years.

The London Slimes [Times] has reached a new low in criticism of the ODES and the New Statesman like unto it. Sharrock in the Tablet and an anonymous writer in the Listener have seen the root "No twisty thoughts." Harvard has printed the translation minus the apparatus and the seal text. I do not see any reason to forgive them, unless it will arouse someone to the deplorable condition of U.S. universities.

If you are ever in Ann Arbor, you might cheer D[onald]. Pearce 1317 Minerva Av., you could discuss style with him.

cordially but anonymously yours

Miss Mastrangelo is busy seeing ALL the "terza pagina," all the advertised writers in Italy, and having no end of a time. Her heart is in the right place.

if Mr Wang is looking for a career or even a livelihood.

When Byzantium fell in A.D. 1205 or thereabouts, the greek emperor lost control of the gold coinage, but the prefect's edict, already 700 years old (approx) lasted on and was still functioning when Kemal took over. This is the <book of> guild regulations. It has been printed in english and french, but I have not yet got hold of a copy.

The point is that NO ONE in the occident knows ANYthing about chinese trade guild organizations.

There is an open and exciting field of research. It takes a life-time to perfect one's prosody, but one can start research at once on any subject.

reached a new low: cf. Confucius, 191.

Sharrock: the British poet and critic Roger Sharrock corresponded with EP from 1955 to 1957 (Beinecke).

Pearce: the Michigan professor Donald Pearce co-edited with Herbert Schneidau Pound/Theobald (1984).

Kemal: Mustafa Kemal Atatürk (1881–1938), founder of the modern Turkish Republic.

143   EP to Wang (TL-1)

[St Elizabeths Hospital]
[Washington, DC]
11 Ap [1956]

Will be
Deelighted to see
Hnbl/Wang
whenever he gets here.
Finale to VISIT, as from
                        of
His Excellency etc.
quite lively/
see no way of shortening unless you omit the first "forever" and show pause by spacing
    sic: He shall live
                    forever.
by no means sure this is any improvement.
Hnbl/Wang gives me credit for knowing a great deal more than I do re/ Chinese.
Know only Fenollosa's notes, and the Classic Anthology and have probably forgotten all I learned from F[enollosa]/ during past 40 years.
    can only impart by example and by a few remarks in my criticism ABC etc.

beware dictionary equivalents/ weight etc/ 2000 years different emotional tone/ relation to social or unsocial order.

?? may be it was a night-club ??

144 *Wang to EP (ALS-2; Beinecke)*

Apt. 9, 242 Mulberry
n. y. 12, n.y.
October 8, 1956

Caro maestro [Dear master],

Chao called me about a week ago concerning the plan which you and he had discussed. After listening to what he intended to do, I suggested that we should perhaps start a journal in English to facilitate the exchange of Chinese and American thoughts. It should cover Chinese literature, art, music, economics, medicine, cooking, etc. The expenses of such a publication should be kept at the minimum. Chao and myself will try to enlist patrons to support the publication—with your help. We will also get responsible and capable contributors to write about the topics in which they excel. What think you of this suggestion?

Yesterday I called upon the two young ladies from Texas. They are charming and patrician, as compared with the typical New York product of Brooklyn, Staten Island, etc. Miss Marcella Spann had the good fortune of attending a school where an intelligent instructor was given the freedom to teach what he considered to be the best instead of the "great books" recommended and prescribed by the college authorities. I read the reading list of her Comparative Literature course. It was a challenging but not overwhelming list. Among the authors included there were Shakespeare, Voltaire, Confucius, Pound, Joyce, Eliot and Wyndham Lewis. There were no Feodor "Idiot" Dostoevski, no Thomas "Magic Button" Mann, no Joseph "Jungle Jim" Conrad, and above all, no John "Archangel" Milton. I always pray for the day that there will be another 秦 始 皇 (the first emperor of Ch'in Dynasty BC 221–210) who burnt all the reference books and literary "masterpieces" that had cluttered up the libraries and buried alive in mud all the ancient and doddering scholars. My cry is let there be another 秦
始
皇!

For eugenics' sake, please tell me what the best books on money issue are.

I plea to translate the complete poetical works of 王 維 [Wang Wei] of 太 原 (Tai Yüan, Shensi), T'ang Dynasty poet and one of my ancestors. 王 維 is generally known as WANG WEI in English, but I think it should be spelt as WANG FEI or WANG FAY. Which name sounds better to you in English?

May I visit you again within three weeks?

Kindest regards to Mrs Pound—
[signed] 桑

P.S. Enclosed a new poem. Please suggest possible improvements!

Marcella Spann: see Glossary on Spann, Marcella.
Dostoevski: Fyodor Dostoyevsky (1821–81), *The Idiot* (1868–9).
Mann: Thomas Mann (1875–1955), *The Magic Mountain* (1924).
Conrad: Joseph Conrad (1857–1924), *Lord Jim* (1900).
WANG WEI: see Glossary on Wang Wei.

145   EP to Wang (TL-2)

[St Elizabeths Hospital]
[Washington, DC]
11 Oc [1956]

Note the most efficient method used by E.P. for putting over authors: Joyce, Eliot, W. Lewis.

This was not done by starting NEW mags/ but by entering and strengthening mags/ already there and which had printers and mild distribution etc.

Ergo, for consideration C[hao] & W[ang].

NOTE that an excellent venzuelan

Francisco Rivera (no relation of Primo)

is at 2604 Fulton Av. Berkeley, Calif.

he invites, what he cant have, contribution from E.P. for a new magazine, strictly literary.

starting with St J. Pearse, which is excellent in so far as it is respectable, non-committal, guaranteed to keep OFF and away from all vital issues sticking to culture.

I suggest yu send him yr/poem, / say that a group of Han [Chinese]/ could greatly strengthen their mag/

(opinion of competent, if anonymous critic)

You cannot put over chinese interests save a CULTURE <u>at this</u> moment.

It is no TIME to start anything by plunging into the abyss of Chinese politics as of 1956.

Ergo, say you have been ASKED to inquire if the mag/which Rivera recommends would devote 8 pages monthly to the best chinese tradition.

You can call his attention to the Chinese World for 1 Oct. Confucius' birthday issue.

Say that some chinese scholars cannot affiliate with the Ch. World at this time.

But that they could presumably come to focus on a scholarly or poetic review of autochthonous nature.

Rivera has not given name of mag/ nor of poetry edtr. It should at least provide outlet for C. and W.

not committing them to inconvenient or impolitic views as to immediate events.

Alzo/ the gt/ tradition comes via the written word. There are millions of $ ready to yatter about art/ Metropolitan museum Hsüan-tsung etc.

Whatever you are able to do in 20 years time/ a START/ with 8 pages or even 4, at no expense to C & W. can be solidly made IF Rivera can swing it: i.e. a section under advisement of C & W.

Chao even moving forward as from Chiang [Kai-shek] and the Ch[inese]. World.

without going into opposition, always with due respect to respectable elders

Chao endorsing what is good in Chiang, W[ang]. observing the virtues of Chao that he happens to approve, and restraining himself temporarily re/ points of difference.

Gli uomini vivono in poshi [Men live in small groups]. IF three effective issue [s] of X. appear it cd/ be drawn to the attention of [Achilles] Fang and [Joseph] Rock.

one can only procede BY INDIVIDUALS. name, cognomen and address (when the hell-hounds aren't on the trail of the protagonists)

I shd/ more relish NAMES than general subjects, such as cooking (needing specific demonstration and certainly dealt with in the restaurant ads/ in Ch/ World, not to say their sumptuous representation of pantomime)

Hawley can be considered AFTER you see whether Rivera can be useful.

which i request you do AT once by airmail.

yes, of course glad to see you in 3 weeks, one week, or whenever you can raise the car fare/ no need of special permission etc. on regular days, Sat/Sun/Tu/Th/

no one likely to be here whom you shd/avoid.

I shall be interested in prompt reports on progress/i.e. toward a LIST of specific individuals who can write in a way to cause readers to READ re/ the Celestial tradition.

Many find Fang unreadable. Others are bloody well bored at hearing about the dullest european philosophers, or having chinese light correlated to european obfuscation etc. Cooking is to EAT. economics are likely to be KILLED, I mean any ref/ to them shd/ be made AFTER the seed of kulch has at least sprouted an inch or two.

benedictions.

Rivera: in his reply of 22 October 1956 Francisco Rivera states that he "is NOT directly connected with any literary magazine" (Beinecke).

Chinese World: in 1958 David Wang became a reporter and translator of the San Francisco bilingual newspaper.

Hsüan-tsung: Tang emperor Xuanzong or Tang monk Xuanzang.

Rock: see Glossary on Rock, Joseph F.

146 *Wang to EP (ALS-1; Beinecke)*

c/o Dartmouth Club
37 E. 39th St.
n. y. 16, n.y.
Dec. 5, 1956

Enclosed you will find a copy of Rivera's letter. I am not sure if he is mad or he is only mad at you.

I have been prevented from coming to see you mainly because of an urgent matter which developed in my apartment. My present roommate, a Jew of Polish descent, has rummaged my collection of nationalist literature. And, I believe, he has come across such lines as

"Decadence sets in
When kikes and niggers
Became overseers," in my writing.

I tolerated him up to very recently because I needed someone to share my rent after Bob Sharp, my former roommate, had left for his truck-driving job and because he asked to stay on after he had sublet my apartment during the summer. Now I have to keep an eye on him until he is out of this place. I asked him to move out yesterday, and he begged to stay on till the 1st of January.

I don't understand why Kasper does not devote more energy to uprooting the polluting elements in the United States.

I may have to use force to evict this nasty little Jew, Karler (Korowitz). I wonder if I can get some help in this respect.

Sempre [as ever],
Hsin

Rivera's letter: see Letter 145 n.
Kasper: see Glossary on Kasper, John.

147 *EP to Wang (TL-2)*

[St Elizabeths Hospital]
[Washington, DC]
[January 1957]

For a little serious conversation re/points not covered during Wang's visit.
O.K. eugenics/ very necessary /
endocrinology not kikietry.
spot distractions /
WHIB. Wheat in bread party.

a concept the incult should agree on/
and comprehensible at all levels.
Unfortunate that J. K[asper]. shd/ be on local line, not on universal slogan /
What they get diverted FROM is issue of money.
& tax SYSTEM.
both of which need INTELLIGENCE on the part of anyone who is generating
resistance.
ergo there are items for aristos.
all the mutt can object to is the AMOUNT of the taxes.
NO publicity will be given these issues by the Meyerblatt and similar sewers.
AND very few people either understand or are LIKELY to understand them.
the secret doctrine is necessarily secret NOT from desire to monopolize it.
Does R[alph]. R[eid]. yet understand ANYthing about history?
his ethic seems O.K.
Has Wang himself digested the Sq $ series?
A magazine shd/ be organ of something.
hence q. proper to want a manifesto.
let me see draft of it as soon as posbl/
WHEN possible avoid american tendency to split/
cannot admit corruption/ that we agree on.
BUT should not exclude useful parts of a mechanism
such as production facilities.
keep eye out for paper-MANUfacturer /
only material component
i.e. human component in material process who has NO interest in worse
letters <rather> than in better.
from econ/ angle
He alone WANTS more printed matter to be in course of becoming
without regard to its being monotonous
to him 100 books selling 1000 each are as good as one book that sells 100 thousand.
he don't OBJECT to someone he don't understand doing something good.
i.e. QUA paper manufacturer.
Basic principle autarchy and local control of local affairs unfortunately
weakened by issue that cannot be universally accepted.
WHICH is universal to any sane human being. it eliminates Miltons and Ikes.

J. K.: see Glossary on Kasper, John.
Meyerblatt: Eugene Isaac Meyer (1875–1959), American banker and owner of Washington Post and
    Washington Times-Herald.
R. R.: Ralph Reid, a regular visitor, contributed "Opus 1, no. 1" and "excerpts from F. L. Wright" to
    Edge, 5 and 7.
Ikes: in an undated letter to EP, Wang writes: "I had never dumped Dulles with Eisenhower:
    I consider him to be one of the few Conservatives left in Ike's regime of 'modern Republicanism' "
    (Beinecke).

148   *EP to Wang* (TL-1)

[St Elizabeths Hospital]
[Washington, DC]
[February 1957]

Baller, 1892 and 2nd/ edn. 1907 printed Wang iu p'uh's

王
又
樸

comment on, or expansion of, the Sacred Edict, but does not give translation of
Iong Cheng's [Yongzheng's] text.

It would be advisable for Hsin to make THE authoritative translation, BOTH
because I shd/ like it, and because Stock cd/ print it, AND because it cd/ be
useful in disciplining bullyumaire floundstions etc.

VERY hard to distinguish lyric poets sufficiently to discipline publishers (even
when the latter are better than crablice).

16 pages, a convenient length.

Three respectable Emperors / wd/ be useful to get 'em back on the map
and the respected W[ang]. iu-p'uh was a credit to the 王 [Wang] family

re/ Hsin's question of a week or so ago / more expensive to maintain twins
AND a putative father, than to maintain twins alone.

this may not be the comfort the unfortunate are asking for.

王又樸: Shanxi Salt Commissioner Wang Youpu's colloquial expansion of Kangxi's "Edict" is
included in F. W. Baller, ed., *Sacred Edict*. Cf. Canto 98/708:

王
又

Ouang-iu-p'uh
      On the edict of K'ang-hsi
in volgar' eloquio taking the sense down to the people.

149   *EP to Wang* (TLS-2)

[St Elizabeths Hospital]
[Washington, DC]
18 Feb [1957]

some Yong Ching [Yongzheng] very damnbiguous/
Salt commissioner [Wang Youpu] much needed. also Wang now.
interesting see where come out Hsin view
                              Ez view.

also some very Gemisto

or if not damnbiguous, various inclusions possible but salt commission <u>was</u> needed.

Wang poems Edg 3. O.K.

Hsin's zillusions re/ celerity of postal service that takes 3 days to get letter from Cong. Heights to Wash/D.C. office comes ON Monday to ask about permit fer ManGawd to git on on the Sunday preceding.

If you dont turn up THIS sunday / will send a few IDEAS, fer yu to try on London Soc. Crediters etccyroar.

I dont spose YOU have copy of TIME fer 9th inst. which no one here has seen or procured?

news of its copying Tempo mendacity arrives from Orstraliar.

ZO Sd

P.S.

Yong Ching

I think him

write

雍

正　　雍

Canto 61 正

W.L[ewis]. for long time/ lot undigested wrong reading matter in gullet / NOT by any means / 正 or 經 [gentlemanly]

mind active, not stop in same mess

but lot mess ergo cf/ Hroobloody/hrussian [Russian]

Sacred Edict/ bilingual for Wang's comment

Chinese only for Iong Ching [Yongzheng]

2nd edtn Shanghai 1907/ Presbyterian Mission.

Baller trans/ the Wang

Gemisto: the Byzantine philosopher George Gemistus Plethon (*c*.1355–1452) is listed in Canto 98.

Wang poems: "Tang & Sung Poems," *Edge*, 3 (February 1957).

:EP's seal with which he signed letters. It has his Chinese name 保 恩 德 (Bao En-de; Preserve Grace-virtue).

Canto 61 雍 正: Yongzheng 雍 正 (r. 1723–35) of Canto 61.

正 *or* 經: Phrase taken from Yongzheng's expansion of Kanxi's "Sacred Edict" in Baller. Cf. Canto 98/711:

"Parents naturally hope their sons will be gentlemen."

正 cheng

經 king

150　*EP to Wang (TLS-1)*

[St Elizabeths Hospital]
[Washington, DC]
26 Feb [1957]

Dear Wang

I dont understand the reference to Duke, N.C. Certainly did not express disapproval as know nothing about the place.

There are a couple of other N.C. institutions crawling with liberaloid egg-heads, pinko-commisants etc.

What might be more use is recent commendation of Wang by Dr W. C. Williams, 9 Ridge Rd. Rutherford,

who is far more unlimited in expressions of approval than E.P. ever is,

tribute all the better in being spontaneous, and I dont think W. C. W. knows that I know you. He had seen yr/ poems in print.

Perhaps he could be used to sway the commanders.

[signed] E. P.

Williams: in a letter of February 1957 William Carlos Williams (1883–1963) told his college pal EP: "I do enjoy EDGE—the last translations from the chink by/of David Rafael Wang are worth the trip half way round the world to have encountered" (Beinecke). For Wang's collaboration with Williams, see "The Cassia Tree," New Directions, 19 (1966); rpt. in Collected Poems of William Carlos Williams, vol. ii, ed. Christopher MacGowan (New York: New Directions, 1988). The EP/Williams relation is chronicled in Pound/Williams: Selected Letters of Ezra Pound and William Carlos Williams, ed. Hugh Witemeyer (New York: New Directions, 1996).

151 EP to Wang (TLS-1; Beinecke)

[St Elizabeths Hospital]
[Washington, DC]
[February/March 1957]

Dear Hsin

The foregoing for use on idiots or others.

IF I were recommending anywhere in particular I wd/ tell you to apply to what I think is called Washington U. east shore Maryland, in reach of the nashnz's keppertl.

There is at least one literate there, and he says the faculty is not lousy, which is mostly the case in murkn beaneries.

You might drop an enquiry to

Tom Jones

113 Maple Av

Chestertown, Md.

He is interested in Corneille / in disagreement with Monsieur Reid I believe/ but that doesn't in least imply that he wd/ agree with Hsin.

BUT, damn it, a human being, literate, on ANY campus is a reason for at least enquiring into local facilities.

Why THE hell don't anyone go see D. D. Paige <141 E. 44th St.>, who does know something about N.C. tho I dont think he was at Duke.

Hold on/ I think it is the U.N.C. that stincgks. At any rate dont know anyone there/ ask PAIGE.

As to Pindaric urge . . . it led Pin to rhetoric, or @ least that was my impression.

[signed] Z

Washington U.: in spring 1958 Wang enrolled at the University of Maryland.

Tom Jones: in a letter to EP of 1 November 1956, Tom Jones introduces himself as "president of the Mount Vernon Literary Society of Washington College, in Chestertown, Maryland" (Beinecke).

Reid: Ralph Reid. See Letter 147 n.

D. D. Paige: see Letter 28 n.

152   *Wang to EP (TLS-2; Beinecke)*

[New York]
14 Marzo [March 1957]

IMPORTANT clarification:

Hsin has no Pindaric urge—at least what E.P. calls the Pindaric urge.

Hsin, not being a genius, realizes his own limitations.

As Hsin sees it,

the greatest Narrative poems have been written by Homer, Chaucer, and Po Chu-Yi;

the greatest love poems by Propertius, Catullus, and Ovid;

the greatest Imagiste poems by Li Po and Wang Wei;

the greatest Religious poems by Yeats and, perhaps, Blake;

the greatest poems on Ethics and Morality by Dante;

the greatest Dramatic poems by Shakespeare;

and the greatest Political poems by E.P. and Tu Fu/

What is actually left for Hsin to write but a subject in which he can excel others?

The point is that no one has written anything DECENT about sports except Homer (in snatches). And if you try to write artistically about the speed, the color, and the sound and fury of boxing, you'll find it more difficult than writing about the ethos of Confucius. HAN and T'ANG dynasties emphasized sports besides the arts. MING and CH'ING dynasties relegated athletics to an inferior position. The Greeks were aware of the importance of exercise. But the modern Chinese have neglected it. The consequence: the Chinese became effeminate weaklings bullied by the West. The great Chinese novels, The One Hundred and Eight Bandits (or Water Margin) 水 滸, and The Dream of the Red Chamber 紅 樓 夢 illustrate two different concepts of the CHINESE HERO. In the former the men are real Chinese, i.e. virile and lusty; in the latter the hero is a Proustian type degenerate a la France. Before the Yuan Dynasty the artists were also men; after the Sung Dynasty the poets and painters were intellectual molly-coddles, as found mostly in France and the United States today.

(Incidentally, these two novels are better than anything [Henry] James has written.)

E.P. is a great tennis player, per esempio [for example]. If E.P. were an effeminate, he would not have written <u>Personae</u> and <u>The Cantos</u>. AND you know what Kung thought of the athletic Tze-Lou and Julius Caesar of the athletic Antony.

[signed] 燊

Po Chu-Yi: see Glossary on Bo Juyi.
水滸: a masterpiece of fiction about 108 outlaws (*c*.1370) attributed to Shi Naian (*c*.1296–*c*.1372). See *Outlaws of the Marshes*, trans. Sydney Shapiro (1980).
紅樓夢: a masterpiece of fiction depicting the decline of a powerful family and the tragedy of two young lovers (1754) by Cao Xueqin (*c*.1715–*c*.1763). See *A Dream of Red Chambers*, trans. Yang Hsien-yi and Gladys Yang (1978).

153   *EP to Wang (TLS-1; Beinecke)*

[St Elizabeths Hospital]
[Washington, DC]
21 Mar [1957]

HSIN/
wot is the min chih party / it's [its] badge not in ideogram /
people's WHAT party, there being 5000 chihs.
I take it Ching mei, is the keppertal of the ex-republic of the U.S. and a Washington delegate of the elegant plum bank might be of a district, or of WHAT?
The lady wot sez <she wuz> Idaho and mormon, dont appear malevolent, but the paper DEcidedly unsegregated.
whether useful <place wherein> to suggest that Ez is against certain diseases of thought that have afflicked various races / there being a lot of non-semitic jews, etc.
I don't know
You probably know by now that the gal [Anne Lebeck] is (or is said to be 26 of age) etc.
she thanks me fer prospect of printing you/ but you have not been expansiVO on the ambience or chances/
Got to be kept separate from the distinctive quality of Edge/
the min chih has a red badge but it dont look hroosian red/ said to have scared old Mr whazzisname. bolshies in Mathews dic/ have other labels/ not min chih
old Lampmen kusses Bill W[illia]ms/ BUT you realize that for 50 years there have been almost NO amerians writing to say what they think, 99.9999% writing to try to get past a copy desk.
hence the value of Bill W.
Mrs Ponsot refers to the "copy cathedral"
her blurb says "so far they have 5 children."

Ouan soui [Cheers]
[signed] Z

min chih party . . . Ching mei . . . lady: see Letter 155.

old Lampmen: Rex Herbert Lampman, an inmate of St Elizabeths, began corresponding with EP after his release in 1953.

Mrs Ponsot: Marie Ponsot, New York poet whose first book was *True Minds* (San Francisco: City Lights, 1956).

154   EP to Wang *(TLS-2; Beinecke)*

[St Elizabeths Hospital]
[Washington, DC]
7 Ap [1957]

Not clear if Hsin turned down by ONE bloodyversity or turned down altogether/

More I see it, and remind of what in Cantos I had forgot, more I see REMARKABLE Manchus /

a subject which the HSIN could treat carrying dynamite to blow the buggahs off their bloody bugrocratic elevations.

I admit that the dynamite in trans/ of Odes has got silent treatment

BUT it may seep thru in another 40 years/

Va. Poetry Soc. in yester, aware of timelag.

The Manchu DYnasty / looks like an innocent subject, all safely past etc.

新 [Make it new]

to git some PERsonality into chinKIstory / as Psellos into Byzantine FEEmales.
What the devil is the

夫
身

wise guy, big shot?

[signed] EP

REMARKABLE Manchus: the remarkable Qing emperors Kangxi and Yongzheng (Kang Hi and Yong Tching) of Cantos 60–1 and 98–9.

Psellos: the Byzantine theologian Michael Constantine Psellus (*c.*1018–78) was the author of *Chronographie*.

155   Wang to EP *(ALS-2; Beinecke)*

Apt. 9, 242 Mulberry St.
New York 12, n.y.
April 7, 1957

Meant to answer you sooner. But am busy writing the fifth canto of "The Grandfather Cycle" and a full-length play.

One business at a time:

Wrote to D. D. Paige several days ago. Heard rumor that he had left for Europe.

Finally saw Williams as you had suggested. He wanted to write a preface to my grandfather poems and suggested that I should send them to Henry Rago of Poetry, Chicago. He won't be any more help to me on my fellowship applications. Too late: I have been turned down by all the universities for some damn reason I can't figure out.

Am not sure of the etymology of 禾矢. Will have to check in the authoritative 康熙 [Kangxi] dictionary for you.

As for A[nne]. Lebeck, she is already looked after.

Min Chih Party is definitely 民治, a reform party during the reign of Tsè Hsi, the Empress Dowager. It was also known as the movement of Kang and Liang 康梁維新. The young king [emperor] 光緒 [Guangxu], who supported the movement, was later locked up by the Empress Dowager, a vicious old hag.

Mei Ching, not Ching Mei, should be the Chinese version of the "keppertal of the ex-republic of the U.S."

美京 are the ideograms.

Plum: national flower of China. A plum bank ought to be a Chinese bank.

B. Romney is a genuine Mormon: she knows her ancestry well. She still has hundreds of relatives in Utah. Though a bit "villagey," she is decidedly not diseased. She is attached to a French-Canadian, not to any Jewish boy.

Will you quote the whole sentence which includes 夫身? I must know the context to answer accurately.

Greetings to D.P.

[signed] 燊

P.S. Enclosed a short poem about Li Po, with Tu Fu and E.P. in it. Wonder if I should send it to the Edge.

"The Grandfather Cycle": a long poem of 101 cantos of which Wang finished fifteen. Its first four cantos appeared in the June 1957 issue of Poetry Broadside. See the first fifteen cantos in The Human Voice, 2/1 (1966), 31–6.

Romney: Barbara Romney, editor of Poetry Broadside.

156   EP to Wang *(TL-1; Beinecke)*

[St Elizabeths Hospital]
[Washington, DC]
3 May [1957]

No objection to Marcella's having ideas, fancy or otherwise
incline to favor ACTivity/ as anthropologist, instructive to observe activity/ inactivity / vide Mang Tze, less phenomenal, ergo less food provided the observer.

///

Not all things from one man/

of the FEW (damn) bits of sapience from U.S. pragmatik.

"not what you know but whom you know"/

murkns enslaved cause wont communicate with each other/

not necessary to use their intelligence if they have mobilizable $ and enough intelligence to permit extraction or direction of same/

Lee Lady has rustled $20 for Edg/etc. the HOPE of appearing shd/be used as lure tho subscribers are not REQuired to contribute their own compositions.

And Graves (funereal name) can't be expected to consider Sharp a poet who suggested that S/ was being inserted with that label.

However if the young cerement is hopeful, the time not wasted.

Wang at lib/ to try to gaze on the 5 young Ponsot and their paternal painter.

8920 172nd St

Jamaica 32, N.Y.

excuse for intrusion, you are looking for ms/ for EDGE, and want be sure a review copy of her bk/ has been sent to Stock/

yu cd/ even do a paragraph on it, IF you can stand it.

thanks fer trying to contact Miss Tseng.

Of course if Graves was buried in a female german, he wd/ react nihilistically, and the slavs ARE savages and the limitations of the German Anschauung have been noted.

tho I doubt if John Dewey was competent to do so.

fergarzACHE dont think every name I send yu as subject of investigation is assumed to be source of LIGHT

KUANG KUANG MING MING etc.

no nacherly I have not read books "ON" by any of 'em.

<Sandry or Sandri>

if the buggars cant katchee some FACT of use or interest, I prefer to git on with my own chop.

No interest in Frost, Sandbag [Sanburg] or even in Elvis the Pelvis. no objection to others having it.

Lee Lady: Lee Lady (b. 1939) visited EP in 1956–8. After taking degrees in mathematics and Greek, he earned a Ph.D. from New Mexico State University (1972). He was a math professor at University of Hawaii from 1977 to 2001.

Graves: Robert Ranke Graves (1895–1985), British poet, novelist, and critic.

Sharp: Bob Sharp. See Letter 146.

Miss Tseng: in a letter to EP of 2 May 1957 Wang reports: "Mrs. Pao Swen Tseng has already departed for Formosa, according to information supplied by the Chinese Delegation" (Beinecke).

KUANG KUANG MING MING: the phrase from Wang Youpu's expansion of Kangxi's "Sacred Edict" means "enlightened." It surfaces in Canto 99/722.

Elvis the Pelvis: American rock-and-roll icon Elvis Presley (1935–77)

157   *Wang to EP (TLS-6; Beinecke)*

[New York]
4 Luglio [July 1957]

Caro Maestro [Dear Master],

Been busy working on article on modern chinese literature and translating some poems for EDGE. Also doing a bit of work on the Edicts. Heard from Stock, who turned down my "Mr. Universe" poem. Read Stock's own poem in EDGE No. 4 and have a very low opinion of it. It leads me to wonder why so many inferior poets are magazine editors (e.g. Karl Shapiro, Stephen Spender, John Crowe Ransom and anthologists Sheldon Rodman, Rolfe Humphries, Oscar Williams among a host of other mediocrities).

Wonder if E. P. has ever seen an issue of POETRY TAOS. It combines cheesecake with poetry. W. C. Williams showed me a copy of it. Between covers of nude young ladies in technicolor there are sheaves of modern verse.

New York is not completely dead. There is at least one boy I know who's doing some honest work. Tom Sullivan, whom I mentioned in last letter, is hard at work on Brook[s] Adams and Zi[e]linski. He has written some insipid verse in the manner of Edgar Lee Masters, but his prose style is quite decent. His autobiographical sketches remind me vaguely of passages out of Portrait [of the Artist as a Young Man], but he cannot be just dismissed as an imitator of J[ames] J[oyce].

Nora was here. Told about Horton's anti-Kasper campaign. Hsin mistrusts all people with flat heads and big jowls.

The first four cantos of THE GRANDFATEHR CYCLE has [have] already come out in Romney's rag. With her usual woman's incompetence, she has allowed the printer to mutilate my poems abominably. As a result, a whole page of corrections has to be mimeographed. She is now staying at her beau's summer home in Jersey.

Marie Ponsot not heard from. It seems that after I had mentioned about my interest in eugenics, she decided not to see me. After all, the Catholic Church considers eugenics as sorcery.

Saw pore Ann[e] [Lebeck] last night. She insisted that women could be as intelligent as men if they so desired. She wanted to get a Ph.D. some day. Would like to write philosophical articles. Asked Hsin why E. P. has been partial to Marcella [Spann] and less fond of her. Hsin disagreed with her on all points. Adolf [Hitler] knew where women should belong more than any other political leaders. Told her that glorification of the "New Woman" by merky thinkers like Ibsen and GBS [Shaw] has lead [led] to family disunity and political chaos in the West. Shaw as an antidote for Englishmen and westernized Chinese is excellent, but as a "philosopher" is all rot.

Literature is at a low ebb in Red China, but no lower than that in England. From Formosa all kinds of obscenities and vilifications of Chinese Communist leaders have flooded into this country. Chiang Kai-shek is certainly the last person on earth to encourage or inspire any national literature. Imagine Lucky Luciano or Frank Costello as the president of the United States and just see what kind of literature will flourish.

Many verse-songs (樂 府) were written by Tu Fu and Po Chu-Yi. Some of them were inspired by the cruder songs of the Chinese people. I have translated two of them. "I Joined the Army" and "The Song of the Boat-Puller of the Tyrant Yang" are enclosed. Hope il maestro will read them over and give Hsin some criticism.

Po Chu-Yi, who used to tear up his verse whenever his washerwoman failed to understand and appreciate it, is now enjoying an unprecedented popularity in Red China. Definitely one of the top ten or fifteen greatest Chinese poets, he is regarded by the Chinese Communist writers to be at least as great as Tu Fu and even greater than Li Po. As a narrative poet, he is comparable to Chaucer. Next to Tu Fu, he was the T'ang poet most interested in political matters. Since il maestro has translated Li Po, Tao Yuan-Ming, and Hsin's ancestor Wang Wei or Wang Fei (Omakitsu in Nipponese) and read some of Tu Fu, I think it is time that E. P. should take a look at Po, who resembles Tu Fu in many ways. His 長 恨 歌 "Song of Unending Sorrow" about Yang Kuei-Fei and Emperor Ming Wang of the T'ang Dynasty is a masterpiece of Chinese narrative verse on a major scale.

Chao told me about E. P.'s recent discovery of Kuan Chung, the great Chinese economist. But Kung learned a good deal more from the Book of Changes (易 經) and the Duke of Chou 周 公, one of my ancestors.

In the near poetic vacuum of the U.S. today, Hsin has found Elvis the Pelvis [Presley] a welcome relief from the constipations of Robert Frost, the diarrhea of Carl Sandbag, and the stinking shit of Shapiro, Schwartz, Rexroth, Tate and other buggers. Elvis at least makes one feel like fucking or busting the noses of some spineless poetic jerks like Richard Eberhart and W. H. Auden and murdering some filthy intellectual scumbags like Adlai Stevenson and/or Anthony Eden.

Believe that la Marcella has shown il maestro Hsin's "The Message of Elvis Presley." Wonder where I can send it.

About Graal in Portugal, Hsin has never heard from him since writing him and sending mass. to him. Who is this person and what does he do in Portugal?

Both Sharp and Hsin had the idea of starting a gym in Washington D.C. These are the facts: (1) as far as I know from checking through health and muscle magazines, there is no health studio in the district itself. The nearest gym is in Baltimore. There must be students at Catholic University and other youngsters who feel like going to a gym for weight-lifting, calisthenics, boxing, etc. Unless there is a serious problem about segregation, Washington should be a good place to start a gym. (2) In a gym you can sell books relating to mental and physical health and also health food. (3) Gyms used to be headquarters of the pre-war Bunds. Young people can get together to exchange ideas and practise target-shooting, which may come in handy later in dealing with the Dulleses and Stevensons etc. (4) There are unsavory characters in bookstores as well as gymnasiums. But the future of real American manhood is more likely to be found swinging on parallel bars than slinking in bookstore corners behind bifocals. (5) If one such gym becomes successful in D.C., a chain of similar gyms can be started all over the United States. In the long run, it will be more effective than having bookstores. Does E. P. agree?

A candidate for running such a gym in Washington has been suggested by both Sharp and Nora. Les Blackaston, whom Hsin has not yet met, has been described as a junior version of Hemingway. What does E. P. think of him? Cheri [Sheri Martinelli] or Marcella [Spann] can be used as the trademark of the gym, and even Chatel can be put to selling health drinks behind a bar and eating all his can food there in perfect safety (without the interference of his landlady).

The blasted firecrackers outside make thinking impossible.

Salute to D.P.

[signed] 燊

Shapiro ... Ransom: Karl Shapiro (1913–2000), editor of Poetry; Stephen Spender (1909–95), co-editor of Encounter; John Crowe Ransom (1888–1974), editor of Kenyon Review.

Rodman ... Williams: Sheldon Rodman, ed., Mortal Triumph and Poems (1932); Rolfe Humphries, ed., New Poems (1953); Oscar Williams, ed., Book of New Poems of 1943 (1943).

Tom Sullivan: David Wang refers to Tom Sullivan as a newcomer to New York and "an admirer of il maestro" (2 May 1957, Beinecke).

Brook[s] Adams: see Glossary on Adams, Brooks.

Zi[e]linski: Thaddeus Zielinski (1859–1944), Polish professor of Greek. Henry Swabey's translation of his "The Sybyl" (Paris: Rieder, 1924) appeared in Edge, 2 (December 1956).

Nora: Nora Devereaux Lyden, a divorced mother with two sons, was brought to EP and his circle by John Kasper.

Luciano ... Costello: New York organized crime bosses Charles Luciano and Frank Costello.

Eberhart: Richard Eberhart (1904–2005), professor and poet-in-residence at Dartmouth College, 1956–70.

Stevenson: Adlai Stevenson was Democratic presidential candidate in 1952 and 1956.

Eden: Sir Anthony Eden (1897–1977), British prime minister (1955–7).

Graal: unidentified.

Elvis the Pelvis: see Letter 156 n.

Dulles: John Foster Dulles (1888–1959), US Secretary of State from 1953 to 1959.

Sharp: Bob Sharp. See Letter 146.

Les Blackaston: unidentified.

Chatel: Jean Chatel, an aspiring novelist, later became a psychiatrist.

158   EP to Wang *(TLS-1; Beinecke)*

[St Elizabeths Hospital]
[Washington, DC]
28 Sp/57

You wd/have got in with yr/godman/BUT it is unconfucian NOT to observe the flight of time/

mebbe as the request to get on Sat/ didn't arrive till Monday they tho[ugh]t it not worth answer.

I had some suggestions.

still have 'em if yu get here.

K[asper]/ probably in ERROR mixing with ignorant / which is different from the crowd.

Guard against sedition. USE the law, even when the tyrants do not.

The theory of the law, the words of the law, until changed by constitutional and legal process.

Note that Kerr and Ritchie are more astute.

CONSTITUTION PARTY

Ritchie combining with Peters who has vast amount of PARTICULAR knowledge.

though stuck in his own generation.

Whether Maverick will open the other part of his mind, I dont know. he has again been allowed to TEACH

which may be a bad sign, BUT he does go into detail and up to date has answered question and LOOKED at texts.

HAS NOT yet grasped sense of stamp scrip/but may be demurring to find out if I know what the hell I am talking about.

yrz

Kerr and Ritchie: Gordon Kerr, an instructor at Aberdeen University, informed EP of the success of his "Pound campaign" (15 June 1953, Beinecke). Eleanor Ritchie at Berkeley described to EP admirers' discussions of his poems (6 November 1956, Beinecke).

Maverick: see Letter 135 n.

▦ : see Letter 149 n.

159   *EP to Wang (TLS-1)*

[St Elizabeths Hospital]
[Washington, DC]
11 Jan 58

Appeal to N.H. Pearson, 233 N.G.S. Yale Station, New Haven Conn. He has just had member of family in nervous breakdown/ so is distracted at moment.

So keep him in reserve until real danger of deportation/

IF deportable, INSIST on going to Formosa, not to Moscovite dependency

say yu are OBviously not howling for white supremacy/and that study of systematic defamation shd/ be made by some FOUNDATION.

needs 200 researchers ENdowed.

IMPrimatur, and for greater etc. and copies not only to Stock
but to

Chas. Martell, 25 College St. Canton, N.Y.

Wm. Cookson, 5 Cranbourne Court, Albert Bridge Rd. London, s.w. 11 England

Desmond O'Grady, 40 via Pisa, Roma, Italy

Vanni Scheiwiller, 6 via Melzi D'Eril, Milano, Italy.

alzo L Dudek / Delta

1143 Sixth Av. Verdun, Montreal, Canada.

AND Sheri [Martinelli] wants a copy.

yrz

[signed] E.P.

I shouldn't send anything ELSE with it to any of them. Goullart been heard from.

Martell: Charles Martell had short articles on EP published in *The Laurentian* of St Lawrence
University, where he was a student till 1957.

Cookson: William Cookson (1939–2003) founded the Poundian journal *Agenda* and edited *SP*. See
memorial issue of *Agenda*, 39/4 (Summer 2003).

O'Grady: Desmond O'Grady, a poet and a correspondent. In 1960 EP looked him up in Rome and
stayed at his apartment for several days.

Vanni Scheiwiller: see Glossary on Scheiwiller, Vanni.

Dudek: Louis Dudek of McGill University corresponded with EP. CBC aired his "Letters of Ezra
Pound" on 14 September 1957.

Goullart: see Letter 165 n.

160   *Wang to EP (TL-1; Beinecke)*

[New York]

Jan. 14 [1958]

Lemme know fer shoor if thou hast received the Chinese jacket. Sent it by
parcel post with insurance ("swallow's comb" in Chinese). 燕 梳

Yes, already sent copies to England, Italia, and Australia. Am really in deep
trouble. Lost my job with the YMCA as a result of pressure from the ADL [Anti-
Defamation League]. Accused of "anti-Semitism" mainly because of Rattray's
article in the NATION and Ridgeway's article in the IVY MAGAZINE. If
matters are not cleared up, may be forcibly sent back to RED China against
my wishes. Pray that E. P. will at least help by calling Rattray a liar. See no other
way out. Eagerly await E. P.'s instruction.

Will be with Doc Williams on Friday.

Do you have a spare copy of EDGE No. 8? Would like veerrrry much to have it.

Chinese jacket: in a letter to EP of 8 January 1958 Wang writes: "Your Chinese jacket already made
and sent from Hong Kong" (Beinecke).

10

P. H. Fang and the Naxi Rites in *The Cantos*
"I have found your Muen Bpo & KA MA gyu"

Lijiang in remote southwest China has been a hot tourist attraction ever since its inclusion in the list of UNESCO's World Heritage sites (see Fig. 10.1). Many have attributed this distinction to the legacy of the American botanist Joseph Rock (1884–1962), including his monographs and books about the Naxi ethnic group inhabiting the Lijiang area. Some have also linked this honor to *Forgotten Kingdom,* a 1955 book by the Belarus-born traveler Peter Goullart. Few are aware of Pound's contribution to this glory. Among the beautiful lyrics of Pound's final cantos are those about the landscape of Lijiang and the strange culture of the Naxi.

Carroll Terrell and others are not wrong in identifying Rock's "The Romance of ^{2}K'a-^{2}mä-^{1}gyu-^{3}mi-^{2}gkyi," "The ^{2}Muan ^{1}Bpö Ceremony," and *The Ancient Na-khi Kingdom of Southwest China* as sources of the Naxi (Na-khi) passages in *Thrones* and *Drafts and Fragments* (Terrell, 674, 713). But was Rock the first to introduce Pound to the Naxi? Rock and Pound exchanged letters for several years of which one from Rock to Pound (dated 3 January 1956) has been discovered. In it Rock refers to a Naxi native: "My friend Pao-hsien Fang, a Na-khi boy whose parents I used to know for many years in Likiang, Yunnan, sent me a letter written by Prof. G. Giovannini of the Catholic University of America. In the letter Mr. Giovannini told Fang that he had given you two of my papers on the Na-khi . . . among whom I lived for 27 years" (Beinecke).

P. H. Fang, the "Na-khi boy," now a retired Boston College research professor, confirmed in a 2003 interview (see Fig. 10.2) that he was a mutual friend of Rock and Pound and that in 1954 he loaned to Pound inscribed copies of "The Romance of ^{2}K'a-^{2}mä-^{1}gyu-^{3}mi-^{2}gkyi" and "The ^{2}Muan ^{1}Bpö Ceremony." Upon Pound's return to Italy, Fang obviously asked about these monographs, for in a letter to him of 15 July 1958 Pound wrote: "I have found your Muen Bpo & KA MA gyu in my luggage." Also, on 5 August 1958, Pound wrote to Peter Goullart, asking how he could "get copies of [Rock's] Na Khi stuff": "have had to send Fang's copies back to him" (Beinecke). Pound had used Fang's copy of "^{2}K'a-^{2}mä-^{1}gyu-^{3}mi-^{2}gkyi" so frequently that by 1958 its soft cover was worn off and replaced by a hard binder. Fang still keeps this copy with Pound's note in red ink: "Sorry the binder has omitted Rock's dedication to Fang" (see Fig. 10.3). In a January 1959 card to Ezra and Dorothy Pound Fang acknowledged the return of this and the other Rock monograph: "Thank you for these books you sent back and the beautiful binding with your precious signature" (Letter 164).

What do we know about P. H. Fang? How did he get to know Pound? Born to a merchant family in Lijiang, Fang (Fang Baoxian 方 寶 賢, b. 1923) came to America via India in 1945. After taking a master's degree at Ohio State University (1950), he started to work on a Ph.D. in physics at the Catholic University of America in Washington, DC. There he met and married Josefine Maria Riss from Austria, who held a Ph.D. from the University of Graz and would soon start working toward a degree in library science. Among their friends was CUA Professor of English Giovanni Giovannini, who later became their firstborn Paula's godfather.

Early in 1953 Professor Giovannini took P. H. Fang to Pound at St Elizabeths Hospital. The American poet, Giovannini told Fang, had translated Li Bo's poems and Confucius' *Analects*. P. H. Fang was impressed. In the next five or more years he and Josephine (officially spelt that way in the US) visited Pound countless times. More than once or twice they took their daughter Paula and son David with them. On Pound's birthdays Josephine would make a kind of cake she knew Pound was fond of and it was usually Paula who would carry it to where the Pounds received their visitors. In a letter of 6 January 1959 Dorothy Pound wrote of one such visit: "Paula may remember bringing EP his birthday cake at St. E's" (Beinecke).

The Fangs' visits coincided with the moment Pound was trying to bring out an edition of the Confucian Odes with a Chinese seal text and a sound key. With a visitor from China, naturally he would talk endlessly about Confucius, Fenollosa, and Fenollosa's essay on "The Chinese Written Character as a Medium for Poetry." One day, when Pound began quoting Fenollosa and marveling at the Chinese character again, P. H. Fang surprised Pound by remarking that the scholar-priests of his hometown still used primitive pictographs. This was the first time he told Pound that he was from Lijiang on the borders of Tibet. Lijiang was the center of the ancient Naxi kingdom, which flourished from the eighth to the eighteenth centuries. Its landscape, along with a unique culture, had fascinated Rock and Goullart. And it would soon surface in Pound's new cantos in *Thrones* and *Drafts and Fragments:*

> at Li Chiang, the snow range,
>
> > a wide meadow
>
> > (Canto 101/746)

> By the temple pool, Lung Wang's
>
> > the clear discourse
>
> > > as Jade stream
>
> > > (Canto 112/804)

The "earthly paradise" over Lijiang is real, Fang testifies. Starting from 1973 he has been returning to his hometown regularly. The "snow range" remains as majestic and serene as it has ever been; and so do "the temple pool" and the "Jade stream" (see Fig. 10.1). Fang is too modest to consider his role as important, but his visits to St Elizabeths served to open Pound's eyes to a China not only beyond the Chinas of De Mailla and Legge but also beyond those of Carsun Chang and Achilles Fang, resulting in a new direction in the late cantos.

From that point on, whenever P. H. Fang showed up, Pound would ask him to draw a few Naxi pictographs and teach him how to pronounce them. Among the dozen or more Naxi pictographs Fang drew for Pound were those for the "sun" and the "moon." In Canto 112 Pound reproduces two Naxi pictographs, one for "fate's tray" or, as Rock puts it, "a large winnowing tray made of the small bamboo," embodying "a fate, a life," and the other for the "moon" (see Canto 112/805). Although both pictographs occur in Rock's "²K'a-²mä-¹gyu-³mi-²gkyi" and "²Muan ¹Bpö," it is safe to assume that Pound had learned the Naxi sign for the moon first from P. H. Fang.

On those early visits to St Elizabeths, P. H. Fang spent no less time chatting with Pound about his people's strange ceremonies—²Muan ¹Bpö (Sacrifice to Heaven) and ²Ndaw ¹Bpö (Sacrifice to Earth). He must have prepared Pound for Rock's accounts of these Naxi rituals. ²Muan ¹Bpö subsequently found its way into Canto 98 and ²Ndaw ¹Bpö into Canto 112.

In late 1953, with a Ph.D. in hand Fang moved to Dresher (near Philadelphia) to take a job at Philco. In 1954 Rock paid Fang a visit on a trip to the East Coast from Hawaii, where he was a research professor. He had been a friend of Fang's parents. When in Lijiang during the 1920s and 1930s, the botanist had borrowed sums of local silver dollars from the elder Fang, which he had chosen to pay back in the early 1950s by sending checks of American dollars to P. H. Fang at the Catholic University. Before departure on his 1954 visit, Rock took out two of his monographs—"²K'a-²mä-¹gyu-³mi-²gkyi" and "²Muan ¹Bpö"—and inscribed them to P. H. Fang. Believing that these papers would answer most of Pound's queries about the Naxi script and rites, Fang sent them to St Elizabeths through Giovannini.

In early 1956 Fang moved back to DC to start on a research job at Catholic University. When he resumed his visits to St Elizabeths, Pound would keep him longer for his Naxi lessons. He would pick a word here and a word there from "²K'a-²mä-¹gyu-³mi-²gkyi" or "²Muan ¹Bpö" and ask P. H. Fang to pronounce them and explain their meanings. P. H. Fang's copy of "²K'a-²mä-¹gyu-³mi-²gkyi" bears some of his glosses and corrections for Pound. On page 9, for instance, above the phonetic symbol "Yu-" is the English word "sheep" in Fang's hand. From the Naxi pictograph for "shepherd," a figure with a sheep's head, Pound could have guessed what "¹Yu-" in Rock's "¹Yu-boy" meant. P. H. Fang's gloss points to Pound's insistence on making certain what each part of a Naxi compound signified. In describing the pronunciation of the

Naxi word for "cuckoo," Rock states that "The word ³gkye-²bpu is the most difficult to pronounce." Next to this is given in Fang's hand "eng geek." No doubt, it was at Pound's urging that Fang facilitated the "unpronounceable" word. On that same page, Fang corrects a mistake in Rock's description of the Naxi pictograph for "three months of spring." His copy shows that "four" in "four horizontal lines" is crossed out and changed to "3." Going through Rock's monographs with Pound, P. H. Fang must have facilitated far more unpronounceable words and corrected far more inaccuracies than those that have been recorded.

To this day, P. H. Fang holds that Lijiang was brought alive to the West less by Rock than by Goullart and Pound. To him Goullart's and Pound's Lijiang is more palpable and joyful than Rock's. After reading *Forgotten Kingdom* he wrote to Goullart to say how grateful he was for the "obvious affection" shown there for his native land. For Pound's efforts to turn Rock's "limited resources" into poetry, Fang was similarly full of admiration. In December 1958, after reading the Naxi cantos of *Thrones*, he got so thrilled that he wrote: "I wish more cantos from you will resurrect 麗 江 [Lijiang], after the Revolution [of 1911], Republic, the People's Republic, Commune etc." (Letter 164). A year later he sent Pound another card, stating "my beloved country and my beloved village will be immortalized through your pen and your words" (Letter 166). By then Pound had stopped communicating with the outside world. Nonetheless, his dialogue with the native from Lijiang was destined to endure. The memorable Naxi passages in the final cantos should be viewed as his responses to P. H. Fang's appreciative greetings (see Fig. 10.4).

Fig. 10.1. "By the temple pool, Lung Wang's / the clear discourse / as Jade stream" (Canto 112) (P. H. Fang)

Fig. 10.2. P. H. and Josephine Fang with Zhaoming Qian, 2003.

Fig. 10.3. EP's note to P. H. Fang. (P. H. Fang)

Fig. 10.4. The Fangs to EP and DP, 1959. (Brunnenburg)

161   *The Fangs to EP and DP* (ACS; Beinecke)

[Washington, DC]
[December] 1957

Greetings
From Our House
to Your House . . .

[signed] The Fangs 方
寶
賢
上

162   *EP to P. H. Fang* (ALS-2; PHF)

[Brunnenburg]
[Italy]
15 July [1958]

Dear Fang

I have found your Muen Bpo & KA MA gyu in my luggage. Are you in a
hurry or do you merely want to know they are safe.

Sorry for confusion. Greetings to G. Giov[annini]. & La Dr[ière]. auguri [best
wishes] for the most recent edition of the Fang.

Cordially
[signed] E Pound

G. *Giov[annini].*: Giovanni Giovannini (1906–85), professor of English at the Catholic University of
    America. His notes relating to visits with EP, 1952–56 are kept at the Lilly Library.
La *Dr[ière].*: see Letter 75 n.

163   *EP to P. H. Fang* (ANS; PHF)

[Brunnenburg]
[Italy]
Aug. 1958

Sorry the
binder has omitted
Rock's dedication
to Fang.
Ez Pound

164   P. H. Fang to EP (ACS; Lilly)

[Washington, DC]
[January] 1959

Dear Poet,

Thank you for these books you sent back and the beautiful binding with your precious signature.

Is the design of 八 卦 [hexagrams] in this greeting card appropriate?

I wish more cantos from you will resurrect 麗 江 [Lijiang], after the Revolution [of 1911], Republic, People's Republic, Commune etc.

Please let us hear from you!

Merry Christmas & Happy New Year

Paul, Josefine
Paula, David, Maria,
Anna, Peter, John-Michael
Fang

165   EP to P. H. Fang (TLS-1; PHF)

[Rapallo]
[Italy]
25 Ag [1959]

Dear Mr Fang

I have at last got hold of Rock's "Ancient Kingdom" with its fine photographs. Have you his Vienna address?

Can you urge him to contact the Forschungsinstitut in Frankfurt?

The widow Frobenius is a friend, and my name useful there.

also can he stop at my daughters.

Mary de Rachewiltz, Schloss Brunnenburg-Tirolo

MERANO Italy,

My son in law is doing nicely in Egyptology, and should be useful in contacts in Rome. Not that Rock needs them. BUT the more we correlate the better.

Goullart's book is very lively. You could also ask Rock about Goullart who stayed with him in Li-Chiang.

cordially yours
E. Pound
[signed] EP

The widow Frobenius: see Glossary on Frobenius, Leo.

Goullart's book: *Forgotten Kingdom* (London: Murray, 1955) by Peter Goullart of Belarus, who lived in Lijiang from 1939 to 1947. Goullart and EP corresponded in 1958–9 (Beinecke).

166   *P. H. Fang to EP (ACS; Brunnenburg)*

[Washington, DC]
[December] 1959

We followed your work with gratitude: my beloved country and my beloved village will be immortalized through your pen and your words.

[signed] 方
寶
賢

Appendix
Ezra Pound's Typescript
for "Preliminary Survey" (1951)

Understanding of the Chinese language has been perhaps retarded by the assumption that because the ideogramic signs do not inflect, the spoken language, which children are said to acquire so much more readily than their <foreign> elders, is not inflected.

It is however permitted us to speculate whether the <early> creators and inscribers did not behave rather as we do when speech is not quite precise enough, that is when we add a map or a diagram to make a more exact communication.

It is even permitted us to suppose that the original chinese speech was not only inflected but also agglutinative. Enlightened speculation would make use of Leo Frobenius' "Childhood of Man" (1909, Lippencott, translated by A. H. Keane, late v.p. of the Anthropological Society of Gt Britain); of Fenollosa's notes and of Bernhard Karlgren's examination of early oracle bones, this last <as control and> to keep the follower of Fenollosa from becoming too wildly fanciful.[1] The Frobenius will be more illuminating to those who know also his later Erlebte Erdteile Bd/ 7, Frankfurter Societats Druckerei, Frankfurt, a/M 1927.[2] But on the supposition that the <spoken> language might be both inflected and agglutinative let us try to put ourselves in the place of a primitive man in the animalistic era. He wished to make the least sound possible, the sounds least likely to startle his game. 64 out of the 466 sounds in Mr O. Z. Tsang's dictionary begin with ch, the commonest bird sound.[3]

If we were presented with all the forms of the greek verb lambano, listed as separate words, and indicated by pictures of the various possible subjects of the verb, greek wd/ be even more discouraging to beginners. Neither is it necessary to assume that the primitive mind uses just our kind of category. Years ago in studying the Japanese Noh it became appeared that the authors had categories of their own, not ours; hence the suggestion that the graph "tree" plus "each" [格][4] might be translated "organic category."

[1] See Leo Frobenius, *Childhood of Man*, trans. A. H. Keane (London: Seeley & Company Limited, 1909); *Fenollosa/Pound, The Chinese Written Character as a Medium for Poetry: A Critical Edition*, ed. Haun Saussy et al. (New York: Fordham University Press, 2008); *Dictionary of Old and Middle Chinese: Bernhard Karlgren's Grammata serica recensa alphabetically arranged,* ed. Tor Ulving (Göteborg: Acta Universitatis Gothoburgensis, 1997).

[2] Leo Frobenius, *Erlebte Erdteile* (Parts of the Earth Experienced), 7 vols. (Frankfurt: Frankfurter Societäts-Druckerei, 1925–9).

[3] O. Z. Tsang, *A Complete Chinese–English Dictionary* (Shanghai: Lin Nan Middle School, 1920).

[4] Going through Pound's manuscript in 1951 Achilles Fang inserted about half of the characters surveyed. They are placed within square brackets.

Let us grant that Karlgren is right in saying that spoken chinese preceded the ideogram. This wd/ have little effect on a translation of the ODES composed long after the ideogramic system had developed but it wd/ have definite bearing of the formation of chinese speech. Again, standing beside the hunter, he is not greatly concerned with the sex of the game. He calls his companion's attention to it, and the companion can observe whether it be single or plural, but verb can inflect, and the so mysterious chinese pronouns may also inflect in indication of ~~its~~ <the object's> position, its farness or nearness.

Let us again approach our 64 ch sounds

chu, chueh ch'i chi chih ching chiang cheng chung chiung

We know that King Wan gave great attention to choosing his CHIH 止, and a struggle toward an exact philosophic terminology will have led us to consider this the point of rest, the centrum circoli of Dante's vision in the Vita Nuova.[5]

The chih whether we write it with the hitching post sign or with the leaf bursting from the branch is undoubtedly ON the spot. Despite exceptions a good many ch sounds can be read as indicative of place or of motion.

The ideogram is uninflected, yes, and it shows what need not be shown to the companion in the forest, that is, whether an altar or a tool or a grass shoot is being prepared or approaching, with chueh or chieh.

The chung is the middle in profundity, the weight drawing to the centre.

The careful reader will want fuller examples, which I shall try to give without prejudice, having first indicated a few more general suggestions.

yü toward or approaching, yu grasped

yuan, the yon at rest, yih the wilderness beyond it.

For agglutinative suggestions we may begin with ang up, iang down from above, ao possibly high ung possibly weight. I am for the moment neglecting the question of tone, as it happens by chance to be omitted from Mr Tsang's excellent dictionary. It never yet did a problem any harm to have it approached from a different angle. The root problem will be whether tone functions as inflection or as a clear distinction between quite different concepts, or with nuances or both. (as for example Li strength, and Li measure, the latter including i rectitude)

A certain number of ``an'' certainly agglutinate into words implying tranquility. Further examination will show how much is related and how much fortuitous.

The mysterious WEI might seem to have no common fount for its fifty meanings, but starting from a root picture of leather most of these meanings can be found in association with either the thong or the curtain, or to have leathery qualities. Eighteen KO (leather) ideograms are on the contrary, with two exceptions, apparently heteroclite.

Starting in the midst of the CH sounds we find

CHAO out of 20 we have six knives (let us say bright knife blades) 2 claws and one lance.

Chao, omen (dots separated by something listed as legs rad/ not under pa); summon (cutting voice)

ideogram chao or hua, search, paddle, to oar; beckon (hand plus knife-blade voice) bright (sun blade); dawn (whence ch'ao court, a.m. attendance at court etc.)

enlighten, etc. fiery gla[n]ce, summons.

---

[5] Cf. *Confucius*, 232: "*There is no more important technical term in the Confucian philosophy than this chih (3) the hitching post, position, place one is in, and works from.*"

claws: bamboo claw, a skimmer or ladle.

basket for catching fish (to claw fish, seems unlikely, and the sign is more probably allied to cho or chao to cover).

first, begin[n]ing, Chu (or chao) clear, bright.

announcer, edict

hasten to visit, pierce.

We have clear indication of the root meaning to cut, and slight possibility of combination with AO (to examine later) in CH'AO

eleven rather uninteresting ideograms, 4 containing shao (few) and three nest. Nest with knife, attack; idem with strength, toil at, fag; quarrel; ridicule (court voice); seize, take ladle out (vide chao, ladle) fray, slight epidemic, ch'ao or chao paper money.

TEN CH'ÊN circumflex

1. [塵] dust, stirring of earth beneath the deer's feet
2. [晨] dawn
3. [櫬] coffin, especially the inner one
4. [瞋] stare scornfully, glare
5. [臣] minister of state (pictorially the big eye, sonorously ? the "big noise")
6. [蜃] large clam, a sacrificial vessel
7. [襯] inner garments, lie beneath, give alms, patronize. The congeries clear in the pictogram, dress and relatives or affection.
8. [趁] avail one's self, take advantage, follow, GO TO MAEKET
9. [辰] a day, a time, 7 to 9 a.m., 5th of the 12 stems, third moon, seasonable animals
10. [陳] (printed chen in text) arrange, set in order, spread out. I shd/ say rather SHAKE into order. And the old stale, that which needs to be shaken.

The pictorial link is <radical> sign 9 which appears in the composition in 2, and in 6, sacrificial vessel, as well as in Chen (not circumflex) pregnant, in chên [振] circumflex rouse, idem 22 rich, wealthy, give [賑], and under the cloud rad/ in the SHAKE sign, [震]

Which brings us again to our CHENG focus.

CHENG, CHÊNG, and CHING

Let us break the alphabetic order to look at <the> two very interesting CHENG ideograms. The better known (to perfect, bring to focus) shows the sun's lance coming to rest on the precise spot. The other a mouth over the mysterious jen (gen) ninth of the ten divining stems in no case to be mistaken for the similar sign meaning a king. T. lists a "Six Jen" as a book of magic regarding the lucky stars.

We have, in the sound, locative CH verb in its intensive form. The graph is fruit not of the animalistic era but sabic, our precursors have passed from the realm of magic to that astrologic observation we may as well say astronomic. There can be <no> hesitation in admitting that CHENG has to do with motion.

CHÊNG with ê circumflex

The best known ideograms are: [正] to correct, govern, reality lawful regular (chih rad/) 10th in T's list

[政] GOVERNMENT, to rule, chih in composition with going along radical. 8th in T's list.

And for clarity we will number the rest.

1. [丞] an assistant
2. [乘] to ride, take advantage of opportunity
3. [偵] spy out the attentive man looking at chên (inquire) the great ideogram from the Book of Changes translated by Z. D. Sung, firm and correct, to have a shell and a direction.[6]
4. [征] attack, invade, levy taxes
5. [徵] summon, testify, prove, enlist, proof, evidence
6. [拯] rescue, aid by hand (watch the ideograms which contain the aid component)
7. [挣] get free from, make an effort
9. [橙] the common orange
11. [澄] with the water rad/, clear, limpid, settle
12. [蒸] fire rad/ vapor, distill, bring forward, multitude mist, a prince, to decoct, bring forward. A confusing lot until one gets to the root of the picture: the WINTER SACRIFICE, which includes the sign (no. 1.) for an assistant)
13. [争] to contest, wrangle, quarrel (this ideogram is included in 7, 14, 16, 17, and 20) I suspect someone's ear was unattentive at some moment during the past 5000 years, and that there is a pull from ANG (up)
14. [狰] a fabulous leopard with five tails and a horn.
15. [症] chronic malady
16. [睁] look angrily, open the eye
17. [筝] harpsichord, a kite (?ang), an aerial harp fixed to a kite.
18. [蒸] To steam, boil, vapor, hemp torches, all, numerous, you have guessed that this grass head ideogram contains "winter sacrifice."
19. [誠] SINCERITY, the perfect word, the sun coming to rest on the precise spot verbally.
20. [諍] To remonstrate (word and contest)
21. [證] witness, evidence. Word and sacrificial dish as found in teng (complete, record)
22. [鄭] plain, prairie, a feudal state under Chou.

CHIEH [介]. to lie between, assist, good.

I think we have here CH, one, two, that is the IEH equals erh, sequence, increase, with the hand root using both, and the limit meaning from the idea of sequence the verbal idea of place

CH, i, erh.

CH'IEH

The same, with perhaps greater emphasis on the ONE, TWO, idea, whether to separate or to put together. In both the united and divided forms, the same concepts, water penetrating between, comb sequence, eyelashed on-to'd.

---

[6] Z. D. Sung, *The Symbols of Yi King* (Shanghai: China Modern Education, 1934).

CHIEN.

The list of ideograms almost an essay on the nature of HEAVEN. Place, unity, equity. There is but one EN in Tsang's dictionary. Taking

I, the unifier

ERH, the second

ê circumflex, as a divider

the A in CHA might seem difficult.

It is associated with the thorn stroke, and starts in simplest form meaning sudden. Most of the meanings follow that indication, the bursting into bud, the derived meaning in fasten, not the thorn pin.

If the CHIEN group of ideograms gives us an essay on the nature of heaven, we have here, with the wrn holding the wranglers in suspense, several in indications of early concepts of government, or to put it differently the sound gives the general, and the picture the more detailed indication of what part of government, or good order is indicated or emphasized.

CH'ENG

two ideograms: elevated, dignified

[称]: call, designate, praise, RAISE, take up, plead, weigh. A steelyard. Growing grain or crops rad/ with hand gripping what? I suppose the steelyard or at least beam or handle of primitive balance.

Adjectivally: suitable, fit.

The vowel in the up indicator is decidedly undecided, f ê circumflex feng is a mountain peak or summit.

As to the relative durable durability of vowels and consonants we may have to wait Carlo Scarfoglio's long meditated work on comparative philology.[7] Toward which the present scattered notes might with luck make their small contribution.

CH'ÊNG

ê circumflex and separate

1. [城] city, town, citadel, to raise or build a city.
2. [懲] warning, precaution, correction, chastise
3. [承] support, uphold, contain, confess, succeed, inherit, promise, be honoured (aid element, winter sacrifice origin)
4. [撐] prop up, support, a leaning post
5. [程] the 1/100th part of an inch, rule, pattern, limit, period, task, to measure, to estimate.

I wish the calligraphers wd/ decide whether the lower right hand component of this and the next sign is a jen [壬] or a wang [王]. At any rate we have the grain rad/ with an orifice and a wang (not a jen) as printed in Tsang.

6. [逞] exhaust, extreme limit, be pleased with, hasty, presuming, exhaust.
7. [騁] to gallop a horse.

---

[7] The Italian journalist Carlo Scarfoglio translated into Italian EP's *Classic Anthology Defined by Confucius* (Cambridge, Mass.: Harvard University Press, 1954). See his *L'Antologia classica cinese* (Milan: All'Insegna del Pesce d'Oro, 1964).

Does our orderly eng in government [政] include the up concept, as it very well might? The NG terminal is decidedly active in any case, in the verbal inflection conjectured. BUT the chinese verb does not inflect according to the latin specification that the verb indicates time. Our hunting precursors lived in the eternal present, as with Frobenius african who denied that they had any "fables" such as Aesop's brought by the whites. They, the dark tribesman, told what the little antelope was doing AT THE MOMENT of the narration, not in a dim lost era.

34 CHING, 1. well [井], 10 ax [斤]

    2. [京] capital, a high peak a mound, ten million, exalted

    3. [兢] cautious, watchful (two on tip toe?)

    4. [剄] cut one's own throat

    5. [剠] to brand the face (capital plus knife)

    6. [勁] strong, stiff, hard.

    7. [境] region, district, condition of life

    8. [徑] bye-way, diameter, radio radius, adj. district, prompt.

    9. [情] heart-azure (vide infra) passions, feelings, facts, an affair

   11. [旌] banner, signalize

   12. [景] sun above capital: view, scenery, regard kindly large.

   13. [晶] three suns, clear, crystal.

   14. [津] ferry, overflow (water-pencil)

   15. [經] run thru, straight across, creek joining two places, fountain.

   16. [睛] iris of eye, pupil, eye-ball

   17. [矜] pity, value respect, boastful, elated, handle of spear

   18. [竟] finish, examine thoroughly, at last, only

   19. [競] strong, violent, two hsiung under two li (erect, stand up rad/)

   20. [箐] (or ts'ien) bamboo rad? creels, cage, cross-bow.

   21. [青] cleaned rice, sperm, expert

   22. [經] the warp, classics, regulate, already, past

   23. [罄] jar, vessel, exhausted, all

   24. [荆] thorn, bramble

   25. [菁] flower of the leek

   26. [警] warn

   27. [鏡] mirror

   28. [阱] pitfall, hole

   29. [靖] quiet, tranquil, standing azure

   30. [靚] ornaments, paint the face, darken the eyebrows.

   31. [静] grasp the azure, peaceful, quiet, meditate in quiet ponder.

   32. [頸] (of keng) the neck or throat

   33. [驚] frighten, startle

   34. [鯨] whale, huge (dark fish)

We may have to give up Morrison's "azure" and accept O. Z. Tsang's "green, blue, black, grey" for this radical, CHING [青], which occurs in 5% of our CHING. The Ching Nu is the Goddess of Frost.

The ax cuts, the well and the pit are excavations. The sun's ax is its brightness, a ching cut is a clean cut the ax rad/ occurs in the delightful picture cut the cackle (tuan) in the Chin Declaration (in the Great Learning).[8] The NG component of height is clearly present in one, and possibly present in five items of little collection.

CHING does not belong to the locative CH verb inflection. conjugation of the locative verb CH.

17 CH'ING (azure or green-black-blue-gray in five of them)
  1. [傾] turn upside down, squander, test, smelt, incline
  2. [清] cool, cold, refreshing (our azure combines here with ice, infra with sun, water and word)
  3. [勍] strong powerful (capital-strength)
  4. [卿] high official
  5. [慶] blessing, happiness, good, congratulate
  6. [擎] to lift, to raise
  7. [晴] weather clear after rain (sun-azure)
  8. [檠] stand for lamp, bow or dish
  9. [清] pure, clean, purify (water-azure)
  10. [磬] musical stone (onomatopoeic, but also indicating clear tone) but note carefully that the ideogram is also used for gallop a horse, and empty, exhausted. vide supra
  11. [蟶] Narrow clam or muscle
  12. [証] witness, prove, verify by evidence
  13. [請] invite, pray (word-azure)
  14. [輕] light, dissipated, easy, mitigate, take off edge. This is a monkey-puzzle on carriage rad/)
  15. [青] azure etc.
  16. [頃] head inclined, 100 mow, and instant (ladle-head)
  17. [黥] tattoo faces of criminals (capital black)

CHIO [角, 桷, 腳, 覺] and CHIU are extraneous to our verbs in CH, i.e. both to location <(tumulus)> and to cut.

Of 3 CHIUNG, the first with a secondary meaning of peak wd/ seem to be <the first> CHIU mound, tumulous plus NG

and the third CHIUNG [迴] is locative (far off, remote)

CHO 17 uniformally expressing the idea: to lay hold of with the pictogram whowing what does or is done to, no connection with CH verbs be at, or cut [琢].

CHOU [周]

The great dynastic name, given as verb: provide, extend, make a circuit; adjective: enough, close, secret; bend, revolution, circumference. Certainly associated with idea of motion.

[8] Cf. *Confucius*, 77: "ideogram of the ax and the documents of the archives tied up in silk."

19 ideograms in a mutilated copy of Tsang picture as with grass indication: wrinkles mostly what lies close together, and in some cases what revolves. On the whole it seems to belong to our CH locative. Various CH'OU can be associated with the CH cut idea without great strain, and by ref/ to the pictograms. The first CH'O to stab, is a clear case.

CHU, to go out of

THE GREAT GENATIVE, root of a tree lying

above ground, BAMBOO (the radical)

A half hundred ideograms in the CHU list, a rule, a lord, to halt to go out of, several of them clearly indication: origin, others baffling till we come to the clue in the 14th. "root of a tree lying above ground," that picture unites the heteroclite for the eye. The bamboo radical indicates a particular result of root, something from which a thing goes, or on which it stays, a SOURCE. This CHU is definitely of the locative verb.

As with WEI, leather, we have apparently heteroclite meanings.

We have also in our own language traces of similar not-ambiguities. To hide, conceal, to give a hiding. The leather curtain, the lash, the thong that binds, the showing a whip to a dog in produce respect or fear. So with the 32nd CHU, beat down, build, erect, flap, the picture is dulcimer (bamboo radical) over a tree. The ambiguity of up, down, flap, are all equal to verb "y to bamboo," i.e. to do what the bamboo does or is under for. The "dulcimer" includes "work" and a sign (I shd/ say for motion) that has no defined meaning as a separate ideogram. 41. punish, eradicate

CHU 2

We root in the ground to root up, and we are said to be rooted when we stop and stand firm.

The CHU list is too long to reproduce here, but the earnest reader can enjoy himself with it if he be so minded.

In tracing our CH conjugation we may even end with the idea that to "be at" or move, and to CUT have something in common. We "cut along," we depart, part and split. The ax makes a clean cut and separates. An active and an intransitive CH are not inconceivable.

CHÜ, with the umlaut is not going to fit very neatly into scheme so far outlined. We find however a carpenter's square, utensil, arrange. If chü (umlaut) enters our scheme at all it must be pre- it must have to do with preparation. Someone else must determine whether the cauldron preceded the altar. In the boiled sacrifice they are the same. An element which Tsang gives as meaning: great, huge, combines with the arrow sign to make the carpenter's square. A saw is found lower in the list, also some saw tooth mountains. The saw may be onomatopoeic.

I leave chü with judgement suspended.

CHÜ however does seem, in 24 ideograms fairly consistent in indication either preparation or unpreparedness; the preparation distinguished in the pictograms to show whether the preparation is in the cook house or the field, or by the pestle, for unprepared perhaps I shd/ write irresolute, hesitant (feet rad/). Both CHÜ and CH'Ü umlaut seem heteroclite, all one can observe is that if the groups seem without nexus, the individual words also seem without very comprehensible centre to their divergent meaning ascribed to them singly. Whether one shd/ postulate various lost terminal consonants, and leakages of meaning from other groups I do not know. I see nothing here to help define the CH verb.

CHUAN however seems fairly consistently to include the idea of turn, indicated definitely in 5 out of 13 ideograms, and for the most part directly relatable to either the CH of motion or of cutting.

Most of the 13 CH'UAN are clearly "connect" with pictogram of what (string, stream, beam) with a couple of violent exceptions, possibly emphasized chu'an, chu(boat) ang.

CHÜAN and CH'ÜAN <umlaut>, the first fairly heteroclite, the second definitely indicating curvature which is also indicated in the pictograms, two of 12 chüan and 6 of 11 chüan (small circle, wriggle of snake)

CHUANG, CH'UANG, idea of weight, strength, bed is frequent.

CHUE, CHUEH, CHÜEH umlaut) CH'ÜEH (umlaut), this suffix EH is the latin ex, horn, projection, husk

The chue is ambiguous in sound, but the pictogram contains "out of."

Chüen and Ch'üen connect with the chüan and ch'üan.

CHUI

CHUI tempts to several false analogies: how do we connect sew, beat, hammer and awl?

I think the clue is in the simple radical for short tailed bird. The bird has a sharp beak and pecks, some hammers look not unlike certain birds. The thread and (?) four stitches is the pictorial explanation of what happens with that particular piercing. Clay walls are hammered together but I do not think this is the primary association between the divergent senses of the sound chui.

CHUI belongs in the leather and root class. The verbal sense carries over quite clearly into at least three ch'ui: to beat, and two kinds of mallet, differentiated in ideograms.

The CHUN and CH'UN groups (lips and spring) are independent and extraneous from our locative or cut conjugations but CHÜN umlaut has clear indication of place above, latin super or altus, as with the water rad/ deep sea, italian mare alto. The third chun, even, equal must be taken as "level up to" and chun water level or plumb-line is one wd/ say its relation. The verbal sense of the 15th chun can only be traced thru its noun, hornless deer (bind, seize, collect). But superior, ruler, high (with mountain rad/) etc. belong, I shd/ say without question to our verb CH.

CH'UN umlaut might seem scattered were it not for the graphic signs. Grain heaped in an enclosure; the chief place above the sheep; the dress on the noble; granary, flock and skirt for a lady.

CHUNG we have already located as the perpendicular axis potently locative, the weight that draws to the centre, with ch'ung.

The single CH'OU is an eloquent picture of grind with the teeth (teeth and foot), and augur to bore a hole.

Let us now return to our omitted CH forms.

CHÊ circumflex, 19 ideograms

1. wise (hand, ax, mouth) clear cut, know intuitively cutting clean into.

The sense of cut (CH) is clear in a number of cases, in others the pictogram indicates the primitive association with cutting (five axes, a knife). The wagon rad/ is given two sounds chê and chü umlaut, and the ideograms with two signs assigned them always raise doubts. There is however a conjunction of wagon and cut in No. 1 & 17, the track of the wheels, a cut in primitive life as distinct from the hoof-prints. Among the meanings of 18, cover, hide, screen, intercept. The sound gives a general sense, the pictogram indicates the particular (more or less) object acting or acted upon. Various che take their sense from the wagon, indicated in their graphs. In four CH'Ê circumflex we have four very nice illustrations of cut and of ê as ex.

No. 1 remove and through, cuts both ways.

2. pull, drag, haul, tear (remove by wagon) I think the original sounds for ax and cart have melted together

3. remove, reject.

4. clear water, connecting with the "through" sense in No. 1 as indicated by similar ideogramic adjunct to the radical.
   THREE CHEN

1. pregnant; 2. even, uniform, place evenly cf/ chun water-level or plumb line; 3. pillow, cross bar at back of a carriage.
   29 CHÊN circumflex, EUDAIMON, the ANVIL
   The list looks heteroclite enough at the start.

1. (chen in index, shen in its own page in Tsang) men and horses in large company, crowd.

2. heart rad/ fearful

3. to rouse, restore, terrify, save (a hand that moves up or down?)

4. pour, add, deliberate.

5. I, me, we, subtle, incipient (pictogram, moon and eight over heaven)

6. kind of tree, target.

7. hazel

8. sink deep

9. curious, jewel, treasure.

10. examine

11. boundary, raised paths, terminate.

13. truth, immortality, pure (the eye looking straight)

14. ANVIL, stone and divination sign

15. propitious, spirit and the great sign of CHANGES, the shell and the direction

16. the steelyard (up, down, cf/3)

17. needle, to probe (bamboo rad/)

18. gentry, the literati, graduation, the girdle, to bind. (shên in text chên in index)

19. utmost, highest, attain

20. look at, examine

21. UNCORRUPTED, the great sign in I King, the shell and divination sign, the carapace and a direction.

22. rich, wealthy, to give.

23. bar behind carriage, to move, turn (indicated in pictogram)

24. deep in wine

25. pin, needle (metal rad/) sting, probe, pierce.

26. a mart, a great trading town, to repress, to keep in subjugation, to ward off an evil influence.

27. ideogram mound and wagon: rank and file, battalion, set in array

28. To SHAKE, VIBRATION the 51st sign of the CHANGES. Here is our key, to couple with ANVIL

29. bird like a secretary falcon.

One is tempted to connect Chun with the CH of location, or motion, and up and down with the steel-yard.

But the predominant number of meanings of the <u>sound</u>, which is even onomatopoeic, if you like, centre round the anvil, the hammer of Thor falling upon it.

Chên is the thundering heaven and CHIEN the calm or the righteous.

Even we say a horse chestnut for something larger that looks like a chestnut, and bull has similar connotations.

Again the old rule of english philology that the oldest words are those that have diametricly opposite meanings that is, that need gesture to indicate which way they depart from a median.

There are M. graphs that do NOT indicate any reason for their pronunciation. It takes no wild fantasy to get sheep over big meaning excellent. This ideogram is pronounced as mei, as for the lure of a lady's eyebrow, and the meaning fills up and extends over the space between graph and sound.

It is not our job to say what our precursors ought to have done, but we can try to find out why they did it.

MENG circumflex is uniformally dark in 4 cases.

   1. [夢] dreams (grass net over evening) 2. sun below horizon, 3. setting moon (moon blind kitten)

   4. [氓] people are graphcd as "lost families," ideogram in combination: rascals, gypsies, or in phrase, take census of the people.

   5. [猛] severe, cruel: eldest dog or animal

   6. [艋] small boat or junk etc. of all the dark ships, greek and latin.

   7. [萌] direct reverse to brightness, bud represented as grass over MING (sun and moon) to shine.

<u>J</u>

Tsang gives under a hundred J words the most known being JEN, man, and JÊN, circumflex, manhood. There are two clear ideas, or two sides of the generative heat, hard and the soft, masculinity, femininity, a considerable number of J come over directly in various gen- english or latin origin, generation, gentle, etc.; the values ascribed to i, an, and, ung (activity) hold good in a number of cases.

<u>P the divider, pair and peer</u>

In several hundred P ideograms we find knife after knife, not the violent ax that says "ch." PAN is the quiet equitable cut, the half. One does not expect a universal answer, the P idea shd/ be tested not as cut but as division, and as comparison. If PIH, North, is written with a ladle or dipper, that may be sky sign, but does not give indication of sound. P as in part.

PA, P'A, PAI start us off with such neat fits into our scheme that one expects ructions further down the list. The sense of P is divided not cut. The knife radical is TAO and the radicals differ from the meaning of the sound root to good purpose, that is they permit the graph to make the distinction which the gesture or the visible implement can make in the pre-graph era, thus whether the partition is made by cutting or wrapping. Rake and harrow divide by even measurings, or approx even with primitive instruments.

Not only the Pa of eight and six, the evenly dividing numerals, but the agglutinated I and AN follow our conjectured line, I, unity, equitable.

PAI, white is, I think according to Aristotle, the colours united. Pai meaning plain white silk enters an interesting phrase "the three pai," purple, black and yellow silk used as presents, the ceremony being as important as the actual colour. Spread out seems to escape our classification, hand and net over ning (to be able) but note the ulterior guide that Tsang offers us as to usage, this PAI means, to arrange, and pendulum (certainly the equitable divider).

Branch, PAI with water rad/ means also to appoint, to allot. Cypress is written tree-white, white it is not, but it is of all trees the most united, the most that is a single upright, the most neatly bundled.

P'AI we note is not PA'I and may shed light in several directions, it allows us to proceed on supposition that the A is separative and the I implies what ought to be. The FEI rad/ incorporated in 1 and 3 first with observant man rad/, and secondly with hand, shows two uprights with three prongs turned outward. With hand this gives, place in order, exclude, a line, a row. The PAN fit neatly, note that PAN, remove, transport is pictured separate by boat, the hand is combined with PAN, an affair, definitely not with ch'uan, and the shou rad/ being here a peaceable pole. And I think we might formulate, or almost frame the hypothesis that the IMPLEMENT is graphed, because it is what you can graph, whereas the action is sounded.

If that holds we have made considerable progress if not in tracing the process probably followed in creating the chinese language, at least in putting together a mnemonic gadget that might help occidental beginners, occidentals at the start of their chinese studies.

Full list of all cases wd/ require making a dictionary but the cases of PAN emphasize that values ascribed both to P and to AN, division serene, semicolons indicate that the meanings belong to different ideograms: board, plank; class, troops; slice, petals, carpels of an orange; beautiful eyes the black and white clearly divided.

Secondary derivative meanings, i.e. those growing from the implement can, with a little good will, be followed in Tsang or any other competent dictionary.

P'AN, I think the dissillable emphasizes or tends to verbal connotation, thus PAN half, P'AN to halve. PANG rather more so, class, party, assist. The only way you can divide by silk is to bind. PANG is used for bivalves, oysters and clams. P'ANG is onomatopoeic for the noise of stones crashing, and the association with that emphasis may give the meaning of heavy to the "rainside," i.e. heavy rain P'ANG, etc.

PAO, to divide by wrapping A O, ab alto

1. shooting start, clearly from above
2. defend, guardian, feed.

3. recompose

4. precious, a coin. The enfolds, and wraps are shown in the graphs. Sometimes with humour, and suggest that the modus of formation of hail stones was known. Cannon contains horse, possibly with magnifying sense guessed at in our treatment of M. Whether the leopard is PAO from the division of colour in his pelt, I don't know, the wrapping claw suggests felinity in the graph.

P'AO as the preceding and possibly, more so, nothing to rebut, in the graph for plane we have both the knife and the curl (of the shavings) and the A O, ab alto; and also in foam with the water rad/ The lion's roar is mouth and roll, and I suppose properly onomatopoeic when spoken gruffly ... PEH, North, we have already noted.

PEI, nothing to weaken our significance of the P, but a graph occurring repeatedly, as in indication of lower part that needs further study. EI needing analysis

Reins, two cords with wagon between them.

Up to Pei, the P was running almost too smoothly one cdn't believe that things wd/ run as neatly as that. Pei pejorative disturbs, and only in the first P'EI do we get a possible "out," if the E equals a latin ex, then P'EI UNequal is all right, and the E considered as contradiction to I's equity fits such meanings as bank up with earth, but bothers one in mate, equal, unite, though not in secondary. One must hang up EI for examination in conjunction with other starts.

On through 44 PI with nothing to derange conjecture as to meaning of P, but various puzzles, as for example, whether the pejorative and apparently contradictory, as against the equitable divisions, does not mean the "divided from equity" the which to be determined by gesture, graph or context.

The graph of PEI, low, beats me, unless it comes from draining a field, and "cause" to come from man attending to irrigation.

In some cases where the P association is obscure the graph sustains it by the twin moons, or some other.

In trying to get at the real meaning of a chinese sound the difficulty does not, in numerous cases, arise from my hooking together a lot of words that a prudent man would permit to stay separate. Nor does the tone solve all troubles of ambiguity.

MIAO temple, MIAO sprouts, MIAO blind are differentiated by tone, but blind and small are not. And in dozens of cases the ambiguity or direct contradiction is between the meaning ascribed to the same ideogram. As indeed we speak of something well laid out, or of laying him out.

MING brightness and MING darkness are both listed with even tone, though their ideograms are absolutely distinct. If we suppose that the sound holds it the idea wd/ seem to be that which they both can emerge from.

The four MIEH might seem more or less coherent, the EH being violently separative in destroy, the splints pictured in 2. the no, none, light minute, showing grass instead of bamboo, and 4 the same spikes following blood rad/ meaning stain with blood. But ten MIEN seem without nexus, the last, the rad/ meaning visage contains the absolute contradiction: front, to front, to face, to show the back. Is it possible that M sounds in the aggregate can have any such common basis of meaning as the fork that so persistently occurs in Y words?

The M words are discouragingly heteroclite. If they refer to any great category it must be of things like light that go on and off, that are and are not, or that, like the light, increase and diminish but do NOT branch, fork

repeated element set side by side, i.e. there must have been some idea of parity in division in the mind of whoever decided the graph before it reached us.

PI means lame, and demands that P signify separation from the I

But P'IEH also means lame, and is certainly clearer and more emphatic P——I—— EH which latter is certainly separative. There are among the intervening words cases that need examination, but PIEH, separate; and (2) down stroke to the left in writing, reject, are, as one wd/ expect strongly separative. The divisions implied by the 21 PIEN are, as wd/ be expected, more tranquil. Of course in the field of quite secondary and derivative meanings nothing is going to prevent a discrimination in "law" to branch off and mean the hurry of man when the law is after him. But the P significance will, I think, seem extraordinarily constant to anyone familiar with the vagaries of philogical associations, and up to this point even more so than the implications of the forked twig of the Y. An appendix of details can be provided if any reader be conceived as having the patience to read it. There is one rogue of PIEN "bring lower" to connect with as yet undetermined group of "low" (graph quite different).

So far we seem to come upon, in a good deal of penumbra, the primitive mind sorting out things as related in the following opposites

hither and yon	CH
light and dark	M M
the hard and soft	J
the branching and converging	Y
the wrapping and separating	P

There must be an up and down, a quiet and unquiet, and various other associations, some of which we have hinted. In fact the anvil, and leather, which is perhaps all the reader can stand at one sitting. We have also noted the opposites In and OUT, and the dichotomy of oneness and twoness.

YA in its simplicity is the forked stick or crotch that has come down in our own Y, what opens also shuts and the main radical in 16 ideograms is "teeth" verbal sense being: what the teeth do, as in Ode "we are the king's claws and teeth" it extends to the law court, and a bird's "open and shut" is the neat beak. The buds come out like bright teeth.

YAI, the toothed cliff, precipice 2: to suffer, procrastinate videlicet to Y, to diverge. YANG, the great UP, etc.

1. YANG [仰], to look up
2. [佯] pretend, dissemble, man and sheep (problem, divagate or trace of early mask, VERY early, in fact the ram mask not the commonplace.
3. [央] MIDDLE, listed under the Ta (great) radical and having no connection with its significance, can it be an inverted Y with an indication of grasp, or bind at the join? i.e. quite emphatically an indication of middle.
4. [怏] discontented, uneasy (heart plus the preceding)
5. [恙] illness. Permissible to ask if the upper component is variant on sheep, which it resembles or if it is a Y on one bar crossed by two others.

6. [揚] RAISE, lift, battle –ax, high forehead.
7. [暘] Rising sun
8. [楊] aspen
9. [樣] KIND, sort, pattern, style, again the embedded Y pictured as in 5
10. [昳] misfortune, bad phase of moon plus middle
11. [泱] wide spread, disturbed, water plus idem
12. [洋] ocean water sheep, vast, wide spread
13. [煬] smelt, fire-spread, or fire plus the components of I (change) are divided by a bar.
14. [癢] itch (disease names outside general considerations)
15. [秧] young shoots of grain
16. [羊] SHEEP or GOAT, the Y of the horns thoroughly visible.
17. [陽] male, sun, south or sunny side (spread) of hill north bank of river.
18. [鞅] martingale, leather and middle
19. [颺] to be tossed about, winnow, set forth, publish wind rad/ with sun bar and not sun, I i.e. the change sign plus the horizontal divider.
20. [養] to bear, nourish, bring to support, tame, develop, itch, something like a sheep but with forked bottom as well as top Y, over the eat sign.

We have in Y a good deal to indicate fork out, a little to support the notion that yang indicates upness. The change sign with added stroke does not occur save in composition. How far is the Y idea going to carry into other Y compounds? It appears graphicly in only one pictogram of YAO

unless one wants to see an inverted Y cut off, in 1 and 3 bent distorted, weak and (3) fresh looking, young, tender pleasing, untimely, calamity: which wd seem rather like forcing the meaning m as almost anything might be cut off by the upper thorn stroke.

2. is the great Yao, high, eminent, lofty.
4. bewitching, phantom, I can't rule out a long chance that sign I may be the dowser's twig.
5. handsome, witching, elfs, fairies
6. lofty mountains, wife's parents.
7. the Yao mountains in Honan.
8. high peaks
9. RADICAL small, tiny
10. feudal labour of serfs
11. yao OR chiao, boundary, go round.
12. drag, pull, pluck a flower, snap off, pictogram hand-tiny-strength (dels aussors entrecims ["from the high forked tips" (Arnaut Daniel/EP)])
13. move, shake, wave, trouble, discomposed.
14. the very poetic ideogram sun, wings, bird light of the sun, glorious
15. (OR miao) tree over sun, obscure, mystery
16. viands, mixed

18. beautiful stone, gem, green jasper, as adjective with pond means a fairy pond

19. profound, secluded, obscure: little strength under a cave.

20. kiln, pit for burning bricks: fire and barred Y under cave roof or cover.

21. ideogram in index but not in T's text, lower element as in Yao stone and serf lobour (10)

22. glorious, light of orient sun rising, with wings

23. loins, waist (sense of middle conveyed in pictogram)

24. bale out (hand scooping up from hollow vessel)

25. desire, meet, coerce necessary, essential. HSI (West) rad/ over woman, which appears as component in loins (23)

26. medicinal herbs, administer idem

27. yao OR nüeh (umlaut) tiger rad/ harsh, cruel, calamity oppress. (? onomatopoeic, as of course the triumphant greeting of the sunrise could be in different emotional tone).

28. rustic ditty, false report, evening moon over clay dish component as in 10, 13, yao stone, 22.

29. distant, foot and tracks rad/ with rt/component as in 28.

30. invite, interrupt when in the way

31. lock or key

32. general name for kites, sparrow-hawks etc.

The conjectured AO, high, is clearly present in a number of these YAO; the idea middle is present in others.

omitted no. 17: mix.

YEH?? dark as the devil's oxter?

leaf, arm-pits, profession, dimpled cheek, carry food to labourers in the field, choke; can there be any focus or nexus in 19 YEH?

The first YEH: and, still, also, besides a simple graph of something that might be a tent flap, or by stretch of imagination the flap of an arm is sleeve (such as primitive man does not wear?)

yeh 2.

You can take leaf as lateral, if you like, and the ideogram given in dictionaries as "leaf" you can, as well, take as shade. There are 4 yeh that fit gathering under armpit, or 5 if you count no. 1.

No. 9 contains the embedded Y and a gloriously divided top, a tree with fork: occupation, profession, the divided parts above the organic or organized tree. And from the sense of merit, listed among this yeh's meanings, you can, with perhaps excessive phantasy, suppose a title of honour. The dimpled cheek seems to start as a disagreeable black soot, found again in one of the yen.

And the YEH rad/ meaning head also means page of a book. Will the remaining 17 word sounds starting with Y shed any light on this one? Is EH separative indicating what branches off from, as leaf from forked twig or arm from body? This wd/ satisfy the 9th pictogram in the yeh list.

59 YEN for ire and fire.

At least if there is any nexus between these YEN it wd/ seem to be in the fire sign, the pictogram indicating how this is applied, whether for banquet or for the "2 accensio sanguinis circum cor."

It wd/ be rash to say that for beneath every Y word in chinese there is the idea of the forked sign, in this case the forked tongues of the flame, the words from the mouth. Nevertheless where two diametrically opposite meanings are given for one ideogram, or where the same components appear as is two YEN on the heart radical, differentiated only by the radical being given in two different forms, one must look for an idea that BOTH could come out of.

In the first of two YI, we have: rush together, disperse (the second is a fish hawk or the cackling of geese).

YIA is a river bank. YO indicates music and jollity, the most used showing a tree bursting into the fine white teeth of its blossom. The 4 pictograms indicate whether a winged foot or a flute serve as joy's exponent.

The YEN and the YIN

the word and the tone

35 Yin which apparently run from lewd to gums, yet do not present great difficulty to unification. YIN 16 is "warm genial aura, breath of nature, generative influence of heaven "ideogram air and cause (man in enclosure) 2 and the abbreviated pictures pretty well guide one as to direction and modus of this influence with the forked Y idea coming to the surface now and again.

YIN is emphaticly the INNER, it is the partner of the YANG the feminine as against the masculine, but always the inner, the YIN (tone) is the build up over the sun yin 29 (treasure or silver) if we take it the hidden. The 12th ideogram is given the alternative sound of AN, peaceful, composed.

6, 17, 18, lewd, soak, sink are all nicely and satiricly pictured.

Note that the YIN shade is dark because inner as in contrast to the outer PEH (north) cold and darkness. And looking at the points of the compass we must follow associations of suavity of the South; NG the energetic or active sun coming up from the earth in the East, HSI in relation with the low gentle light of the sunset. With P in the North, and the operant pivot CHUNG in the centre (the chinese give these as the FIVE points of their compass, a symptom of their solid sense as distinct from the infamies passing for intelligence in the occident.

I think we shd. probably translate NÊNG circumflex as the capacity to do a thing quietly and K'ê (circumflex) to imply simply the requisite energy for an operation.

As to the humours of the ideographers painting YIN: the husband's house, relation by marriage, shows a female with a man in a box (or at least enclosed, I dare say the corral is the more ancient form of enclosure).

We must watch the jên (or gên) in composed YIN 6, lewd, 17 soak, 32 long drenched in rain. Here the graph is clear; whereas in 18 & 23 there appears to be a WANG (king) under the HSI of the sunset. More than one foreigner has the decorum of the chinese, their reticence. I do not know whether the Jên has any relationship with the primitive altar signs now rendered "moreover."

YIN is the south bank of the river, as against YANG the North side (vide supra) the ideograms for YIN to be pregnant (7) and 22, abundance can almost be read by their pictured syllables NAI, to be, with the child inside it, and nai to be more in the dish or over it. The pictogram for YIN, heir, posterity suggests a matriarchal epoch.

YING, the radiance, resonance

The ideograms are the earliest comment we have on the mentality which inherited the chinese phonetic associations. The word vibration may seem alien to cave man mentality, but the ideogram for YIN (tone) is a build up, an orderly build up over the sun.

YING No. 1 is "the melody of many birds," birds calling, a simple mnemonic device for the american wd/ be to associate YING, with sing and ring. YIN tone is the ideogramicly the runs resonance. 26 YING ideograms show five with the doubled fire root above a base, two cases of the inverted Y (middle) and seven cases of the shell rad/ doubled in the upper position. The branching off sense of the forked twig inheres in most cases, specified by the graph. The dictionary word in english may not be our idea of a branch off or convergence, thus YING 2, a grave or cemetery might strain our ingenuity in finding either a Y or a radiance were it not for the graph the double fire over covered earth, anyone's guess whether this is phosphorescent hob goblin, animistic awe or trace of corpse burning. But the idea of YING as specified in generalization is present, as it is in 18 fringe, tassel, 20, glow-worm.

YING 3 concubine, 4, an infant, a suckling, here the nü (umlaut) female surmounted by the two opulent shells in primitive maternity, and the lactic emanation. Other YING give shadow, reflection (not the Odes, where it occurs for reflected image in water), 8 mid sun, dazzle, reflection 6 influence. 17 the awn of grain follows 16 tassel, profit, go out to welcome. 11 ocean is a graph indicating mermaids, and in combination Fairy land named in the dictionary. Column or pillar is ideogramicly spelled Tree plus YIN, to be more above the "dish" base depicted.

Encampment, 12 is the doubled fire over two connected squares of a plan, and the oriole shows the double fire in upper position. 10 is cherries, the Y might be the forked stems, and with mouth it?? Tsang notes "cherry lips."

If all the YING do not accord with our present way of considering radiation or Y division, most of 26 ideograms can help us in figuring out how they "got that way" and what sort of fringe is intended. Onomatopoeic attractions stretch fundamental associations, i.e. apparent exceptions can sometimes be easily accounted for in this way, as the very learned Karlgren often indicates in his gloss to the Shih, in particular cases.[9]

YU, the hand's Y closes.

The hand, that by tradition grips the moon (or, quite possibly, a moon clouded piece fat-covered meat) is present, upper left, in 10 of 40 YU, though the hasty looker might miss it in 10, more, especially blame, murmur (ascribed to a radical under which Tsang lists only three words)

YU the simple prolongation or protuberance of the central upright line from the field rad/ differs in tone from YU, to have, although tonal changes often FAIL to occur where today's western reader would think they were most needed to prevent phonetic ambiguity.

Another curious, and possibly QUITE irrelevant fact is that the sequence of graphed radicals often seems to result in the change of aspect of our conjectural phonetic radicals at

[9] Bernhard Karlgren, *Glosses on the Book of Odes* (Stockholm: BMFEA, 1964).

some definite point in the list of homophones so that all or most of one lot are above the division line. This may be pure chance or an hallucination of the present commentor.

1. YU [佑], aid, man rad/ and right or gripping hand
2. [侑] man plus have, or as one chooses, man and hand gripping? meat, meaning to wait on.
3. [優] Man standing beside the 15th YU, meaning melancholy, but here the combination given as abundance, distinguished actor.
4. agree (ger/ stimmt) i.e. it grips
5. [又] more, again
6. [友] friend, graphed by hand above the preceding, but the tone is that have (17th YU) evidently the grip, hand clasp, predominates in primitive idea of friendship, whatever or rather whenever the polite bow over one's own clasped hands supervened.
7. [右] the right (as in right hand, the gripping hand, cf. YU 1. the hand that holds the weapon the TSO hand, with the work rad/ being that used one supposes in artisanship where both hands are needed.
8. [囿] park, the enclosed having, to pen up.
9. [宥] excuse, indulgent, the covered hand.
10. [尤] moreover, and the ideogram is not to be mistaken for a combination of legs running, the upper left element is the hand. The only case so far where tonal change seems to some sort of orders is in the YU 5, 10, i.e. this one and 17, have.

The little Commercial Press dictionary translates YU 10 as best,[10] still more, so that in the order 17, 5, 10 we wd/ have a sort of progress; have, more, still more (if not a superlative best, at least degrees of have.)

11. [幼] youth, delicate, graph: little strength.
12. [幽] umbrageous, space between peaks of mountain filled with "small" (leaves)
13. stack of grain graph showing it under cover (thatch) and stacked round a Y inverted, as suggest at least Tyrolese customs whatever may have been modus in early China)
14. [悠] far, sorry
15. [憂] melancholy
16. [游] go on water, quickly, to a distant place.
17. [有] HAVE
18. the reed of a loom
    YU 4
21. [牖] a lattice
22. [猶] plan, like, a monkey

---

[10] *Chinese–English Dictionary*, ed. Zhang Tiemin et al. (Shanghai: Commercial Press, 1933). EP's copy (with the inscription: "To my friend Ezra Pound, From Lyons, Milan January 1938") is kept at the Burke Library of Hamilton College.

23. [猷] plan, meaning same as preceding, save that the sign is not used to mean monkey, i.e. like, simulacrum. The graph is in fact, the headman and his dog.
24. [由] follow, means, enter by, pass thru graph FIELD with projection.
27. elaborate graph given to mean clouds in three colours, flee in alarm
28. [祐] protect, spirit or descending light and right (hand)
29. flourish, luxuriant, a ditty.
    evening moon and silk (cords) over clay bowl (of musical instrument)
30. [莠] weeds
31. 32. long for, watch
33. [誘] lead on, seduce, word rad/ and weed component
34. flatter, containing inverted Y
35. far distant, distort the foot and trench rad/ carrying the to or thru Yü umlaut three stroke sign
36. [遊] saunter idly
37. [郵] post office etc. mound plus suspend
38. [酉] one of the 12 branches, ripe, mellow, graph looks like a bottle, and is composed of HSI (west) plus one horizontal stroke)
39. [釉] enamel, glossy
40. [黝] ash colour, black rad/ and little strength.

Out of 40 YU we have a number of cases where the Y of the gripping hand is clearly present, others where the meaning is clarified by the graph, and still others that it wd/ be decidedly rash to pronounce on until we have made further examination, both of the tone groups and of varied components

YÜ (umlaut) 78 characters

Can any communication be made with 78 homophones, or can 78 words have a common basis? Before we start feeling superior to man in the animalistic phases, remember that we say aye aye! and pronounce it "I," we speak of in of the ins and out and of an inn.

The 78 YÜ, umlaut, have clear tonal divisions jewel, rain, fish, wings, I, give etc. are not all sounded identically BUT the tonal distinctions do NOT fall into the divisions you or I make were we inventing a new esperanto on a logical basis.

We are in fact, in the case of YÜ, umlaut, faced with one of these very early grunts that need gesture to show its meaning, or, in later phase, the pictogram or other written sign. And, in the main, YÜ umlaut is far from being our worst monkey puzzle. Me, give, in, at thru, I myself (Nos. 1, 2, 3) are all explicable homophones if we are speaking and making a gesture. A group of YU umlaut begin with 4 which is listed under the jen (man) rad/ but is clearly graphed ju (yo enter). this rad/ is clearly graphed in various compound ideograms and with similar components, moon (flesh) knife, or two chevron stood on end and pointing left, which seems to be used loosely for the knife element elsewhere) sometimes in crowded compound the little top projection to the left of the ju seems to have been obliterated.

Sometimes the graph indicates what sort of interior is intended. In the slang of at least three languages and indication of interior (videlicet "inside," "dedans" "dentro" are used as polite synonyms for jail. On dit "je ne voudrais pas vous dire, Monsieur, mais...il...eh...il est dedan."

And one also uses the word "towards" for "something towards" with indication of going well.

The simplest general term for YÜ umlaut is "to, or toward," that is to say it starts from the sense of the two arms of the Y converging, in a visible number of cases.

One wd/ suppose that various primitive words have melted together, but I suspect the necessary starts are fewer than one wd/ at first suppose. The wings of the rain are in upper tone. The fish is in, and I suppose the primitive fisherman found it enough to point to the water.

The 78 YÜ umlaut need Karlgrens researches into archaic sound, that is to say, some of them do, others do not. Incidentally the idea of Cornelia's jewels seems to have preceded her.

Three YUAN mean: eyes without luster; a plant whose boiled flowers stupify fish when thrown in the water, and (3) the drake of the mandarin duck. The plant ideogram is grass over YÜAN (No. 1) umlaut.

The moon and curl appearing as upper element of YUAN 1 and #3 occur in five cases of WAN under a cover, these rads/combined can have nothing to do with AN as the combination does not occur in any case of chan, tan, suan, san, pan, nan, luan, kuan, juan, kan, jan. An can be left till we analyze WAN, with small prospect of solving its implication. It does not occur by itself, but only in composition.

YÜAN, umlaut, 28 cases

I don't know that these will convince the tough minded of the sense of AN suffix implying calm, calm of the yon, the far, the circumference of the heavens, the great sea turtle with cosmic associations.

YUAN in a number of cases has clearly to do with circling, enclosing, it means first, in a sign given alternate sound of WAN, it means the squirming of snakes, all of which may draw the mind to the original figuration of the encircling heaven, AN, the calm circumference. The antipathetic yüan might be discussed in an appendix one doesn't want to lose the main idea in too much minor detail.

YUEH, the moon, producing in graph with metal and lance YUEH No. 4 a large ax or halberd, obviously shaped like a fullish crescent, with moon

YUEH No. 1 I suppose the action of such an ax, meaning specificly to cut off the feet. Yueh 3, the name of a couple of provinces.

The YING and the MING

YING is definitely given as the "sound of many birds." MING is the voice of one bird. It seems unlikely that single consonant shd/ have the general homogeneity, or say the degree of homogeneity found in Y, the sound whence both vowels and consonants branch off. And indeed the first trials of M words seem interesting, from their divergence, but discouraging. Let us see if we can sort of a few M root. Ming is bright, the sun and moon, the total light process; MEI and MENG are in certain cases dark, from definite black ink to young ignorance. MA presents several probably fortuitous to common european words, the italian ma (but) ma and old lady MA means horse, and nothing phoneticly to do with a male horse, but the sound is indubitably initial in mare.

MEI is perhaps the simplest chinese M, starting with black ink, and indicated by graph in derivative, as the black eyebrow, the connotations of female eyebrow, the door's eyebrow, the streams eyebrow (all useful for budding poets), the tree branches over the eye. And where MENG has the sense of youth or stupid, the graph indicates the young animal (rad/ pig, that can enter compound cat) say kitten with grass over it, that is before its eyes are open.

Perhaps the most elusive M connotation corresponds to the latin mag- and maj-

GLOSSARY

ADAMS, BROOKS (1848–1927). Great-grandson of John Adams and brother of Henry Adams. He was the author of *The Law of Civilization and Decay* (1895) and *The New Empire* (1902). EP praises his "cyclic vision of the West" in *Carta da Visita* (1942) and draws on his *Law of Civilization and Decay* in Canto 100.

AGASSIZ, LOUIS (1807–73). Swiss-American geologist and naturalist. He was the author of *Recherches sur les poissons fossiles* (1833–43) and a contributor to the *Natural History of the United States* (1857–62). He is listed in *ABC of Reading* (1934) and Cantos 89, 93, 94, 100, 103, 107, and 113.

ARIGA NAGAO (1860–1921). Japanese scholar of international law. He served as an interpreter for Ernest Fenollosa during Mori's lectures on Chinese poetry. EP acknowledges that *Cathay* (1915) is "For the most part . . . from the notes of the late Ernest Fenollosa, and the decipherings of professors Mori and Ariga" (*Personae*, 130).

BENTON, THOMAS HART (1782–1858). US senator (1821–51). He is listed in Cantos 88 and 89. A part of his *Thirty Years' View, 1820–1850* (1854–6)—"Bank of the United States"— appeared in the Square Dollar series.

BLACKSTONE, WILLIAM (1723–80). British jurist. In *Guide to Kulchur* (1938) EP lists his *Commentaries on the Laws of England* (1765–9) as one of the essential books "dealing with history and philosophy of law" (352).

BO(BAI) JUYI 白 居 易 (772–846). Tang government official and poet. Fenollosa's "Hirai and Shida" notebook (Beinecke) records one of his masterpieces (*Pipaxing* or "The Lute Ballad"), which EP marked "Po Chü'i, 9th century, 772–846." For Bo Juyi's career and poetry in translation, see Burton Watson's *Po Chü-i: Selected Poems* (2000).

BYNNER, WITTER (1881–1968). American poet and translator. He first met EP in 1910. In 1917 and 1921–2 he toured China. Among his translations from the Chinese are *The Jade Mountain: A Chinese Anthology: Being Three Hundred Poems of the Tang Dynasty 618–906* (with Kiang Kang-hu, 1929) and *The Way of Life According to Laotzu* (1944).

CAIRNS, HUNTINGTON (1904–85). American scholar. His books include *Leibniz's Theory of Law* (1947) and *The Limits of Art* (1948). As general counsel for National Gallery of Art (1946–65), he also served on the Harvard Dumbarton Oaks administrative committee (1951–4). His correspondence with EP (1948–60) is housed at Beinecke and Lilly.

CHIANG KAI-SHEK 蔣 介 石 (1887–1975). President of the Nationalist Chinese government (1928–49). He assumed command on outbreak of war against Japan in 1937. EP was critical of Chiang's reliance on foreign loans, a policy, as he saw it, based not on Confucianism.

CONFUCIUS or K'UNG FU-TZU (Kong Fuzi) 孔 夫 子 (551–479 BC). Chinese philosopher. Unsuccessful in his political career, he spent his late years editing classics and teaching disciples from all parts of China. Confucian thought appealed to EP as humanist discourse. He translated into English the first three of the Confucian Four Books: *Da xue* as *Ta Hio* (1928) and *The Great Digest* (1947); *Zhong yong* as *The Unwobbling Pivot* (1947);

and *Lun yu* as *Confucian Analects* (1951). Confucianism plays an important role in *The Cantos*. EP's Confucianism is treated in Mary Paterson Cheadle's *Ezra Pound's Confucian Translations* (1997) and Feng Lan's *Ezra Pound and Confucianism* (2005).

CUMMINGS, EDWARD ESTLIN (1894–1962). American poet and prose writer. He and EP first met in 1921. Excerpts from *Eimi* by Cummings (1933) are included in EP's *Active Anthology* (1933) and poems by Cummings are presented in EP's and Marcell Spann's *Confucius to Cummings* (1964). The Pound/Cummings relation is detailed in Barry Ahearn's *Pound/Cummings: The Correspondence of Ezra Pound and E. E. Cummings* (1996).

DE MAILLA, JOSEPH-ANNE-MARIE DE MOYRIAC (1669–1748). French Jesuit. EP depended mainly on his multivolume *Histoire générale de la Chine* (1777–85), a translation of a Qing (Manchu) expansion of the Chinese history compiled by Zhu Xi (see below), to make Cantos 52–61.

DE RACHEWILTZ, BORIS (1926–97). Italian archeologist and Egyptologist. In 1946 he married EP's daughter Mary Rudge (b. 1925). His *Papiro Magico Vaticano* (1954) and *Massime degli antichi Egiziani* (1954) play a role in Cantos 91 and 93.

DE RACHEWILTZ, IGOR (b. 1929). Brother of Boris de Rachewiltz. He studied Chinese, Mongolian, and Asian history at the University of Rome (1948–51) and the Instituto Universitario Orientale, Naples (1952–5). He worked at the Australian National University at Caberra until retirement in 1994.

DEL MAR, ALEXANDER (1836–1926). American historian. He headed the US Bureau of Statistics from 1866 to 1869. Parts of his *A History of Monetary Crimes* (1899) and other works appeared in the Square Dollar series.

DU FU (712–70). Tang poet. He and Li Bo (701–62) are often considered the two greatest poets in China's literary history. The Du Fu/Li Bo relation is treated in Sam Hamill's *Endless River: Li Po and Tu Fu: A Friendship in Poetry* (1993). For Du Fu's work in translation, see Burton Watson's *Selected Poems of Du Fu* (2002).

FENOLLOSA, ERNEST (1853–1908). American orientalist. After a twelve-year sojourn in Japan he became the curator of oriental art in the Boston Museum of Fine Arts (1890–7). His *Epochs of Chinese and Japanese Art* was published posthumously in London in 1912. In 1913 his widow Mary Fenollosa entrusted to EP his notes and manuscripts, which yielded *Cathay* (1915), *"Noh" or Accomplishment* (1917), and "The Chinese Written Character as a Medium for Poetry" (1919).

FROBENIUS, LEO (1873–1938). German anthropologist and archeologist. He led twelve expeditions to Africa between 1904 and 1935. His works include *Unter den unsträflichen Athiopen* (1913) and *Erlebte Erdteile* (Parts of the Earth Experienced), 7 vols. (1925–9). He and EP met in 1927. He is listed in Cantos 38, 74, 87, and 89.

GUAN ZHONG 管仲 or GUANZI 管子 (c.725–645 BC). Ancient Chinese statesman and economist. He served as prime minister to Duke Huan of Qi. His teachings are recorded in the work *Guanzi*. For its first thirty-three essays in translation, see Allyn Rickett's *Guanzi: Political, Economic, and Philosophical Essays from Early China; A Study and Translation* (2001).

HAWLEY, WILLIS MEEKER (1896–1987). Hollywood book-seller and sinologist. He supplied the Stone-Classics texts of *The Great Digest* & *The Unwobbling Pivot* (1951). He also provided EP characters for *Rock-Drill* (1955) and *Thrones* (1959). The EP/Hawley relation is treated in Mary Paterson Cheadle's *Ezra Pound's Confucian Translations* (1997).

HORTON, T. DAVID (b. 1927). American poet and publisher. A graduate from the Catholic University of America, he was a regular visitor to EP at St Elizabeths. At EP's instigation he and John Kasper co-founded the Square Dollar series of inexpensive paperbacks.

HU SHI 胡 適 (1891–1962). Chinese poet and scholar. Educated at Cornell and Columbia, he championed the modern Chinese literary language based on vernacular. His works include *Outline of Chinese Philosophy* (1919) and *Chinese Renaissance* (1934). He was ambassador to the US from 1938 to 1942.

KARLGREN, BERNHARD (1889–1978). Swedish sinologist. His works include *Analytic Dictionary of Chinese and Sino-Japanese* (1923), *Glosses on the Book of Odes* (1946, 1964), and *Grammata Serica* (1957) of which EP owned copies of the first two.

KASPER, JOHN (b. 1929). American publisher. A graduate from Columbia he began visiting and corresponding with EP in 1950. At EP's instigation he and David Horton brought out the Square Dollar series. He later became a Nazi sympathizer and a segregationist.

KIMBALL, DUDLEY. American printer. He founded the Blue Ridge Mountain Press in Boonton, New Jersey. From 1949 to 1951 he worked on EP's Confucian *Odes* manuscript with an English translation, a Chinese sound key, and a seal text.

KING WEN 文 王 (11th century BC). Father to China's third dynasty Zhou. After capture and imprisonment, he continued to fight the Shang, a dynasty eventually overthrown in the hands of his son King Wu. As one of Confucius' ideal model rulers, he is listed in Canto 53.

KWOCK, C. H. 郭 長 城 (b. 1920). Honolulu-born journalist. As editor of *Chinese World* (San Francisco) he requested a message from EP to be printed on Confucius' birthday. The message released in *Chinese World* 23 September 1954 was "Kung is to China as water to fishes." In 1980 he co-founded with painter Walter Leong and poet Gary Gach the Li Po Society of America. He is co-translator with Vincent McHugh of *Old Friend from Far Away* (1980) and translator of *Tiger Rider and Other Chinese Epigrams* (1986).

LAOZI 老 子 (6th century BC). Ancient Chinese philosopher. The Taoist classic *Daode jing* is attributed to him. He is listed in Canto 54. See Stephen Mitchell's *Tao Te Ching* (1988).

LAUGHLIN, JAMES (1914–99). American poet and publisher. In 1936, at EP's instigation, he founded the publishing company New Directions. For six decades he was EP's chief American publisher. The EP/Laughlin relation is chronicled in David Gordon's *Ezra Pound and James Laughlin: Selected Letters* (1994).

LEWIS, PERCY WYNDHAM (1884–1957). English painter and writer. He and EP first met in London in 1909. Together they launched the Vorticist movement in 1914. Lewis is listed in Canto 80/526. The EP/Lewis relation is detailed in Timothy Materer's *Pound/Lewis: The Correspondence of Ezra Pound and Wyndham Lewis* (1985).

LI BO (Bai) 李 白 (701–62). Tang poet. He is often considered one of the two greatest Chinese poets along with Du Fu (712–70). Eleven of his poems are presented in EP's *Cathay* (1915). For his work in translation, see David Hinton's *Selected Poems of Li Po* (1998). For a discussion of Li Bo and Du Fu, see Sam Hamill's *Endless River: Li Po and Tu Fu: A Friendship in Poetry* (1993).

MacLeish, Archibald (1892–1982). American poet and dramatist. He first met EP in Paris about 1923. In 1944–5, he was US assistant secretary of state, and in 1949 he became a Harvard professor. He lobbied for EP's release from St Elizabeths Hospital.

McNaughton, William (b. 1933). American scholar. In 1953 he transferred from the University of Missouri to Georgetown to be close to EP with whom he studied Confucianism and edited *Strike* (1955–6). After taking a Ph.D. at Yale (1965), he helped found Chinese programs at Oberlin, Denison, and Wabash, and the program in translation and interpretation at the City University of Hong Kong, where he taught from 1986 to 1998.

Mencius 孟子 (c.372–289BC). The greatest Confucian thinker after Confucius himself. His teachings are preserved in *Mencius*, the last of the Confucian Four Books. EP discusses Mencius in "Mang Tsze" (*SP*, 81–97). His abridged translation of *Mencius 2*, "Mencius, or the Economist," appeared in *New Iconograph* (New York) in 1947.

Mori Kainan (1863–1911). Japanese scholar of Chinese literature. He gave Ernest Fenollosa private lessons of Chinese poetry in 1899–1901. EP calls his *Cathay* "Translations ... from the notes of the late Fenollosa, and the decipherings of the professors Mori and Ariga" (*Personae*, 130).

Qu Yuan 屈原 (c.340–c.278 BC). Ancient Chinese poet. As minister to King Huai of Chu he was banished to the far south. His works include *Li Sao, Nine Songs*, and *Nine Pieces*. EP's "After Ch'u Yuan" (1914) is a variant on no. 9 of *Nine Songs*. For Qu Yuan's career and poetry in translation, see David Hawkes' *The Songs of the South: An Ancient Chinese Anthology of Poems by Qu Yuan and Other Poets* (1985).

Rock, Joseph F. (1884–1962). American botanist and anthropologist. He lived with the Naxi people in southwest China for twenty-seven years. His works, "The Romance of ²K'a-²mä-¹gyu-³mi-²gkyi" (1939) and "The ²Muan ¹Bpö Ceremony" (1948), play a role in EP's late cantos. The EP/Rock relation is treated in Emily Mitchell Wallace's " 'Why Not Spirits?'—'The Universe Is Alive': Ezra Pound, Joseph Rock, the Na Khi, and Plotinus" (*Ezra Pound and China*, ed. Zhaoming Qian, 2003).

Santayana, George (1863–1952). Spanish-American philosopher, poet, and Harvard professor. After retirement in 1912 he moved to Italy. He and EP met in Rome and Venice in 1939. He is listed in Cantos 80, 81, 95, and 100.

Scheiwiller, Vanni (1934–99). EP's Italian publisher. His father Giovanni Scheiwiller (1889–1965) issued EP's *Confucius: Digest of the Analects* (1937). He published the first Italian editions of *Rock-Drill* (1955) and *Thrones* (1959).

Shun 舜 (c.23rd century BC). Legendary Chinese ruler after Yao and one of Confucius' ideal model kings. He is alluded to in Cantos 53, 56, 58, 74, and 106.

Sima Qian 司馬遷 (c.145–86 BC). Grand Historiographer under the Emperor Wu of Han (EP's Liu Ch'e; r. 140–87 BC). His *Historical Records* chronicles the Chinese history from ancient times to his own day. For Sima Qian's Chinese history in translation, see Raymond Dawson's *Historical Records* (1994).

Spann, Marcella (Booth) (b. 1933). American scholar. She traveled with EP and DP from Washington to Italy in 1958. In Italy she and EP co-edited *Confucius to Cummings: An Anthology of Poetry* (1965).

STOCK, NOEL (b. 1929). Australian journalist, poet, and university teacher in the US (University of Toledo). He founded the Poundian magazine *Edge* (Melbourne, 1956–8) and authored *The Life of Ezra Pound* (1970).

SUN, VERONICA HUILAN 孫 蕙 蘭 (b. 1927). Immigrating from China, Sun worked on an MA in English at the Catholic University of America from the fall of 1950 until the fall of 1952. In 1955 she joined the Ford Foundation in New York. Her letters to EP (1953–7, Beinecke) document when she visited St Elizabeths Hospital, left for New York, and got married.

SWABEY, REVEREND HENRY (1916–96). Anglican vicar in England and Canada. He corresponded with EP at intervals from 1935. His translation of Thaddeus Zielinski's "The Sibyl" appeared in *Edge*, 2 (1956).

TAO QIAN 陶 潛 or TAO YUANMING 陶 淵 明 (365–427). Chinese poet. EP presents his poem "The Hovering Cloud" in *Cathay* and alludes to his prose piece "The Peach Blossom Fountain" in Canto 84/558: "T'ao Ch'ien heard the old Dynasty's music | as it might be at the Peach-blossom Fountain." For Tao Qian's career and work in translation, see A. R. David's *Tao Yuan-Ming, AD 365–427* (1983).

TUCCI, GIUSEPPE (1894–1984). Italian orientalist. In 1933 he helped found the Italian Institute for the Middle and Far East (IsMEO). He was the author of *Indo-Tibetica I* (1932) and other books.

WANG SHOUREN 王 守 仁 or WANG YANGMING 王 陽 明 (1472–1529). The most important neo-Confucian philosopher after Zhu Xi (1130–1200). For a discussion of his neo-Confucianism, see Tu Wei-ming's *Neo Confucian Thought in Action: Wang Yang-ming's Youth* (1976).

WANG WEI 王維 (699–759). Tang government official, poet, painter, and musician. EP's "Epigraph to 'Four poems of Departure'" in *Cathay* (1915) is a variant on a short lyric by him. For Wang Wei's career and work in translation, see Pauline Yu's *The Poetry of Wang Wei* (1980). For the EP/Wang Wei relation, see Zhaoming Qian's *Orientalism and Modernism* (1995).

WILSON, THOMAS JAMES (1902–69). American publisher. Educated at University of North Carolina and Oxford, he served as the director of Harvard University Press from 1947 to 1967.

XU SHEN 許 慎 (c.58–147). Ancient Chinese lexicographer. His *Shuowen Jiezi Dictionary* (Explication of Graphs and Analysis of Characters, AD 100–21) lists 9,353 characters under 540 radicals. It started the tradition of etymological analysis.

YAO 堯 (c.23rd century BC). Legendary Chinese ruler and one of Confucius' ideal model kings. He is honored in Cantos 53, 56, 58, 74, and 106.

ZHU XI 朱 熹 (1130–1200). Song neo-Confucian philosopher. He prepared the Confucian Four Books. His *Outline and Details of the Comprehensive Mirror* yielded De Mailla's *Histoire générale de la Chine*, the main source of Cantos 52–61. He is listed in Cantos 80 and 99.

ZHUANGZI 莊 子 (c.369–286 BC). Ancient Chinese philosopher. His teachings are preserved in *Zhuangzi*. EP's "Ancient Wisdom, Rather Cosmic" (1916) is a variant on Li Bo's recreation of *Zhuangzi*, 2.13. For *Zhuangzi* in translation, see Burton Watson's *Chuang Tzu: Basic Writings* (1996).

INDEX

Items appearing as illustrations and notes are indexed in bold: e.g. 86 **i**, 168 **n**. An asterisk following a surname indicates an entry in the Glossary.